The Royal Commission
on Ancient and Historical Monuments in Wales

An Inventory
of the Ancient Monuments in

Brecknock (Brycheiniog)

The Prehistoric and Roman Monuments
Part ii: Hill-forts and Roman Remains

Her Majesty's Stationery Office

Printed for Her Majesty's Stationery Office by Acolortone Ltd., October 1986, Dd. 737394. C10.

Table of Contents

List of Figures

Figures 31, 35, 39, 44, 52, 79, 87, 101, 104, 111, 125, 128, 132, 139, 152, 157, 161, 172, 176 have been supplied by Mr. D. R. Wilson, and are reproduced by permission of the Committee for Aerial Photography, Cambridge University.

Chairman's Preface

This publication forms Part ii of the first Inventory volume planned for the county of Brycheiniog, *Anglice* Brecknock. The volume will deal with the Prehistoric and Roman monuments of the county, Part i being an inventory of Neolithic and Bronze Age sites and all undefended settlements of probable pre-Norman date, and the present Part describing those enclosures which can be classed broadly as hill-forts or related structures, and all Roman remains.

Altogether 77 monuments are described in detail in this Part, and the staff concerned have investigated nearly 100 sites during the course of the work. There is also a thorough examination of the probable routes of Roman roads in the County. In the course of fieldwork for this volume many previously unrecorded, small undefended enclosures of varied form have been discovered throughout south Brecknock and the Commissioners have directed the newly established National Archaeological Survey to conduct a detailed survey of these sites and the landscapes in which they occur. Many of the results of this work will be incorporated in Part i of this volume. As the fieldwork and research on the subject of this part have been completed and two reasonably unified and substantial themes are represented, the Commissioners feel justified in publishing this material in advance of the descriptions of monuments of earlier or undefined date.

This book is divided into two main sections: Hill-forts and Roman Remains. Each section has its own introduction in which the morphology of the monuments and their probable historical context is discussed. The Roman section is further divided into subsections dealing with various kinds of military or civil sites. The Hill-fort section is not subdivided as classifications are not as clear-cut, a problem considered in the introduction. The monuments of each section or subsection are numbered separately, so that future discoveries, missed in the present survey or brought to light by excavation, can be easily added by extending the numbers in each division. To assist to some extent in identifying the appropriate category to which a monument belongs, each section has been allocated two or three index letters which precede every number throughout the Inventory. Within sections and subsections the monuments are arranged in National Grid order as explained in the introductory remarks labelled Presentation of Material.

The Commissioners decided to exclude lists of finds from volume I of the Glamorgan Inventory because of the time involved in preparing them, their lack of completeness and the possibility that compiling such fell outside the scope of the Commission's Warrant. However, as portable objects of the periods dealt with in this part are few in Brecknock and the compilation of a list of them has involved no significant amount of staff time, the Commissioners have decided to include them on this occasion.

The inclusion of a monument in the list of those recommended as 'most worthy of preservation' follows the practice adopted by the Commissioners for Glamorgan.

Corrections or criticisms of the contents of this volume will be welcomed with a view to their possible inclusion in some future edition; they should be sent to the Secretary. Properly accredited persons may consult the records of the Commission at the headquarters at Edleston House, Queen's Road, Aberystwyth, Dyfed.

The contents of the volume are Crown Copyright, including most of the illustrations. Copies of these can be purchased through the Secretary of the Commission.

February 1985   R. J. C. ATKINSON

Editorial Note

The final form of the Inventory is the result of detailed discussion between the Commissioners and their staff. In the case of this Part, C. H. Houlder has acted as Editor. The work was compiled and written in its entirety by D. M. Browne. Particular mention must be made of the roles of certain other members of the Executive Staff during the investigations. Foremost among these was Dr. A. H. A. Hogg, former Secretary of the Commission, who devised much of the field-work scheme and was involved actively in the surveying both before and after his retirement. W. E. Griffiths, C. H. Houlder, D. K. Leighton and B. A. Malaws also made significant contributions to the surveying.

The maps and figures were drawn by the illustrating staff, B. A. Malaws and J. B. Durrant and the photographic work was by I. N. Wright.

Report

To the Queen's Most Excellent Majesty

May it please Your Majesty

We, the undersigned Commissioners, appointed to make an *Inventory of the Ancient and Historical Monuments and constructions connected with or illustrative of the contemporary culture, civilisation and conditions of life of the people in Wales from the earliest times, and to specify those which seem most worthy of preservation*, humbly submit to Your Majesty the following Report, being the seventeenth on the work of the Commission since its first appointment. This Report will accompany the second part of the first volume of the Inventory of Monuments in the County of Brecknock.

2. It is with deep regret that we record the death of our former Commissioner Sir Idris Llewelyn Foster and our fellow Commissioner Dr. Raymond Bernard Wood-Jones.

3. We have also to record the loss by retirement, on expiry of term of office, of our former Chairman Dr. Hubert Newman Savory, of the late Sir Idris Llewelyn Foster, and Dr. Arnold Joseph Taylor as well as the resignation of Professor David Gordon Tucker. We desire to record our grateful thanks to these for their excellent service.

4. We have to thank Your Majesty for the appointment of Professor Richard John Copland Atkinson to be Chairman of this Commission in succession to Dr. Hubert Newman Savory for a period of seven years from 1st January 1984, under Your Majesty's Royal Sign Manual dated 10th May 1984.

5. We also have to thank Your Majesty for the re-appointment under Your Majesty's Royal Sign Manual dated 10th May 1984 of the following Commissioners from the 1st January 1983: Mr. George Counsell Boon for ten years; Professor Edward Martyn Jope for three years; Professor Dewi-Prys Thomas for four years; Professor David Gordon Tucker for two years; Professor Glanmor Williams for eight years; as well as the appointment of the following Commissioners from 1st May 1983: Dr. Michael Ross Apted and Dr. Ronald William Brunskill, each for five years. We also have to thank Your Majesty for the appointment under

Your Majesty's Royal Sign Manual dated 30th July 1984 of the following Commissioners from the 1st June 1984: Professor David Ellis Evans, Dr. John Geraint Jenkins, and Mr. Jenkyn Beverley Smith, each for a period of ten years.

6. We have pleasure in reporting the completion of our enquiries into the Hill-forts and Related Structures and Roman Remains in the historic county of Brecknock, which we have retained as the framework of our report in preference to the administrative units which came into being in 1974. We have recorded 77 Monuments. Nearly 100 sites were visited.

7. We have prepared a full Inventory of these Monuments which will be issued as a non-Parliamentary publication.

8. We desire to record our special thanks for valuable assistance from the owners and occupants of land where monuments exist; also from Mrs. E. Alcock; Dr. J. L. Davies; Professor J. K. S. St. Joseph; Mr. R. E. Kay; Mr. Alistair Pearson; Mr. J. A. Taylor; Mr. D. R. Wilson.

9. We desire to express our acknowledgement of the good work of our executive staff; their names, and indications of their particular contributions, are included in the Inventory volume.

10. We humbly recommend to Your Majesty's notice the following monuments as most worthy of preservation:

Hill-forts and Related Structures

HF 1 Craig y Rhiwarth
HF 2 Clawdd British
HF 4 Craig y Ddinas
HF 5 Gelli-nedd
HF 6 Rhyd Uchaf
HF 7 Llwyncelyn-fawr
HF 9 Y Gaer, Defynnog
HF 10 Twyn y Gaer
HF 11 Twyn-y-gaer
HF 12 Enclosure N.E. of Ffinnant Isaf

HF 14 Corn y Fan
HF 18 Enclosure on Cefn Cilsanws
HF 19 Enclosure on Coedcae'r Ychain
HF 20 Enclosure E. of Nant Cwm Moel
HF 21 Y Gaer
HF 22 Enclosure S. of Nant Tarthwynni (I)
HF 23 Enclosure S. of Nant Tarthwynni (II)
HF 24 Enclosure N. of Tyle Clydach
HF 25 Enclosure in Coed y Brenin
HF 26 Coed y Caerau
HF 27 Enclosure W. of Nant Cwm Llwch
HF 28 Plas-y-gaer
HF 29 Coed Mawr
HF 30 Slwch Tump
HF 31 Twyn Llechfaen
HF 32 Coed Fenni-fach Camp
HF 33 Pen-y-crug
HF 35 Twyn-y-gaer
HF 36 Gaer Fach
HF 37 Gaer Fawr
HF 39 Coed Pen-twyn
HF 40 Penffawyddog
HF 42 Enclosure N.W. of Pantywenallt
HF 43 Tump Wood
HF 45 Coed y Gaer
HF 46 Enclosure W. of Allt yr Esgair
HF 47 Allt yr Esgair
HF 48 Enclosure near Caeau
HF 49 Earthwork on Cockit Hill

HF 50 Castell Dinas
HF 53 Pendre
HF 54 Enclosure E. of Pen-yr-allt
HF 55 Hillis
HF 57 The Gaer, Aberllynfi
HF 59 Llys-wen Enclosure
HF 62 Crug-y-gaer
HF 63 Coed Cefn
HF 64 Crug Hywel

Roman Military Works

RF 1 Fort at Caerau, Llangamarch
RF 2 Fort at Y Gaer, Brecon
RF 3 Fort at Pen-y-gaer
RMC 1 and 2 Marching camps on Y Pigwn
RMC 4 Marching camp at Beulah

Roman Roads

RR 1 Lengths of *Sarn Helen*: between Coelbren and Cefn Gwenynawg; between Plas-y-fan and the A4215; S. and E. of Felin Camlais.

Roman Civil Sites

RV 1 Site of the probable Roman villa at Maesderwen, Llanfrynach.

All of which we submit with our humble duty to Your Majesty.

(Signed) R. J. C. ATKINSON (Chairman)
M. R. APTED
G. C. BOON
R. W. BRUNSKILL
D. E. EVANS
J. G. JENKINS
E. M. JOPE
J. B. SMITH
D.-P. THOMAS
G. WILLIAMS
J. G. WILLIAMS
P. SMITH (Secretary)

List of Commissioners and Staff

During the preparation of this volume (1970-1985) the following Members, appointed by Royal Warrant, have served on the Commission:

William Francis Grimes, C.B.E., M.A., D.Litt., F.S.A., F.M.A., Emeritus Professor of Archaeology in the University of London and formerly Director of the Institute of Archaeology. (Chairman, retired 1979.)

Hubert Newman Savory, M.A., D.Phil., F.S.A., formerly Keeper of Archaeology in the National Museum of Wales. (Appointed Chairman 1979, retired 1983.)

Richard John Copland Atkinson, C.B.E., M.A., F.S.A., Emeritus Professor of Archaeology in University College, Cardiff. (Appointed Chairman 1984 for seven years.)

Michael Ross Apted, M.A., Ph.D., F.S.A., formerly Assistant Chief Inspector of Ancient Monuments of the Department of the Environment. (Appointed 1983 for five years.)

George Counsell Boon, B.A., F.S.A., F.R.Hist.S., F.R.N.S., Keeper of the Department of Archaeology and Numismatics in the National Museum of Wales. (Re-appointed 1984 for ten years.)

Ronald William Brunskill, M.A. Ph.D., F.S.A., Reader in Architecture in the University of Manchester. (Appointed 1983 for five years.)

David Ellis Evans, M.A., D.Phil., F.B.A., Jesus Professor of Celtic in the University of Oxford. (Appointed 1984 for 10 years.)

Sir Idris Llewelyn Foster, M.A., F.S.A., formerly Jesus Professor of Celtic in the University of Oxford. (Re-appointed 1981, retired 1983; died 1984.)

John Geraint Jenkins, M.A., D.Sc., F.S.A., F.M.A., Curator of the Welsh Industrial and Maritime Museum. (Appointed 1984 for 10 years.)

Edward Martyn Jope, M.A., B.Sc., F.B.A., F.S.A., Emeritus Professor of Archaeology in the Queen's University, Belfast. (Re-appointed 1984 for three years.)

John Davies Knatchbull Lloyd, O.B.E., D.L., J.P., M.A., LL.D., F.S.A., formerly Chairman of the Ancient Monuments Board for Wales. (Appointed 1967, retired 1973; died 1978.)

David Morgan Rees, O.B.E., M.A., F.S.A., formerly Keeper of Industry, National Museum of Wales, and Keeper in charge, The Welsh Industrial and Maritime Museum. (Appointed 1974; died 1978.)

Jenkyn Beverley Smith, M.A., F.R.Hist.S., Reader in Welsh History in the University College of Wales, Aberystwyth. (Appointed 1984 for ten years.)

Arnold Joseph Taylor, C.B.E., M.A., D.Litt., F.B.A., P.P.S.A., F.R.Hist.S., formerly Chief Inspector of Ancient Monuments and Historic Buildings. (Re-appointed 1980, retired 1983.)

Dewi-Prys Thomas, B. Arch., F.R.I.B.A., M.R.T.P.I., Emeritus Professor and formerly Head of The Welsh School of Architecture, Cardiff. (Re-appointed 1984 for four years.)

David Gordon Tucker, Ph.D., D.Sc., C. Eng., Emeritus Professor and Hon. Senior Research Fellow in the University of Birmingham. (Re-appointed 1983, retired 1984.)

Glanmor Williams, C.B.E., M.A., D.Litt., F.S.A., F.R.Hist.S., Emeritus Professor of History in the University College of Swansea. (Re-appointed 1984 for eight years.)

John Gwynn Williams, M.A., Emeritus Professor of Welsh History in the University College of North Wales, Bangor. (Re-appointed 1977 for ten years.)

Raymond Bernard Wood-Jones, M.A., B.Arch., Ph.D., F.S.A., A.R.I.B.A., formerly Reader in Architecture in the School of Architecture of the University of Manchester. (Re-appointed 1973 for ten years; died 1982.)

Staff

During the preparation of this volume (1970-1985) the following have served as Staff of the Commission:

Secretary

Mr. A. H. A. Hogg, C.B.E., D.Litt., M.A., F.S.A. (to 1973)
Mr. P. Smith, B.A.. F.S.A. (Investigator to 1973)

Principal Investigators

Mr. C. H. Houlder, M.A., F.S.A.
Mr. W. G. Thomas, M.A., F.S.A.

Investigators

Mr. C. S. Briggs, B.A., Ph.D., F.S.A. (from 1973)
Mr. H. Brooksby, F.S.A.
Mr. D. M. Browne, M.A., M.I.F.A. (from 1975)
Mr. M. Griffiths, B.A., D.Phil. (from 1981)
Mr. W. E. Griffiths, M.A., F.S.A. (to 1980)
Mr. D. B. Hague, A.R.I.B.A., F.S.A. (to 1981)
Mr. S. R. Hughes, B.A., M.Phil., F.S.A. (from 1973)
Mr. D. K. Leighton, B.Sc. (from 1983)
Mr. A. J. Parkinson, M.A., F.S.A.
Mr. D. J. Roberts, N.D.D. (from 1981)
Mr. C. J. Spurgeon, B.A., F.S.A.
Mr. H. J. Thomas, M.A., F.S.A.

National Monuments Record Staff

Mrs. S. L. Evans (from 1977)
Mr. N. J. Glanville (from 1983)
Mrs. E. T. Richards (to 1978)
Miss H. A. Sherrington (Malaws), B.Lib. (from 1977)

Field Recording Staff

Mr. B. A. Malaws (from 1984)
Mr. D. J. Percival (from 1984)
Mr. R. F. Suggett, B.A., B.Litt. (from 1984)

Illustrating Staff

Mrs. L. M. Aiano, B.A. (to 1976)
Mr. C. Baker (to 1973)
Mrs. J. B. Durrant (from 1979)
Mr. J. D. Goodband (to 1983)
Miss D. C. Long, B.Sc. (from 1984)
Mr. B. A. Malaws (to 1984)
Mr. M. Parry, A.S.A.I. (from 1984)
Mr. D. J. Roberts, N.D.D. (to 1981)
Mr. I. Scott-Taylor, S.I.A.D. (from 1984)
Mr. G. A. Ward (from 1973)

Photographic Staff

Mr. D. M. S. Evans (to 1979)
Mrs. F. L. James (from 1983)
Mr. R. G. Nicol
Mr. C. J. Parrott (to 1983)
Mr. I. N. Wright, A.I.I.P. (from 1979)

Administrative and Clerical Staff

Miss B. M. Davies (to 1973)
Mr. P. St. J. L. Davies (to 1974)
Miss C. A. Griffiths
Mr. D. M. Hughes (from 1978)
Mrs. L. M. Jones (from 1980)
Miss S. E. Nicholson (to 1980)
Mrs. C. L. Sorensen (to 1978)
Miss D. M. Ward
Mr. E. Whatmore (to 1978)
Miss E. M. Williams (1980)

List of Ecclesiastical Parishes, with incidence of Monuments

This list corresponds with the map on p. xxii, and indicates the ecclesiastical subdivision of Brecknock into parishes as it stood c. 1850, before any of the changes of names and boundaries which have taken place for administrative purposes (cf. map on p. xxiv and list on p. xxv).

Ecclesiastical parishes are noted at the end of Inventory entries, distinguished by the letter (E) when the monument concerned stands in a civil parish of a different name (C). Spellings used are as shown on the left, generally agreeing with those used on O.S. maps current in 1970. The only departures from this practice (other than cases simply involving hyphens or capitals) are indicated by the addition of the map spellings in square brackets. The Welsh forms, which follow the recommendations of the Board of Celtic Studies, are given on the right only when they differ from those already adopted for use in this Inventory.

No.	Parish name used	Correct Welsh form	Monument Nos.
1	Aberllynfi		HF 57, HF 58, RU 1
2	Aberysgir [Aberyscir]		HF 12, RPC 3
3	Allt-mawr		—
4	Battle	Y Batel	—
5	Bronllys		—
6	Builth	Llanfair-ym-Muallt	—
7	Cantref		HF 28, HF 29
8	Cathedin [Cathedine]		—
9	Crickadarn	Crucardarn	—
10	Crickhowell	Crucywel	HF 64
11	Defynnog [Devynock]		HF 8, HF 9
12	Garthbrengi [Garthbrengy]		—
13	Glasbury	Y Clas-ar-Wy	—
14	Glyntawe		—
15	Gwenddwr		—
16	Hay	Y Gelli	—
17	Llanafan Fawr		HF 17
18	Llanafan Fechan		—
19	Llanbedr Ystrad Yw [Llanbedr Ystradwy]		HF 64
20	Llanddeti [Llanddetty]		HF 21, HF 42, HF 43
21	Llan-ddew		—
22	Llanddewi Abergwesyn		—
23	Llanddewi'r-cwm		HF 38
24	Llanddulas [Llandulas]		—
25	Llandeilo'r-fân		HF 2
26	Llandyfaelog Fach [Llandefaelog Fach]		—
27	Llandyfaelog Tre'r-graig		—

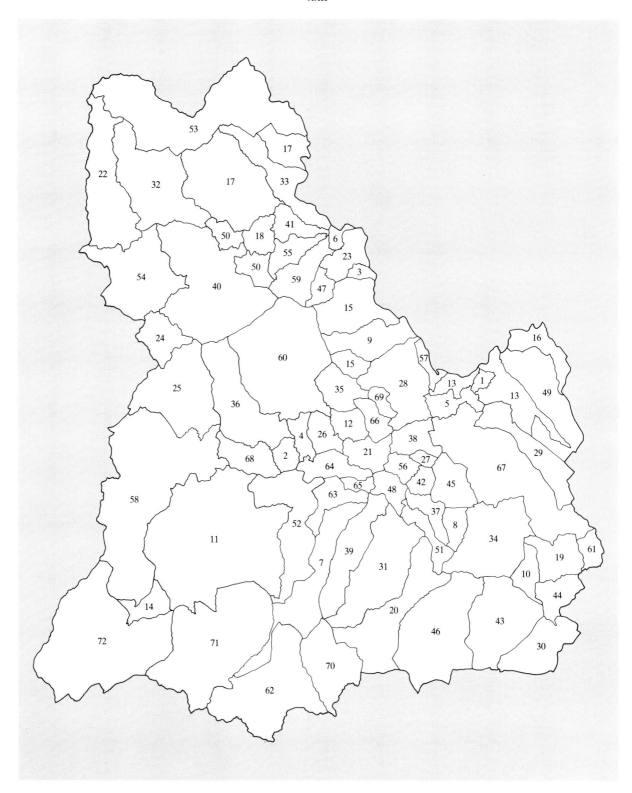

2 Ecclesiastical parishes: the numbers on this map correspond to those in the list of ecclesiastical parishes on p. xxi

No.	Parish name used	Correct Welsh form	Monument Nos.
28	Llandyfalle [Llandefalle]		HF 34, HF 56
29	Llaneleu [Llanelieu]		—
30	Llanelli [Llanelly]		HF 60, HF 61, HF 62
31	Llanfigan	Llanfeugan	HF 22, HF 23, HF 24, HF 44
32	Llanfihangel Abergwesyn		—
33	Llanfihangel Brynpabuan		
34	Llanfihangel Cwm Du		HF 41, HF 45, RF 3
35	Llanfihangel Fechan		HF 35
36	Llanfihangel Nant Brân		HF 13
37	Llanfihangel Tal-y-llyn		—
38	Llanfilo		HF 51, HF 54, HF 55
39	Llanfrynach		HF 25, HF 26, RV 1
40	Llangamarch [Llangammarch]		RF 1, RMC 4, RPC 1, RPC 2
41	Llanganten		—
42	Llangasty Tal-y-llyn		HF 47
43	Llangatwg [Llangattock]		HF 39, HF 40
44	Llangenni [Llangenny]		HF 63
45	Llan-gors [Llangorse]		HF 48, HF 49
46	Llangynidr		—
47	Llangynog		—
48	Llanhamlach		HF 31
49	Llanigan		—
50	Llanllywenfel [Llanlleonfel]		—
51	Llansanffraid [Llansantffraed]		HF 46, HF 47
52	Llansbyddyd [Llanspyddid]		HF 6, HF 7, HF 10, HF 27
53	Llanwrthwl		—
54	Llanwrtyd		HF 3
55	Llanynys [Llanynis]		—
56	Llan-y-wern [Llanwern]		—
57	Llys-wen		HF 59
58	Llywel		RMC 1, RMC 2
59	Maesmynys [Maesmynis]		—
60	Merthyr Cynog		HF 14, HF 15, HF 16, HF 36, HF 37
61	Partrishow	Patrisio	—
62	Penderyn		HF 4
63	St. David Brecon	Aberhonddu	—
64	St. John the Evangelist Brecon	Aberhonddu	HF 30, HF 32, HF 33, RF 2
65	St. Mary Brecon	Aberhonddu	HF 30
66	Talach-ddu		—
67	Talgarth		HF 50, HF 52, HF 53
68	Trallwng [Trallong]		HF 11
69	Trawsgoed [Trawscoed]		—
70	Vaynor	Y Faenor	HF 18, HF 19, HF 20
71	Ystradfellte		HF 5, RMC 3
72	Ystradgynlais		HF 1, RCS 1

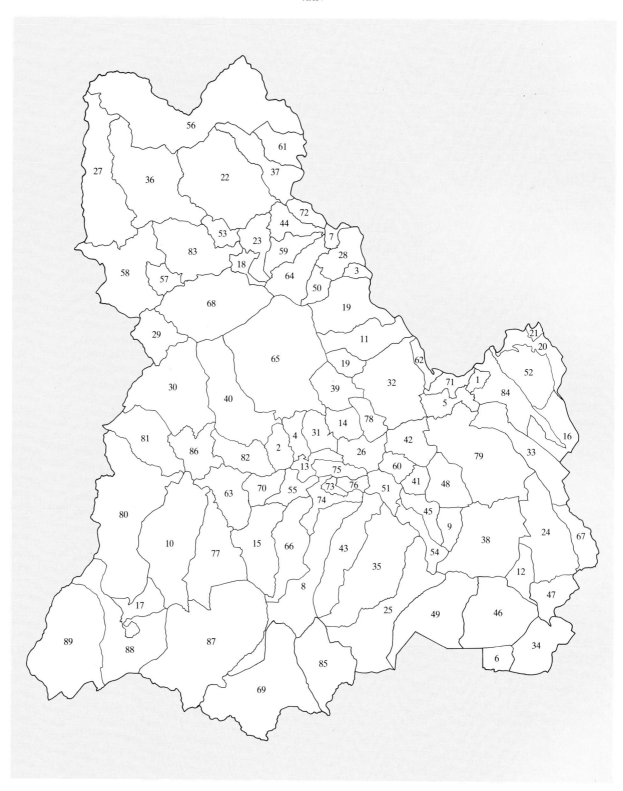

3 Civil parishes: the numbers on this map correspond to those in the list of civil parishes on p. xxv

List of Civil Parishes, with incidence of Monuments

This list corresponds with the map on p. xxiv, and indicates the civil subdivision of Brecknock into parishes as it stood at the end of 1970. Some boundaries and names have undergone changes since the original adoption of the ecclesiastical pattern for secular administrative purposes (*cf.* map on p. xxii and list on p. xxi), and modifications continue to be made.

Civil parishes are noted at the end of Inventory entries, distinguished by the letter (C) when the monument concerned stands in an ecclesiastical parish of a different name (E). Spellings used are as shown on the left, in general agreeing with those used on the O.S. 1:100,000 Administrative Areas map, 1971. The only departures from this practice (other than cases simply involving hyphens or capitals) are indicated by the addition of the O.S. spelling in square brackets. The Welsh forms, which follow the recommendations of the Board of Celtic Studies, are given on the right only when they differ from those already adopted for use in this Inventory.

No.	Parish name used	Correct Welsh form	Monument Nos.
1	Aberllynfi		HF 57, HF 58, RU 1
2	Aberysgir [Aberyscir]		HF 12, HF13 RPC 3
3	Allt-mawr		—
4	Battle	Y Batel	—
5	Bronllys		—
6	Bryn-mawr		—
7	Builth	Llanfair-ym-Muallt	—
8	Cantref		HF 28, HF 29
9	Cathedin [Cathedine]		—
10	Crai [Cray]		HF 9
11	Crickadarn	Crucadarn	—
12	Crickhowell	Crucywel	HF 64
13	Fenni-fach	Y Fenni-fach	HF 32, HF 33, RF 2
14	Garthbrengi [Garthbrengy]		—
15	Glyn		HF 8
16	Glyn-fach		—
17	Glyntawe		—
18	Gwarafog		—
19	Gwenddwr		—
20	Hay Rural	Y Gelli	—
21	Hay Urban	Y Gelli	—
22	Llanafan Fawr		—
23	Llanafan Fechan		—
24	Llanbedr Ystrad Yw [Llanbedr Ystradwy]		HF 64
25	Llanddeti [Llanddetty]		HF 21, HF 42, HF 43
26	Llan-ddew		—
27	Llanddewi Abergwesyn		—

No.	Parish name used	Correct Welsh form	Monument Nos.
28	Llanddewi'r-cwm		HF 38
29	Llanddulas [Llandulas]		—
30	Llandeilo'r-fân		HF 2
31	Llandyfaelog Fach [Llandefaelog Fach]		—
32	Llandyfalle [Llandefalle]		HF 34, HF 56
33	Llaneleu [Llanelieu]		—
34	Llanelli [Llanelly]		HF 60, HF 61, HF 62
35	Llanfigan	Llanfeugan	HF 22, HF 23, HF 24, HF 44
36	Llanfihangel Abergwesyn		—
37	Llanfihangel Brynpabuan		—
38	Llanfihangel Cwm Du		HF 41, HF 45, RF 3
39	Llanfihangel Fechan		HF 35
40	Llanfihangel Nant Brân		—
41	Llanfihangel Tal-y-llyn		—
42	Llanfilo		HF 51, HF 54, HF 55
43	Llanfrynach		HF 25, HF 26, RV 1
44	Llanganten		—
45	Llangasty Tal-y-llyn		HF 47
46	Llangatwg [Llangattock]		HF 39, HF 40
47	Llangenni [Llangenny]		HF 63
48	Llan-gors [Llangorse]		HF 48, HF 49
49	Llangynidr		—
50	Llangynog		—
51	Llanhamlach		HF 31
52	Llanigan		—
53	Llanllywenfel [Llanlleonfel]		—
54	Llansanffraid [Llansantffraed]		HF 46, HF 47
55	Llansbyddyd [Llanspyddid]		—
56	Llanwrthwl		—
57	Llanwrtyd		—
58	Llanwrtyd Without		HF 3
59	Llanynys [Llanynis]		—
60	Llan-y-wern [Llanwern]		—
61	Llysdinam		HF 17
62	Llys-wen		HF 59
63	Maes-car		—
64	Maesmynys [Maesmynis]		—
65	Merthyr Cynog		HF 14, HF 15, HF 16, HF 36, HF 37
66	Modrydd		HF 6, HF 7, HF 27
67	Patrishow	Patrisio	—
68	Penbuallt		—
69	Penderyn		HF 4
70	Pen-pont		HF 10
71	Pipton		—
72	Rhosferig		—
73	St. David Within Brecon	Aberhonddu	—
74	St. David Without Brecon	Aberhonddu	—

No.	Parish name used	Correct Welsh form	Monument Nos.
75	St. John the Evangelist Brecon	Aberhonddu	HF 30
76	St. Mary Brecon	Aberhonddu	HF 30
77	Senni [Senny]		—
78	Talach-ddu		—
79	Talgarth		HF 50, HF 52, HF 53
80	Traean-glas [Traianglas]		RMC 1, RMC 2
81	Traean-mawr [Traianmawr]		—
82	Trallwng [Trallong]		HF 11
83	Treflys		RF 1, RMC 4, RPC 1, RPC 2
84	Tre-goed a Felindre [Tregoyd and Velindre]		—
85	Vaynor	Y Faenor	HF 18, HF 19, HF 20
86	Ysclydach	Is-clydach	—
87	Ystradfellte		HF 5, RMC 3
88	Ystradgynlais Higher	Ystradgynlais Uchaf	HF 1, RCS 1
89	Ystradgynlais Lower	Ystradgynlais Isaf	—

Abbreviated Titles of References

Ant. J.	*Antiquaries Journal.* Society of Antiquaries, London.
A.P.	Aerial photographs, indicating sortie, date, and frame no., refer to the national air cover available at higher planning authorities. See also C.U.A.P.
Arch. Camb.	*Archaeologia Cambrensis.* The Cambrian Archaeological Association.
Arch. in Wales	*Archaeology in Wales.* Council for British Archaeology, Group 2.
B.B.C.S.	*Bulletin of the Board of Celtic Studies.* University of Wales.
B.L.	British Library, London.
Carm. Antiq.	*The Carmarthen Antiquary.* The Carmarthenshire Antiquarian Society.
C.U.A.P.	Cambridge University Collection of Aerial Photographs.
H.M.S.O.	Her Majesty's Stationery Office, London/Edinburgh.
I.A.	Iron Age.
Inv. Glam.	R.C.A.M. (Wales), *An Inventory of the Ancient Monuments in Glamorgan* (Vol. I, 1976, H.M.S.O.).
T. Jones, *Hist. of Brecknock*	Several editions: Theophilus Jones, *A history of Brecknock* (Brecknock, 1805-9); (Brecknock, 1898); (Brecknock: Glanusk ed. 1909, 1911, 1930).
J.R.S.	*Journal of Roman Studies.* Society for the Promotion of Roman Studies.
Lewis, *Top Dict.*	S. Lewis, *A Topographical Dictionary of Wales* (2 vols., London, 1833).
Lhuyd, *Parochialia*	E. Lhuyd, *Parochialia* (3 parts, *Arch. Camb.* supplements, 1909-11, ed. R. H. Morris).
Manning, *Usk*	W. H. Manning, *Report on the Excavations at Usk 1965-1976: The Fortress Excavations 1968-1971* (Cardiff, 1981).
Margary, *Roman Roads*	I. D. Margary, *Roman Roads in Britain* (2nd edn., London, 1967).
M.P.B.W.	Ministry of Public Building and Works. *Cadw* (Welsh Office) is now the statutory authority.
N.L.W.	National Library of Wales, Aberystwyth.
N.M.R.	National Monuments Record, Aberystwyth.
N.M.W.	National Museum of Wales, Cardiff.
O.D.	Ordnance Datum.
O.S.	Ordnance Survey.
P.P.S.	*Proceedings of the Prehistoric Society,* London.
R.	Roman.
R.C.A.M.	The Royal Commission on Ancient and Historical Monuments in Wales.
Roman Frontier	V. E. Nash-Williams, *The Roman Frontier in Wales* (2nd edn., revised under the direction of M. G. Jarrett, Cardiff, 1969).

R.I.B.	R. G. Collingwood and R. P. Wright, *The Roman Inscriptions of Britain: I, Inscriptions on Stone* (Oxford, 1965).
S	In 'Hill-forts and Related Structures' (HF 1-64), indicates number in H. N. Savory, 'List of hillforts...in Brecknockshire', *B.B.C.S.,* XIV, i (Nov. 1950), pp. 69-75; supplement *ibid.,* XV, iii (Nov. 1953), p. 230 and unnumbered additions to the list in *Brycheiniog,* I (1955), p. 119, *f.n.* 132.
Trans. Cymmr.	*Transactions of the Honourable Society of Cymmrodorion.*
Trans. Radnor Soc.	*Transactions of the Radnorshire Society.*

Presentation of Material

General Arrangement

Part ii of Volume I of the Inventory of Ancient Monuments in Brycheiniog (Brecknock) deals with hill-forts and related enclosures and with structures and finds of Roman date. Part i will deal with pre-Iron Age structures and non-defensive sites of uncertain but probably pre-Norman date.

Monuments Included

Some structures cannot be classified satisfactorily by surface investigation, either because of their condition or because they present unusual features. The decision whether to include such marginal cases in the Inventory can be based only on a subjective judgement as to whether they are more likely than not to be genuine; any uncertainty is indicated in the discussion of classification, and rejected sites are listed at the ends of sections.

Form of Entries

These give a detailed description, illustrated where necessary. This is followed by the name of the parish; where the present civil parish differs from the original ecclesiastical parish both are named and indicated by (C) and (E) respectively. The last line gives the sheet number of the current 1:10,000 O.S. map; the National Grid reference, to eight figures, of the approximate centre of the monument or group; the date of survey, or of the most recent visit if no plan is given. Information on condition is conveyed in the entries. For the monuments described in this volume, the structural materials used were almost invariably obtained in the vicinity and are specified only when this is known not to be the case.

Surveying and Representation

The majority of the sites are illustrated by a plan reproduced wherever feasible at a scale of 1:1000. Most of the hill-forts were the subject of fresh surveys by the staff of the Commission using the techniques described by A. H. A. Hogg in his *Surveying for Archaeologists and Other Fieldworkers* (London, 1980) and his expectations of error apply. Thirty-eight sites (HF 1, 2, 5, 6, 7, 9-12, 18-21, 25-29, 31, 32, 35-40, 42, 43, 45, 46, 48, 49, 51, 53, 54, 56, 62, 63) were surveyed using chain and tape technique only. At four sites (HF 4, 14, 50, 59) some use was made of a theodolite to establish the survey framework, with detail measurement by chain and tape. At five sites (HF 30, 33, 47, 55, 64) a plot was made photogrammetrically from specially commissioned aerial photographs and the details checked in the field and added to by chain and tape surveying. Twelve sites (HF 8, 13, 15, 16, 17, 34, 41, 44, 52, 58, 60, 61) were inspected in the field but not considered worthy of a measured survey. One site (HF 3) could not be visited and is described from air photos. Three sites (HF 22, 23, 24) were visited but not surveyed, the existing O.S. Antiquity Model being considered adequate. Dr. Savory's survey of HF 57 is used in preference to a new survey as the site has been eroded considerably since his excavations. The metric system of measurement was used in most cases.

Sections across all or part of an individual site are given where they enhance the understanding of its appearance and position. Only the larger and more important sites have been contoured, as in most cases it has been felt that the amount of labour involved in undertaking this form of survey was not commensurate with the amount of archaeological information eventually portrayed. The general topographic setting of each site is illustrated by the small relief maps accompanying most descriptions.[1] In a few cases, e.g. HF 7, detail of the natural slopes in the immediate vicinity has been sketched in with the aid of O.S. maps to give an accurate impression of the natural topography.

To illustrate the Roman section the most up-to-date O.S. plans have been adapted after ground inspection. Several published excavation plans and section drawings have also been utilised. Inscriptions have been redrawn from the originals.

ANCIENT FEATURES

Slope

Bank & ditch (Roman sites)

Stone revetment

Line of ill-defined earthwork

Rock-cut feature

Stone rubble

Shelf-edge

Track

NATURAL FEATURES

Slope

Contours in metres above O.D.

River or stream

Crag or cliff

MODERN FEATURES

Road

Track

Outline of disturbance (quarrying, etc.)

Fence, hedge, wall, bank or ditch

Building

4 Conventions used on plans

Numbering of Entries

The book is divided into two main sections: Hill-forts and Roman remains; in the latter section the monuments are grouped according to type. Each group has been assigned letters related to its name (e.g. RF = Roman Forts), used as a prefix for serial numbering of the monuments in the group. The order of sites within the groups is determined by their National Grid references, the O.S. system with which every serious reader will be familiar. The county is considered to be divided from west to east into a series of vertical strips 10 km wide corresponding to the eastings SN 7, SN 8, SN 9, SO 0, SO 1 and SO 2. Sites within any type group are first separated according to the strip in which they occur. Site no. 1 is then designated as the most southerly of those in the most westerly strip. No. 2 is the next site to the north. Sites are assigned numbers until all within the particular 10 km strip are accounted for. The same process is repeated starting with the most southerly site in the next strip to the east and so on until all sites are numbered. To keep the system simple no account is taken of the quarter sheet division of 10 km squares used in O.S. 1:10,000 maps. The strictly numerical system is adopted for its simplicity and in the knowledge that no other ordering attempted in the past has proved more satisfactory.

Names

Most early structures are anonymous, and are indicated on the map merely in descriptive terms. Where a traditional name is known, or a specific modern name is well-established, this heads the entry. In other cases, the name of an adjacent farm, village or natural feature is used for convenience of reference, even though its correct application may be to some other object. Unless there is a good reason for a change the names used by previous writers are retained.

Distribution Maps

The maps which accompany each section are intended primarily to show the distribution of the monuments in relation to relief and drainage. The individual monuments shown on these maps are not numbered, since to do so would obscure the distribution pattern at the scale used. Even one inch to a mile is not a large enough scale to permit the exact location of small sites. The position of any particular monument, however, can be precisely fixed by its grid reference. Conversely, if the six-figure reference of a monument of a particular type is already known, its descriptive entry can be found by use of the Index of Grid References (pp. 188-9); some structures may have escaped record, and information about these would be appreciated (see p. xv).

Parishes

The numbers of the monuments within each parish are given on pp. xxi-xxvii. Separate lists are given for Civil and Ecclesiastical parishes; their boundaries are shown on the maps on p. xxiv and p. xxii. The Civil parishes are taken as at the end of 1970. The boundaries of the Ecclesiastical parishes are those of c. 1850.

Superimposed Structures of Different Periods

Occasionally structures of widely different date are superimposed. In such cases, the structure relevant to the present volume is described in detail, and only a short summary description is given of the other remains.

[1] Contour values and intervals are in feet because at the time of preparation metric contouring was not generally available.

Inventory

Introductory Note

Unfortunately there is not enough evidence available to permit a detailed chronological account of the development of late prehistoric fortified sites in Brecknock. The enclosures can be classified into several different groups (pp. 9-20), but within these groups it is likely that the sites vary in date of foundation and length of occupation. Several enclosures are included in this Inventory which belong on the borders of the broad classificatory term 'hill-fort'[1] but are discussed here because they share some of the characteristics of enclosures that belong unquestionably in the class, and are useful examples of the difficulties in achieving a thoroughly consistent classification.

It is as yet uncertain that any of the Brecknock forts is as early as the first, later Bronze Age, phase of hill-fort building in Wales which as far as we know seems to be confined to the northern Marches.[2] The second major phase of construction is dated from the sixth century B.C. onwards in the Marches, and is considered to be a reflection of warfare between the established population and groups of immigrant warriors and their followers bringing new ideas of fortification. Features of this new tradition, such as deep inturned entrances, are found in a few Brecknock forts but do not necessarily imply either direct penetration by the builders of the Marches forts or the same early date, for it is known that these traits have a long history. Nevertheless, the ease with which the Usk-Llynfi Basin can be penetrated from the nuclear area of Herefordshire must be borne in mind, and the discovery of early sites would not be surprising.

The majority of the small embanked enclosures in Brecknock were probably built by single families or small family groups of a long-established native population. Construction of such homesteads may have begun in the late Bronze Age, and continued throughout the Iron Age and into the Roman period. True forts, larger and with multiple, close-spaced 'dump' ramparts, were probably built at a late phase in the pre-Roman Iron Age by the existing population.

The area was part of the tribal lands of the Silures at the time of the Roman penetration of Wales.[3] The number of troops committed by the Romans against this tribe, and its victory over a legion on one occasion and other successful engagements, imply a substantial population, certainly more than could be represented by the number of defended enclosures known, and it seems likely that many undefended sites must remain to be discovered, probably in the lands that lie below 300 m but above the level of river flooding in the broader valleys.

Evidence for slighting of the ramparts at The Gaer, Aberllynfi (HF 57) may refer to the final conquest of the Silures undertaken by Julius Frontinus c. A.D. 75. Three marching camps probably belong to these campaigns. A fourth, RMC 2, possibly was constructed later, in peacetime. The three forts in the county are all Flavian foundations. At Brecon Gaer (RF 2) the masonry of part of the defences and three of the gates has been restored and may be inspected by the public. It is possible that there remain undiscovered fortlets between these forts and bases outside the county, and a fort in the Wye valley near the eastern border. The fragmentarily known road system must have been founded in connection with the fort network with some later modifications. The three probable 'practice camps' are poorly preserved.

Much of the area probably remained under direct military control throughout the Roman period. Evidence of civilian occupation is slight. There are hints of civil settlements outside the forts. Part of an important fourth century villa is known at Llanfrynach (RV 1) from an eighteenth century excavation but no intelligible surface remains may now be seen. Occupation of a cave is attested in the south-west, but otherwise we are totally ignorant of the native settlement pattern in the period. Evidence of expanded arable cultivation, perhaps in response to demands from the Roman army, has been obtained in cores from Llyn Syfaddan (Llan-gors Lake).

[1] A. H. A. Hogg, *British Hill-forts. An Index* (Oxford: BAR, 1979), p. 1.

[2] For recent summaries of knowledge of hill-forts in Wales, see H. N. Savory in D. W. Harding (ed.), *Hillforts* (London, 1976), pp. 237-291; H. N. Savory in J. A. Taylor (ed.), *Culture and Environment in Prehistoric Wales* (Oxford: BAR, 1980), pp. 287-310.

[3] The uninscribed gold coin of the Dobunni from 'Dinas', Brecknock may not mean that this tribe held any sway in the area. *Monmouth Antiquary,* III, i (1970-1), p. 63. Mr. G. C. Boon is of the opinion that 'Dinas' is almost certainly the house at 05932738, on the right bank of the Usk about 2 km downstream of Brecon bridge, and not Castell Dinas or Dinas Farm suggested by D. F. Allen ('The Origins of Coinage in Britain: A Reappraisal' in S. S. Frere (ed.), *Problems of the Iron Age in Southern Britain* (London, 1961), p. 246) because the additional element in the place-name would not be shed to leave only 'Dinas'. Adapted, with permission, from Mr. Boon's contribution on Dobunnic coinage in B. E. Vyner, *Excavations at Caldicot* (forthcoming).

The Physical Background

The major land forms of modern Brecknock do not differ significantly from those encountered by its inhabitants in the pre-Roman Iron Age and Roman period. According to modern authorities[1] this landscape emerged and was sculpted during the Neogene Period (26-2 million years ago) with subsequent glacial modification.

Three main land forms exist within the county:

1. *Mountains*, the result of late Cenozoic uplift and characteristically rising to over 600 m high with the elevation and ruggedness of individual summits consequent on the degree to which erosive forces have been controlled by the resistance, thickness and dip of the component strata. Two topographic zones,[2] Fforest Fawr and the Brecon Beacons, and the Black Mountains, belong to this category.

2. *Dissected Plateaux*. The general aspect is of rounded uplands dissected by steep, narrow valleys. There has been considerable debate as to how this form originated,[3] whether by sub-aerial erosion or marine planation. Recent authorities have tended towards the view that the plateaux represent marine platforms on which the present drainage pattern developed by extending seawards as the land mass emerged. Sub-aerial erosion has subsequently altered the platforms considerably. Three areas are of this type: The Northern Plateau, part of the High Plateau of Central Wales; the Epynt Plateau, and the Coalfield Fringe.

3. *Valley Lowlands*. The two main zones are the Builth-Llanwrtyd Depression and the Usk-Llynfi Basin.

The strike trends of the rock strata of the landscape were formed long before its final emergence. The extensive folding of the Caledonian orogeny was responsible for the north-east to south-west trend of Mynydd Epynt and the land to the north. South of Epynt, the east-west trend is a result of later movements of the Hercynian orogeny towards the end of the Palaeozoic.

The mountains of *Fforest Fawr* and the *Brecon Beacons* stretching across the south of the county are composed of resistant beds of Old Red Sandstone. They form the northern rim of the South Wales coalfield major syncline with an east-west trend. A string of peaks rises to over 600 m, Pen y Fan being the highest at 886 m. The beds have a long low dip to the south of between 10 and 20 degrees and the capping deposit, the hard conglomerate of the Plateau Beds, gives the mountains their tableland surface[4] behind the spectacular escarpment of their northern edge. Magnificent cirques in the north escarpment and over-deepened valleys are the major evidence of glacial erosion of the Neogene landform. The more developed river valleys running south are all narrow and steep-sided and there is virtually no level land not subject to inundation. A multiplicity of short streams with steep gradients drain the north escarpment. The Neath and Tawe follow structural lines but others, especially those cutting the Coalfield escarpment to the south, do not relate to the underlying geology and are classically superimposed.

Geologically the *Black Mountains* in the east of the county are composed like the Beacons of strata of Old Red Sandstone with a gentle dip to the south-south-east. The prominent north-west escarpment, which is less severely dissected than that of the Beacons, rises to over 700 m and has a north-east to south-west trend. Some peaks of the interfluves of the massif attain over 800 m. Pen Cerrig-calch overlooking Crickhowell is an eroded remnant (outlier) of Carboniferous Limestone capping Old Red Sandstone. Long steep-sided river valleys running south-south-east dissect the plateau-like surface of the mountains into narrow ridges. The stepping and terracing of the tablelands have been caused by erosion of differentially resistant sandstones, as has the ribbing and terracing of the valley sides. The north escarpment shows three major breaks of slope which correspond to different degrees of weathering of the capping Brownstones and the lower *Psammosteus* limestones and thin sandstones. The amount of land in the zone available for arable agriculture is extremely limited.

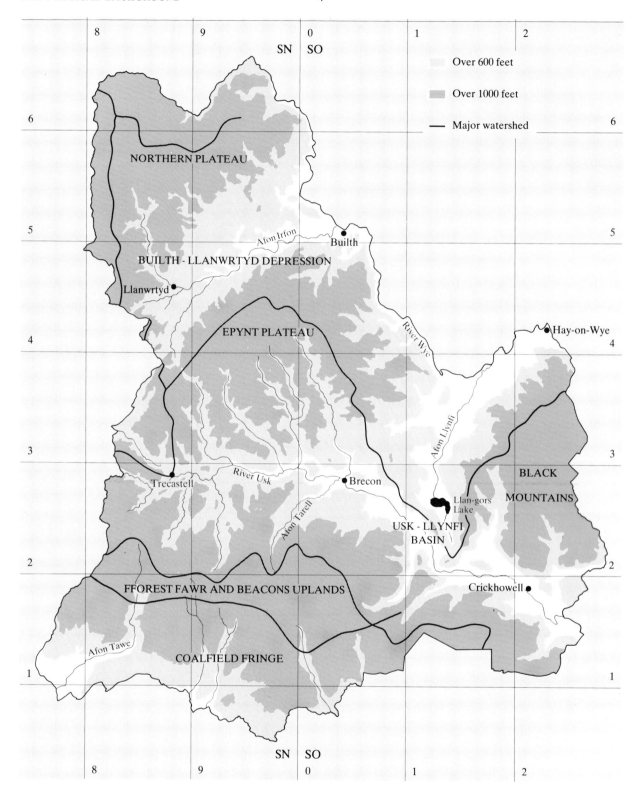

5 Topographical zones

The Ordovician shales, grits and conglomerates of the *Northern Plateau* are considerably folded and the trend of the country coincides with that of the main Tywi anticlinal belt and the smaller Rhiwnant anticline to the north-west. Volcanic rocks outcrop along the crest of the Tywi anticline north of Llanwrtyd, creating rugged crags. The highest ground such as Drygarn Fawr (641 m) and Cerrig-llwyd y Rhestr is formed by strike ridges of conglomerates. A series of consequent streams in narrow steep-sided valleys running south-east dissect the plateau. Glaciation has modified the landscape and the Irfon valley has been especially affected by a major ice-flow from the Pumlumon-Drygarn glacier. The ribbing observed on valley sides and hilltops is due to differential erosion of the rocks, the quartz grits and some mudstones being particularly resistant. Relief, elevation and poor-quality soils are among the factors that have made the region generally unsuitable for crop production.

The upper surface of the *Epynt Plateau* is formed by eroded Red Marls of the Old Red Sandstone. The trends of the crests of the massif (up to 474 m above O.D. at Drum-ddu) conform to the strike of the folded basal Silurian rocks. The underlying structure exerts less influence on the surface appearance of the plateau but the dip of the Ludlow series of the Silurian system of rocks accounts for the steep slopes of the north-west escarpment. The rounded surface of the plateau tilts gently south-east and is dissected by several substantial streams flowing in that direction in valleys deepened by glacial erosion. Except towards their mouths, the valleys contain only very small amounts of flattish land.

At the *Coalfield Fringe* along the southern boundary of the county run escarpments of Carboniferous Limestone capped by steep bluffs of resistant Millstone Grit roughly parallel to the north-facing scarp of Fforest Fawr and the Brecon Beacons. A height of over 600 m is reached at Cefn yr Ystrad north of Merthyr Tudful and other parts of the plateau stand between 360 and 550 m above O.D. The general east-west structural trend is broken by the folding and faulting of the Cribarth disturbance (upper Tawe) and the Neath disturbance. The latter features determine the course of the drainage but elsewhere the streams and rivers cut across the trend of the underlying geology and appear to be superimposed. Valleys have been over-deepened by glacial action, and ice moulding forms are visible in the Basal Grit south of Fforest Fawr. Rock screes created by frost shattering are also evident. Features of the Carboniferous Limestone

areas are swallow holes, depressions caused by the disintegration of the roofs of subterranean caverns. Gorges have also been created in this way. Impressive caves such as those of the upper Tawe valley represent former underground river channels, and modern examples of subterranean rivers include the Mellte near Ystradfellte. Fine waterfalls occur in the south-west of the county at fault lines and where the main stream has outpaced its tributary in incising its bed.

A narrow belt of the Wenlock Series of the Silurian system of rocks extends south-west from Builth along the edge of the Tywi anticline and forms the underlying geology of the *Builth-Llanwrtyd Depression*. The zone is drained by the major subsequent river Irfon running close to the steep north-west scarp of Mynydd Epynt. The landscape between the left bank of the Irfon and the south-east edge of the Northern Plateau is broken, hilly country with rounded summits between about 200 and 300 m above O.D. Several well-developed streams flowing to the Irfon south-east from the Plateau dissect the area. The soils of the region are less naturally fertile than those of the Old Red Sandstone-based valleys.

The *Usk-Llynfi Basin* together with part of the upper Wye valley were the focus of settlement in later prehistoric and Roman times and remain so today. The Basin is formed largely from the relatively easily eroded Red Marls of the Old Red Sandstone with a gentle southwards dip. Glacial erosion has modified the profiles of valleys but there has also been substantial deposition evidenced by till, and fluvio-glacial landforms found include melt-water channels, kanes and kettle holes. Llan-gors Lake, through which the Llynfi flows, occupies a rock basin scoured-out by ice and dammed by glacial deposits. Generally fertile Brown Earth soils have developed on the superficial deposits of the area.

Between its source in the hills of the Carmarthen-shire borderlands and Brecon, the Usk flows in a narrow, steep-sided valley. From the north-west the river receives the waters of the streams following the even more restricted deep valleys cutting across the Epynt plateau. To the south, between the river and the mountain escarpment, is dissected round-topped hill country between about 300 and 400 m above O.D. The flood plain of the Usk broadens between Brecon and Tal-y-bont but, as with most of the valley, this was probably subject to seasonal flooding in ancient as in modern times and was therefore unsuitable for habitation.

The wedge of undulating countryside drained to the north-east by the Llynfi and Dulas rivers has hilltops rising to 300 m and more above O.D., but generally gradients present few difficulties for agriculture, particularly as the Wye valley is approached.

Except at confluences where more gently sloping land is available the peripheral slopes of the Usk valley below Llangynidr tend to have a rather steep aspect.

Climatic and Vegetational History

As Brecknock is essentially an upland, inland county its micro-climates vary according to elevation and aspect. Rainfall increases with altitude so that while the mean annual precipitation for much of the Usk valley lies between 1250 mm and 1500 mm, the Northern Plateau has 2000 mm and over and the highest parts of Fforest Fawr over 2500 mm. Rainfall frequency and intensity can vary considerably within a month and from month to month and year to year within the general pattern, and aspect significantly affects the spatial distribution of the precipitation of any single front, particularly during showery weather.

Increased altitude with its attendant denser cloud cover combine to decrease temperatures and the amount of sunshine in the upland zones. Generally, the higher the land the shorter the growing season. In the upper parts of the Northern Plateau and Fforest Fawr the growing season starts on average over two weeks later than in the lowland. The growing season over 180 m above O.D. is about 260 days or less. The season in several upland valleys can be affected by late local occurrence of frosts.

Only a small amount of direct evidence is available for the climatic and vegetational history of Brecknock between c. 700 B.C. and A.D. 400, and it is presumed in this brief description that the trends were similar to those for which there is evidence in neighbouring counties. During the first half of the last millennium B.C. (late Bronze Age, early Iron Age) there appears to have been a deterioration to cooler, wetter conditions with mean summer temperatures two or more degrees centigrade lower than previously. From the mid-fifth century B.C. to beyond the end of the Roman period the climate became warmer and drier again. Two general effects of worsening climate would have been a lowering of the tree-line and a shorter grass-growing season. The altitudinal limit of viable crop production would be reduced. Peat-formation would have increased in the uplands and soil podsolisation intensified, reducing the quality of pasture.

There is evidence for the increased destruction by man of the valley forests in various parts of Wales during the pre-Roman Iron Age in order to create new pastures and crop-lands. For example, in the upper Ystwyth valley (Ceredigion) in the third or second century B.C. oak forest was being burnt and cleared for crop-raising.[5] This does not mean however that the uplands became totally deforested, for oak forest is attested at the time of the Roman conquest at nearly 400 m above O.D. near Ystradfellte (though how extensive the woodland was hereabouts is uncertain).[6] Nearby, at Maen Madog, the soil found under the Roman road (RR 1) was supposed to have formed under moorland conditions similar to those of today.[7] Other high areas may have supported hazel scrub[8] in the later Iron Age, though during the Roman period native high-plateau woodland may have vanished nearly everywhere.[9] Increasing amounts of grassland, especially in calcareous areas, would favour the grazing of sheep which seem to become more important in the Iron Age.

It is to be expected that agricultural deforestation continued in the Roman period: indeed, there is localised evidence for this in cores taken from Llangors Lake,[10] where a marked change in stratigraphy in the lake sediments occurs from a lower organic mud to an upper, inorganic red-brown silty clay. The cores over this transition show a significant decrease in tree pollens and an increase in those of grass, cereals and weeds. Alder (*Alnus*) in particular showed a notable decline and rye (*Secale*) was the predominant cereal. A mid-third century A.D. date was obtained for the transition (^{14}C 1790 ±60 yr bp, SRR-129, uncorrected). The findings indicate an increase in crop-raising in the lake area. The attendant deforestation contributed to increased soil erosion as the change in nature of the lake sediments showed, and in particular the reduction in alder pollen is interpreted as the result of bringing under cultivation the heavier soils near the lake shore where alder would have grown. The expansion of agriculture onto heavier soil types in the Roman period has been noted in Glamorgan.[11]

It must be stressed that the present evidence allows only the broadest generalisations concerning the history of the economic exploitation of the Brecknock uplands during the Iron Age and Roman times. Local variations in the pattern (including limited upland summer cropping[12] of the hardier cereals) may be expected, and detailed fieldwork, especially excavation, is urgently required before much more may be usefully written.

Material for this section has been obtained from the following: Institute of Geological Sciences, *South Wales* (3rd ed., London, 1970); F. J. North, 'The Geological History of Brecknock', *Brycheiniog*, I (1955), pp. 9-77; T. M. Thomas, 'The Geomorphology of Brecknock', *Brycheiniog*, V (1959), pp. 55-156; D. Thomas (ed.), *Wales. A New Study* (Newton Abbot, 1977); F. V. Emery, *Wales* (London, 1969); J. G. Evans, S. Limbrey and H. Clere (eds.), *The Effects of Man on the Landscape: the Highland Zone* (London, 1975); J. A. Taylor (ed.), *Climate change with special reference to Wales and its Agriculture* (Aberystwyth, 1965); J. A. Taylor (ed.), *Aspects of Forest Climates* (Aberystwyth, 1970); J. A. Taylor (ed.), *Culture and Environment in Prehistoric Wales* (Oxford: BAR, 1980); C. B. Crampton and D. P. Webley: *B.B.C.S.,* XX, iii (Nov. 1963), pp. 326-37, *B.B.C.S.,* XVIII, iv (May 1960), pp. 387-96, *B.B.C.S.,* XX, iv (May 1964), pp. 440-9; F. M. Chambers, *P.P.S.,* 49 (1983), pp. 303-316; R. Jones *et al.,* 'Biological and Chemical Studies of Sediments from Llangorse Lake, Wales', *Aquatic Ecology and Pollution Bulletin,* No. 5, part 3 (Botany Dept., U.C. Cardiff, 1977); J. Turner, *The Iron Age* in I. Simmons and M. Tooley (eds.), *The Environment in British Prehistory* (London, 1981), pp. 250-81.

[1] D. Q. Bowen in Thomas (ed.), *op. cit.,* p. 22.

[2] Thomas, *op. cit.,* p. 57.

[3] D. Q. Bowen in Thomas (ed.), *op. cit.,* pp. 17-22.

[4] North, *op. cit.,* p. 39.

[5] J. A. Taylor in Evans, Limbrey and Cleere (eds.), *op. cit.,* p. 18; evidence of woodland clearance around Tregaron Bog: Judith Turner in Taylor (ed.) (1965), *op. cit.,* pp. 33-8.

[6] *B.B.C.S.,* XX, iv (May 1964), p. 445; for continuity of forestry at some locations see J. Turner (1981), *op. cit.,* p. 275.

[7] *Arch. Camb.,* XCV (1940), p. 211, f.n. 2.

[8] Chambers, *op. cit.,* pp. 309, 313.

[9] Generalising from *ibid.,* p. 313.

[10] Data and interpretation from Jones *et al., op. cit.*

[11] *Inv. Glam.,* I, ii, p. 4.

[12] C. S. Briggs, 'Problems of the Agricultural Landscape in Upland Wales, as illustrated by an Example from the Brecon Beacons', *Upland Settlement in Britain* (Oxford: BAR, 1985), pp. 285-316.

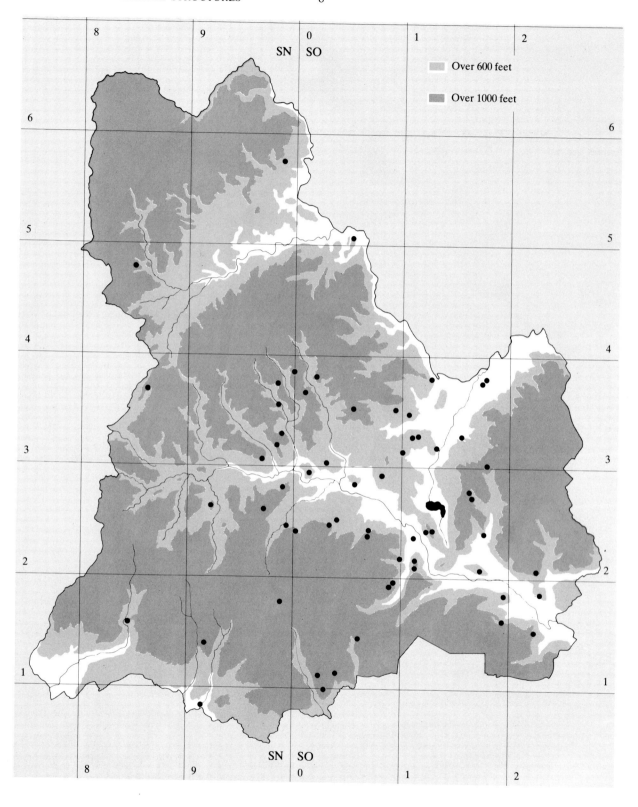

6 Hill-forts and related structures: distribution of all classes

Hill-forts and Related Structures

Documentary Material

The first modern systematic list of the hill-forts of Brecknock was published in 1950 by H. N. Savory,[1] followed by a supplementary list in 1953.[2] This Inventory was based on earlier antiquarian sources such as Theophilus Jones, plans and sections made by E. A. Downman 1909-14, and the author's own fieldwork. Dr. Savory later published a general consideration of the Iron Age in Brecknock[3] which was updated in 1971.[4] The only two excavations of hill-forts (at The Gaer, Aberllynfi (HF 57)[5] and Twyn Llechfaen (HF 31)[6]) were both the work of Savory and these were on the smallest scale. An extensive description of the surface remains of Castell Dinas (HF 50), especially of the medieval castle, has been published by R. E. Kay.[7] As will be seen from the following pages, significant analytic work on these monuments is severely hampered by the lack of extensive excavations, and particularly by the absence of reliable chronological information derived from them. At present, it is not worthwhile to offer more than a few, vague deductions concerning the form and function of the sites. This is, unfortunately, unavoidable; but is preferable to making too facile comparisons with other regions of Wales and the Welsh Marches.

The reference numbers for Savory's lists are given at the end of each entry (e.g. S 1950 b.6 for Twyn-y-gaer, HF 11).

[1] *B.B.C.S.*, XIV, i (Nov. 1950), pp. 69-75.
[2] *B.B.C.S.*, XV, iii (Nov. 1953), p. 230.
[3] *Brycheiniog*, I (1955), pp. 116-125.
[4] *Brycheiniog*, XV (1971), pp. 18-22.
[5] *Brycheiniog*, IV (1958), pp. 33-71.
[6] *B.B.C.S.*, XIX (1961), pp. 174-6; *Brycheiniog*, XV (1971), pp. 18-22.
[7] *Brycheiniog*, X (1964), pp. 15-27.

Hill-fort Locations

The full distribution-pattern of hill-forts and related enclosures now has undoubtedly arisen through a variety of factors some of which are considered below. The large majority of sites are in or on the fringes of the Usk-Llynfi Basin. There is general avoidance of the highest uplands, presumably because they were too exposed. Enclosures on hilltops are clearly sited there for defensive reasons but all are within easy reach of good or medium-quality land and adequate water, and there is no reason why most of these should not have been permanent settlements. Enclosures in non-defensive positions, particularly those on hill-slopes, appear to be sited at the transition between the open uplands and the more wooded valley slopes, indicating a mixed economic strategy. (The enclosures of the southern borderlands of the county are more properly considered as part of the settlement pattern of the Glamorgan valleys; see below.)

Hill-fort Classification

Following the standard adopted for Glamorgan,[1] the distinction between larger and smaller enclosures has been set at an area of 1.2 hectares enclosed. Analysis of the size distribution of the Brecknock sites has not revealed 0.7 ha to be a significant point of division.[2] It is noticeable that there are very few sites (e.g. Pen-y-crug (HF 33)) at which large concentrations of people would have been found, for eighty-five per cent are of the smaller size, in general embanked homesteads for single families or small family groups.

On the basis of size, number of ramparts and strength of position the hill-forts fall into nine classes:

1. Univallate hill-forts exceeding 1.2 ha in area in positions which are naturally strong.

2. Larger univallate enclosures in positions unsuited to defence.

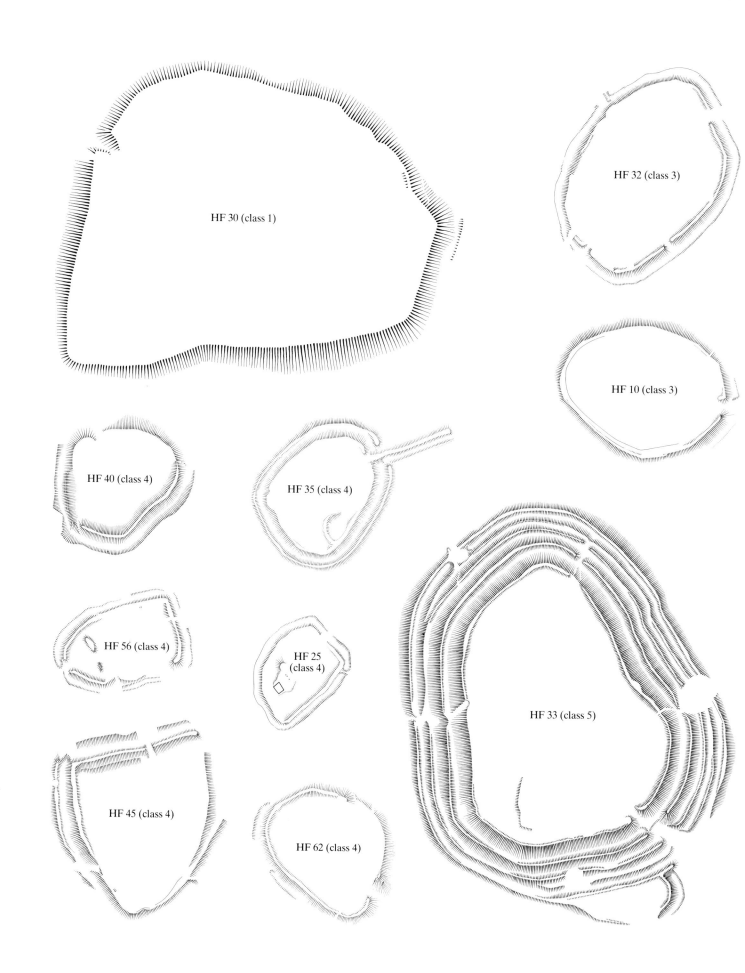

HF 30 (class 1)

HF 32 (class 3)

HF 10 (class 3)

HF 40 (class 4)

HF 35 (class 4)

HF 56 (class 4)

HF 25 (class 4)

HF 33 (class 5)

HF 45 (class 4)

HF 62 (class 4)

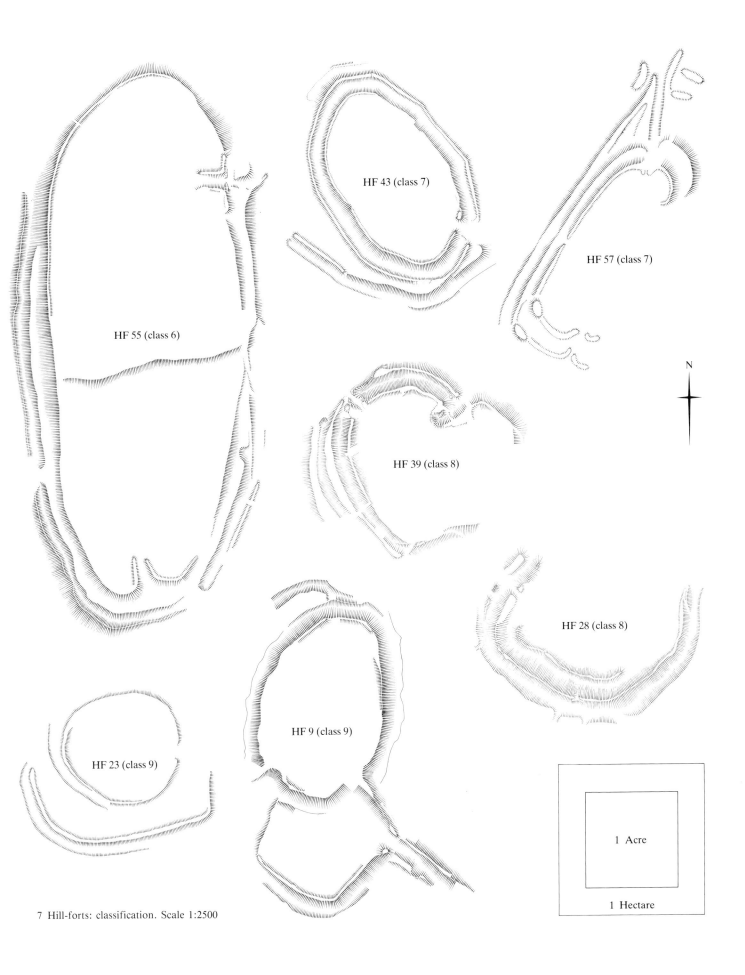

HF 43 (class 7)

HF 57 (class 7)

HF 55 (class 6)

N

HF 39 (class 8)

HF 28 (class 8)

HF 9 (class 9)

HF 23 (class 9)

1 Acre

1 Hectare

7 Hill-forts: classification. Scale 1:2500

3. Smaller univallate enclosures in positions which are naturally strong.

4. Smaller univallate enclosures in positions unsuited to defence.

5. Multivallate hill-forts with close-set defences enclosing more than 1.2 ha in positions which are naturally strong.

6. Larger multivallate forts with close-set defences in positions unsuited to defence.

7. Smaller forts with close-set multiple defences in positions which are naturally strong.

8. Smaller enclosures with close-set multiple defences in positions unsuited to defence.

9. Multivallate enclosures with wide-spaced ramparts.

¹*Inv. Glam.*, I, ii, p. 11.
² *ibid.*

1. The Larger Univallate Forts in positions which are naturally strong (HF 30)

Very large (3.8 ha), and occupying the top of a prominent hill near the geographical centre of the county, Slwch Tump (HF 30) may have housed a considerable population as the base from which economic and political control was exercised over the immediate vicinity. The close proximity of the clearly important site of Pen-y-crug (HF 33) suggests that the two were of different date or function, Slwch Tump possibly the earlier. Unfortunately, besides the substantial, denuded contour defence the visible remains of Slwch Tump are few but include a single entrance protected possibly by short inturns of the rampart. Theophilus Jones suggested that the site may have been bivallate, but this is doubtful (p. 63).

It is likely that the composite sites of Craig y Ddinas (HF 4) and Allt yr Esgair (HF 47) should also be referred in one of their phases to this class. Craig y Ddinas is an inland promontory fort at the head of the Vale of Neath. A curving stone rampart was built across the neck of a long narrow promontory, cutting it off from the rising moorland beyond, and most of the enclosure so defined was protected by sheer natural cliffs. Its area was at least 2.5 ha. Material for the rampart may have been obtained by quarrying in the interior, and an apparently unfinished attempt was made to strengthen the defence across the axis of the ridge by cutting a ditch. Details of the entrance or entrances are uncertain, but access may have been

obtained through narrow, gated gaps between the rampart-ends and the cliff edge. The small enclosure continuing the works to the east may be contemporary with or later than the main site.

Allt yr Esgair is a difficult site to interpret because of the extensive linear quarrying that has disfigured the hilltop and interfered with the ancient works, and because of the afforestation of the eastern half of the fort. The main enclosure bank incorporates the summit of a prominent long ridge and follows a major slope change to the north, so forming an elongated oval of 5.45 ha. Without excavation, considerable doubt attends the possibility that this large univallate structure incorporates an earlier, small univallate fort on the ridge-top; on the other hand it seems probable, though not certain, that the smaller enclosure to the south is a later annexe. Natural cliffs are incorporated in the main enclosure defences on the south part of the west side, while on the east a length of drystone walling, formerly visible, was presumably part of the original structure of the defence, which is elsewhere reduced now to a rubble scarp accompanied in part by a ditch and counterscarp bank. The main rampart material was probably derived from internal quarries. There is no apparent elaboration at the probable entrances. The site is approached and crossed by paths, most of which must be related to the later quarrying, but an ancient ridgeway route may have existed along Allt yr Esgair.

Another site, Myarth (HF 41), should be noted in this context. The indications from early sources are that a very large, essentially univallate, oval structure occupied this hilltop. The rampart seems to have been stone-built, and a single entrance was protected by deep inturns and by simple outworks. It has been claimed that a rectangular guard-chamber of drystone walling, about 1.5 m square, was built into the internal face of the north rampart return, but no trace of this feature is visible today. Such a structure would link the area architecturally with the Welsh Marches; but to speculate upon the implications of such a connection would be unprofitable in the present state of knowledge.

Craig y Ddinas belongs to the settlement pattern of the heads of the west Glamorgan valleys. A sparse population practising a largely pastoral economy which entailed seasonal movements of people and animals is envisaged for this area. A series of small settlements, secure against minor raids and wild animals, but of no great elaboration, is to be expected in the uplands, and sites like Gelli-nedd (HF 5), Craig y Rhiwarth (HF 1) and Glyn Neath (*Inv. Glam.*, no.

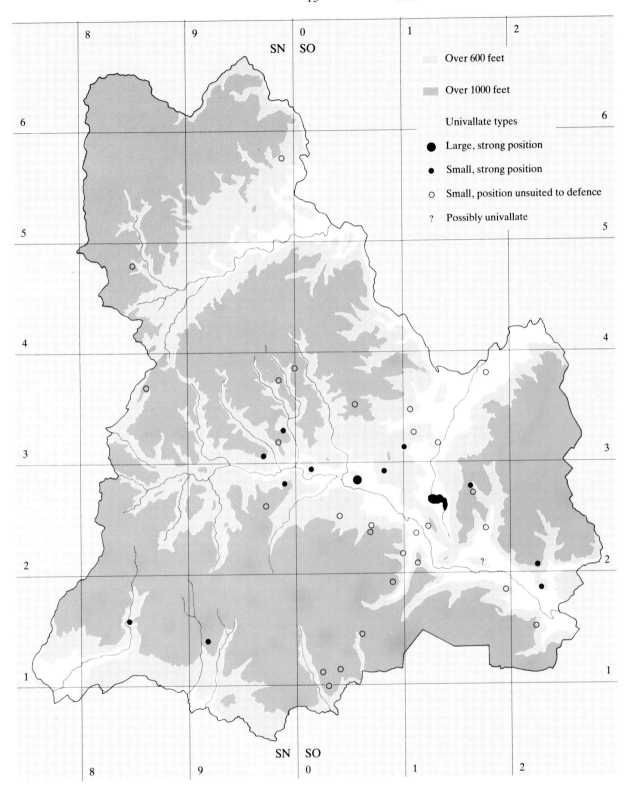

8 Hill-forts and related structures: univallate classes

617) would correspond; but the considerable size of Craig y Ddinas is in this case anomalous, and demands an explanation, for example that it was the base of several family groups linked by kinship, who established and manned the small structures as convenient places from which to control the flocks and herds taken to the higher pastures from late spring to autumn. During this period only small numbers of people, engaged in essential services and crafts not conveniently carried on at the out-stations, would be found at Craig y Ddinas; but the site would fill up as winter approached with returning groups of herders and the animals they intended to over-winter. By contrast, the bleak locations of Gelli-nedd and Craig y Rhiwarth do not suggest sites of all-year-round occupation.

Slwch Tump, Allt yr Esgair and Myarth form a line of forts on prominent hills along the Usk valley. It is tempting to regard these sites as contemporary, probably early, and their fortification as part of a single socio-political process, but there is absolutely no corroborative evidence at present.

2. Larger Univallate Enclosures in Positions Unsuited to Defence

Although no sites in this class can be named there is a possibility that if the outer rampart and ditch at Pendre (HF 53) were additions the fort would fall in this category.

3. Smaller Univallate Enclosures in Positions which are Naturally Strong (HF 1, 5, 10, 11, 13, 31, 32, 51, 63, 64)

Ten sites definitely belong in this class. The site on Cockit Hill (HF 49) could be regarded as a small inland promontory fort but the defensive arrangements are unimpressive. An alternative explanation of the earthwork is that it is an early medieval cross-ridge dyke. If the sub-rectangular annexe at Y Gaer, Defynnog (HF 9) is a later addition, this fort must be included in this category.

Most of the sites are simple ringworks on hilltops with some modification of plan to suit the slope of the ground. They range in area between 0.24 ha and 0.88 ha. At Gelli-nedd (HF 5) and Crug Hywel (HF 64) use is made of natural defences. HF 1 apparently lacks a ditch.

Small-scale excavations at Twyn Llechfaen (HF 31) have provided some data on chronology and structure. Pottery found at the site is considered to indicate a fairly early date in the local Iron Age, probably no later than the third century B.C. It is quite probable that several univallate sites were earlier foundations than some multivallate forts, possibly as early as the sixth century B.C.; but the distinction cannot be taken to be a universal rule, and the form of some is probably related entirely to function, as may be the case with Craig y Rhiwarth and Gelli-nedd. The single homestead with simple defences is a fundamental settlement type in the pre-Roman Iron Age, and such sites would have been constructed throughout the period.

The rampart at Twyn Llechfaen was a bank of clay and clay-and-pebble dumps with a tile-stone facing, the material derived from digging the fronting ditch. A stone revetment or wall may have formed the defence at Coed Cefn (HF 63). At Gelli-nedd a stone wall was constructed partly from material derived from an internal quarry ditch. There are hints of a similar feature at Drostre Bank (HF 51). Walls rather than embankments are a feature of sites on limestone in contrast to those on the Old Red Sandstone, where a wider choice of structural materials was available. At Crug Hywel, a limestone site, the plateau edge was probably scarped and capped with a stone wall, the base of the core of which may have consisted of stones pitched on edge in a shallow trench.

Twyn Llechfaen, Craig y Rhiwarth and Coed Cefn may have had more than one entrance, but generally enclosures of this class have single gateways. The south entrance at Twyn Llechfaen seems to have comprised a simple gap in the bank closed by a wooden gate. At Twyn y Gaer (HF 10) the gap is protected by a short inturn of the rampart on one side, but at Coed Gaer (HF 13) the rampart on one side of the entrance seems to be thicker and curving outwards: if so, out-turning is not recorded for any other Brecknock sites. A more elaborate entrance arrangement exists at Crug Hywel where on the east of the site both the main rampart and counterscarp are inturned either side of a steeply inclined passage-way which narrows to the site of a gate 1.75 m wide at the terminals of the inner rampart. Inturned entrances are of less cultural significance than previously supposed, for they appear to be found in several classes of site.

The entrance at Crug Hywel is approached by a terraced track which may be original, as may the shorter tracks leading to the entrance at Craig y Rhiwarth. The ways approaching other sites are probably more recent.

Near the centre of Twyn Llechfaen a small, flag-paved sub-rectangular floor of a hut was excavated. Associated with it were potsherds, slingstones and an iron object. Trenches in two other parts of the site found no traces of occupation, but overlying the tail of the rampart near the gate was an occupation deposit associated with a posthole, which the excavator took to mark the remains of a lean-to hut. The evidence is consistent with the idea of the site as a defended farmstead containing one or two dwellings for an extended family and some utility structures. Surface remains of huts are few and rarely unambiguous in the Brecknock hill-forts. Thus, Crug Hywel appears to contain the remains of at least four huts, although it is difficult to believe that this site was permanently occupied, in such a bleak position; more probably, it served as a refuge and was occupied during the summer months by herdsmen. The evidence for two huts at Gelli-nedd is unconvincing and there is none at the other sites.

The interior of Twyn-y-gaer, Trallwng (HF 11) is subdivided by a bank and ditch whose relationship to the main defence is obscure. The purpose may have been to separate stock from areas of habitation. Attached externally to the west side of this site in a manner reminiscent of Burley Wood, Bridestowe, Devon[1] was a group of irregular small enclosures defined by tracks and low banks. Scarps beyond these works vaguely resemble the cross-banks at Burley Wood but may be of natural origin. On the slopes south-west of Crug Hywel are two features which appear to be of considerable antiquity, a small semi-circular hillslope enclosure and boulder-revetted terraces, and also the low stone banks of an early field system. However, these external features are not so clearly related to activity at the hill-fort as at Twyn-y-gaer (HF 11). Possibly unfinished sites are Twyn y Gaer, Llansbyddyd (HF 10), and Coed Gaer (HF 13).

The only direct evidence for the subsistence economy of these sites comes from Twyn Llechfaen, which yielded bones of oxen, sheep and pig, but the quantities recovered do not allow a reasonable inference concerning the relative importance of species to be made.

4. Smaller Univallate Enclosures in Positions Unsuited to Defence (HF 2, 3, 8, 12, 15-22, 24-26, 29, 35, 40, 42, 44-46, 48, 52, 54, 56, 58, 62)

Forty-five per cent of all the sites considered under the general terms *hill-forts and related enclosures* fall into this category. They form a disparate group and several are doubtful, but are discussed as examples of the typological problems encountered.[2]

All the sites may be no more than single farmsteads but the larger ones imply more co-operative labour, and while permanently inhabited by one family group (perhaps of higher status) may have acted as the common refuge of several in times of need.

At least fifteen sites are generally assignable to the pre-Roman Iron Age settlement tradition (some possibly originating, however, in the Late Bronze Age), with the possibility of continued occupation or reoccupation in the Roman period. They range in size from 0.12 ha to 0.86 ha, the larger sites usually having a greater defensive capability. Most enclosures lie on hillslopes, some on the edge of a break of slope, but Cross Oak Fort (HF 44) occupies a hillock, Y Gaer (HF 21) and Tredurn Wood (HF 56) are at the edge or tip of a ridge, and Pen-yr-allt (HF 54) and Twyn-y-gaer (HF 35) lie at the edge of a low escarpment in partially defensive positions but otherwise easily approached. The sites are simple shapes, some incorporating natural defensive features in part of the circuit (HF 20, 21, 26 and 54). The strongest part of the rampart is usually set against the easiest approach, so proclaiming that a defensive function was intended. Coed y Brenin (HF 25) and especially Coed y Caerau (HF 26) have drystone front revetments to stony banks. Near the entrance at Crug-y-gaer (HF 62) short lengths of front and rear revetment walling indicate that the stone-built rampart was between 6 m and 6.5 m wide. There are lengths of stone revetment fronting earth and stone ramparts at Penffawyddog (HF 40) and, probably, Coed y Gaer (HF 45). Elsewhere the defences are too eroded to reveal anything of their original structure. Only Nant Cwm Moel (HF 20) and Coed Mawr (HF 29) appear to lack a ditch but at several other sites it is a discontinuous feature; at only Twyn-y-gaer (HF 35) and Coed y Gaer is a counterscarp bank visible. At all places where its site is known, except one, there is a single, simple entrance. Nant Cwm Moel may have had two small entries. Possible single-hut sites are known at four places (HF 22, 25, 35 and 45). At Coed y Brenin (HF

25) a groove about 0.5 m wide, and a few centimetres deep is cut in an irregular rock platform, and represents probably the wall-trench of a roughly rectangular building, possibly of Roman date. A small part of the interior of Tredurn Wood (HF 56) is divided from the rest by a low bank and ditch presumably defining a special activity area.[3]

The long mound projecting from the entrance of Twyn-y-gaer (HF 35) is probably not an original feature and may be a much later pillow-mound. Y Gaer (HF 21) and Tyle Clydach (HF 24) are possibly unfinished sites.

Of the other sites in this category Clawdd British (HF 2) should probably be grouped among the enclosures discussed previously although a medieval date has been proposed, partly from the appearance of the interior which seems elevated and artificial; however, its prominence probably results merely from the excavation of an internal quarry ditch to provide material for the rampart, even though such substantial quarry ditches are not a feature of the other sites. The enclosure is in a desolate area well removed from the main distribution of this type and may have been only seasonally occupied.

Two others in the north of the county, also far removed from the rest of the hill enclosures, are Cefn Trybedd Gwilym (HF 3) and Tŷ-mawr (HF 17). The first, which is no longer accessible (and may not now exist), is included on the basis of its appearance in air photographs. Tŷ-mawr enclosure is badly plough-damaged and is only tentatively included, for it could equally well be associated with attested medieval activity in the vicinity. If these two sites are excluded, then Mynydd Epynt appears to form the north boundary of hill-top and hill-slope forms of settlement; presumably there could have been only a very sparse population in the north, if this was the only type of settlement. The site at Garth (HF 38) might be seen as an unsuccessful attempt to begin the penetration of the Irfon drainage by hill-fort builders from east of the Wye, though this is mere speculation.

Three small sites occur close to each other in the limestone uplands north of the confluence of Afon Taf Fawr and Afon Taf Fechan. Nant Cwm Moel (HF 20) which has been mentioned above, is a very small enclosure, the appearance of which suggests a possible late prehistoric date; but it has a very slight defensive capability, and it is doubtful whether it should be classified as a hill-fort. The same applies to the other two, Cefn Cilsanws (HF 18) and Coedcae'r Ychain (HF 19): the latter is particularly weak and may be unfinished. While there is a tendency to view other sites

in this class as homesteads with at least seasonal occupation, perhaps sites such as the two last named were no more than animal stockades, one element of a mixed economy represented also by open hut settlement and field systems in the uplands nearby. Coedcae'r Ychain appears to be associated with a field system and possibly a hut.

There are other univallate sites within the main distribution area of hill-forts whose surface appearance suggests a possible late prehistoric date; but because of their small area and relatively weak earthworks they fall at the limits of the classification 'defended enclosure'. Ffinnant Isaf (HF 12), Pantywenallt (HF 42), Llwyfen (HF 52), the enclosure west of Allt yr Esgair (HF 46) and Caeau (HF 48) are in this category, all sited on hillslopes. Caeau, however, was constructed by scarping and terracing the hillside to give a more moderate gradient to the interior, and although it has been included here there is doubt as to its status. Likewise, the so-called Gaer in Gwernyfed Park (HF 58) may not have been a 'defended enclosure'.

The oval banks enclosing the churchyards of St. Illtyd's (HF 8) and Merthyr Cynog (HF 15) are described as examples of a more widespread type, the dating and function of which is enigmatic. They appear to be earlier than the nineteenth century, but how much earlier is uncertain: it has been suggested that they are late prehistoric enclosures, reused as religious sites in early medieval times.

5. The Larger Multivallate Forts with Close-set Defences in Positions which are Naturally Strong (HF 33)

Pen-y-crug (HF 33) is the only site in this category, but Castell Dinas (HF 50) is of similar form in part and only just below the size boundary of the class. The location of Pen-y-crug in the geographical centre of the county, its prominent siting and its elaborate works which represent the most developed form of hill-fort architecture, mark it out as probably the most important settlement of its time in the region, for which it may have had a focal administrative function. Its main features are four close-spaced ramparts and a counterscarp bank which follow closely the contours of the hill; they were built by downward construction commencing with the excavation of an internal quarry ditch. This type of construction generally belongs to the last phase of Iron Age hill-fort building and is

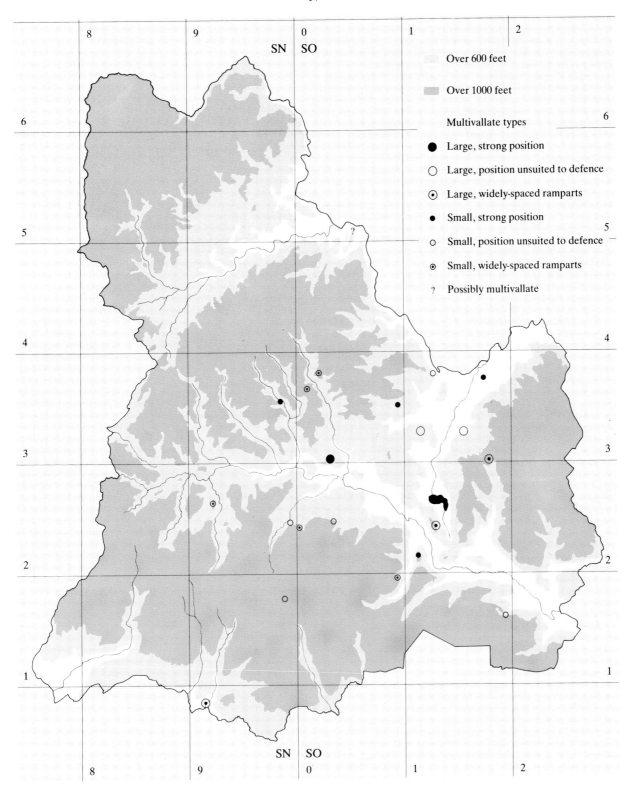

9 Hill-forts and related structures: multivallate classes

associated with sling warfare. Other features at Pen-y-crug are a single entrance protected by inturned ramparts, an external annexe and, internally, the possible remains of an enclosure, perhaps pre-dating the multivallate fort, and a possible hut site.

6. The Larger Multivallate Forts with Close-set Defences in Positions Unsuited to Defence (HF 53, 55)

Hillis (HF 55) occupies a ridge-edge position and has defences on all sides; their strength varies according to the degree of natural protection available. It is nearly twice the size of Pen-y-crug; and this implies that it, too, was an important centre of population although it is not as well-sited tactically. The site has two entrances protected by long inturns. The interior is subdivided by a strong crossbank, which Savory has suggested[4] may represent a Roman or sub-Roman reduction of the utilised area, but it could equally well belong to the pre-Roman period and represent a division of habitations from stock, or a separation of kin groups or families of different social status. While Hillis appears superficially more closely related to the structural style of Pen-y-crug, Pendre (HF 53) may be considered to group with the smaller bivallate sites in weak positions such as Plas-y-gaer (HF 28); it consists of a bivallate system cutting off a broad promontory, the majority of the circuit being formed by steep natural defences.

7. The Smaller Forts with Close-set Multiple Defences in Positions which are Naturally Strong (HF 14, 34, 43, 57)

Pwll-y-cwrw (HF 34) is a dubious site, the supposed earthworks enclosing the upper slopes of the end of a small ridge; they may, however, include a wide-spaced concentric design.

Corn y Fan (HF 14) is conspicuous though small, the triple system of ramparts being considerably out of proportion to the tiny area defended, a feature which might suggest a post-Roman date.[5] Downward construction was the main method employed, and a prominent internal quarry ditch is visible. The entrance approach was between the ends of the outer two ramparts and the crags. There was probably a gate blocking the narrow passage between the end of the innermost rampart and a short length of bank along

the cliff edge.

Tump Wood (HF 43) is set diagonally across the long axis of a prominent hilltop. The main enclosure is bivallate with a single simple entrance. The third rampart and the ditch visible outside may be the remains of an unfinished attempt to construct a *dependent enclosure*,[6] if the open end was not closed by less permanent means, such as hurdling. The fort is approached from the south-east by a possibly ancient track flanked by outworks.

Although not in the strongest of positions, The Gaer, Aberllynfi (HF 57) is probably best assigned to this class. The small-scale excavations here yielded little of use in establishing the period of construction but it was suggested that occupation ceased during or soon after the final Roman conquest of the area. Excavation showed that the visible defence lines displayed only a general relationship to their original courses, a factor constantly to be borne in mind when interpreting other unexcavated remains. Some useful information concerning the structures was recovered at the north-north-east entrance, including details of the stone revetting at the front of the inner rampart, the ditches, remains of gate posts at the narrow entrance gap, and remains suggestive of a moveable bridge; but the excavation was not extensive enough to confirm whether or not this entrance was protected by inturns, as the surface remains suggest. In front was a small annexe or 'barbican', bounded on one side by a slightly sunken track. The main entrance was on the south-south-west and also appears to have been protected by inturns. Evidence of much earlier Neolithic occupation was found.

8. Smaller Enclosures with Close-set Multiple Defences in Positions Unsuited to Defence (HF 6, 7, 28, 39, 59)

Rhyd Uchaf (HF 6) stands well apart from the other sites in this class. It is a peculiar little site with poor defensive capability, the enclosed area being only about 0.01 ha although the three banks occupy a zone up to 22 m wide. Its close relationship with a track and ford may be significant (see p. 164).

The other sites are superficially more alike. They range in internal area from 0.36 ha to 0.89 ha. Two lie on hillslopes; Coed Pen-twyn (HF 39) is set on the edge of a ridge which is easily approached from the north, and Llwyncelyn-fawr (HF 7) consists of defences which run across the common neck of two sloping spurs. In all cases the main earthworks are set against the easiest approaches, so confirming a defensive intention. Llwyncelyn-fawr makes substantial use of natural defences. No downslope works are visible at Plas-y-gaer, but air photographs seem to indicate that a slighter structure once existed to complete the circuit. Similarly, a perishable boundary probably completed the circuit of the defences on the south-east at Coed Pen-twyn. At Llys-wen (HF 59), the downslope defences are noticeably slighter than elsewhere, partly as a result of erosion. An annexe is added to its uninterrupted uphill side and may be contemporary with a possibly unfinished third rampart on the south. Of the two ramparts at Plas-y-gaer the outer dominates the inner, diminishing its defensive potential and so possibly indicating that the outer is a later addition. There are possible signs of unfinished additions to the defences at Coed Pen-twyn. Only their additional defences distinguish these sites from some of the more impressive univallates in weak positions, and the function of the two classes was probably similar; they may even have begun as single-defence enclosures.

Three forms of entrance are known. At Coed Pen-twyn there is a single entry protected by offset inturns of the main rampart. At Llys-wen there is a single, simple gap in the downslope side of the main enclosure. A narrow gap between one end of the ramparts and a ravine was probably the site of the entrance at Llwyncelyn-fawr. A curving, level platform at the end of the outer rampart could have been the site of a gatehouse. More widely-spaced in front of the main works is another bank, probably built to strengthen the defences of the entrance.

A possible hut site has been identified at Coed Pen-twyn.

9. Multivallate Enclosures with Wide-spaced Ramparts[7] (HF 4, 9, 23, 27, 36, 37, 47, 50)

a. Concentric Enclosures

Nant Tarthwynni II (HF 23) is the only truly typical example in the county. It lies on a hillslope in a poor defensive position. The inner and outer enclosures are not connected in any way, and are thus not certainly contemporary; the outer works do not form complete circuits. It is probable that the gaps between the ends of the substantial middle bank and the inner enclosure were closed by some perishable means. The space so enclosed would have formed a suitable protection for livestock, while the inner enclosure would have contained the homestead and other buildings. The location of the site suggests a pastoral function, for the immediate vicinity is unsuitable for extensive crop-production. The small enclosure uphill (HF 22) may have been part of the same complex.

Gaer Fawr (HF 37), in contrast, is in a strong defensive position, and one side is formed by precipitous natural defences. Two ramparts and ditches up to 10 m apart describe an elongated oval, 0.48 ha in area. The outer bank may be a later, possibly unfinished addition. An internal quarry ditch is visible. The form is not typical of the concentric class, but is more akin to the bivallate forts with close-set ramparts in strong positions.

Nant Cwm Llwch (HF 27) probably belongs to this category but the details are obscure. Its position is weak and the internal enclosure tiny, under 0.1 ha.

b. Dependent Enclosures

Dependent Enclosures have not been certainly identified (cf. p. 18 above). The apparently unfinished site of Gaer Fach (HF 36) may have been intended as such, but other possibilities are that the wide-spaced rampart on the nort-east was part of an annexe or additional defence for the entrance. In size and position the site bears a striking resemblance to Gaer Fawr.

The plan of the hilltop part of Castell Dinas (HF 50) probably arises from the modification of an earlier fort to give stronger defences and increase the occupation area. There is doubt about the date and function of the wide-spaced outworks on the slopes west of the main fort. Castell Dinas in its more elaborate form with complex oblique entrance approach seems related to the tradition which also embraces Pen-y-crug.

c. Annexed Enclosures

Y Gaer, Defynnog (HF 9) appears to be the only good example of this class. The annexe (0.35 ha) is set on sloping ground below the entrance end of a strong univallate fort of 0.7 ha. One corner is approached by an embanked track.

The outer stone wall or bank at Craig y Ddinas (HF 4) creates an annexe of only 0.15 ha and may have been intended primarily as an additional obstacle to approach across the neck of the promontory.

The stone-walled annexe of 0.8 ha at Allt yr Esgair (HF 47) seems to have been intended as more than an additional defence work, especially if the identification of a funnel-shaped entrance passage is correct.

In the above cases it is very unlikely that the main, probably original, enclosure was not in use at the same time as the annexe.

[1] A. Fox in S. S. Frere (ed.), *Problems of the Iron Age in Southern Britain* (Institute of Archaeology, London, 1958), p. 48.

[2] *Inv. Glam.*, I, ii, p. 13.

[3] Pen-yr-allt (HF 54) is a possible example of the so-called "satellite" site (*Archaeological Journal*, CXIX (1962), pp. 66-99 (J. Forde-Johnston)), being an outpost of Hillis (HF 55), but this concept has not found general favour (A. H. A. Hogg, *Hill-forts of Britain* (London, 1975), p. 65).

[4] *Brycheiniog,* I (1955), p. 125.

[5] *Inv. Glam.*, I, ii, p. 17.

[6] For this type see A. Fox in Frere (ed.), *op. cit.*, pp. 37-40.

[7] For discussion *Inv. Glam.*, I, ii, pp. 14-15.

Hill-forts: Inventory (HF 1-64)

(HF 1) Craig y Rhiwarth (Figs. 10, 11)

An irregularly oval enclosure stands at 325 m above O.D. on the edge of limestone cliffs forming the E. side of the Tawe valley, 700 m E. of Craig-y-nos. Its rampart, which follows the crests of steep natural scarps on the S. and E. and is set a few metres in from the edges of the cliffs on the W. and N.W., encloses an area of about 0.24 ha. The easiest approach is from the E. The bank is a low mound of tumbled limestone rubble which is partly grass-grown. The outer scarp of the rampart is not more than 0.5 m high generally and the inner face nowhere exceeds 0.3 m. Around the S.E. side the siting of the bank on a natural scarp creates a defence whose outer face reaches a height of 1.7 m. The construction of a field wall has destroyed part of the N. circuit. There is no trace of a ditch. Three simple gaps in the bank mark the sites of

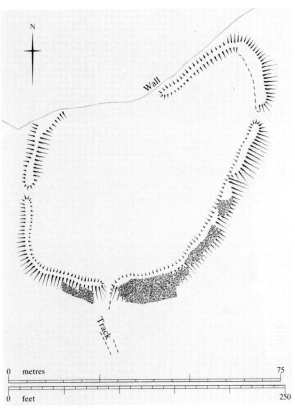

11 Craig y Rhiwarth (HF 1)

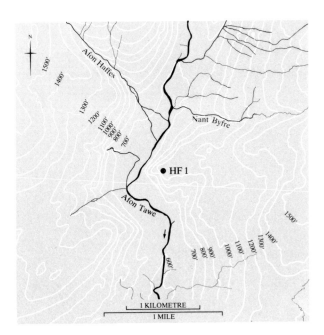

10 Craig y Rhiwarth (HF 1): physical setting

entrances. The breach on the E.S.E. is probably recent. The S. entrance is approached by a track which has been cleared through the scree strewn over an exposed limestone platform. A track across a natural slope approaches the E. entrance at an angle. The grass-covered interior contains no visible structures.

Ystradgynlais (E), Ystradgynlais Higher (C)
SN 81 N.W. (8459 1572)   19 ii 80

(HF 2) Clawdd British (Figs. 12-14)

A small, oval univallate enclosure stands at 307 m above O.D. on the edge of a moderate S.E.-facing slope overlooking the headwaters of Nant y Dresglen, 6.8 km N. of Llywel. The position is defensively weak as the site is overlooked by higher ground on three sides. To the S.E. the land falls sharply and is dissected by streams.

Moorland vegetation and a few trees cover the earthworks which are generally well preserved, although in places cut into by the military who conduct exercises here. On the S. the ditch forms a stream course and elsewhere a boggy hollow. A modern metalled track skirts the N. of the site.

rampart. The latter is most prominent on the W. where its inner and outer scarps are respectively up to 2.1 m and 3 m high. Elsewhere the outer scarp is between 1.2 m and 1.9 m high while on the S.E. the inner scarp is as low as 0.5 m high. The ditch is 2.9 m deep on the W. but becomes shallower eastwards being about 1.6 m deep at the S.E. corner. There is a low counterscarp bank up to 0.8 m high opposite the E. rampart. The most likely position for the entrance is at the S.E. corner where stream erosion has obscured the details. No ancient features are visible on the internal platform.

S 1950 f.7 where it is considered a ring motte. *Brycheiniog*, VII (1961), p. 94 for further consideration of the site as a medieval castle.

Llandeilo'r-fan
SN 83 N.E. (8625 3687)   7 i 83

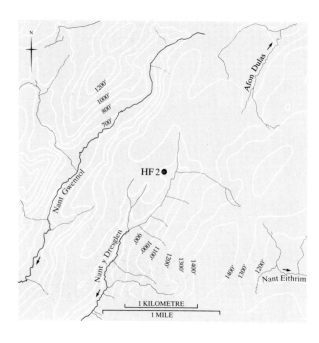

12 Clawdd British (HF 2): physical setting

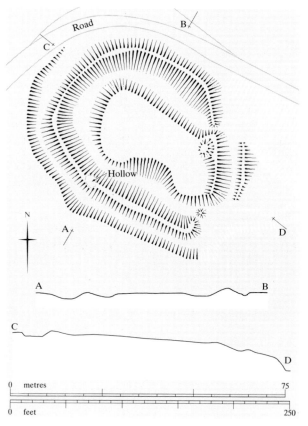

The enclosure measures internally 44 m N.W. to S.E. by 29 m, an area of 0.09 ha. The interior consists of a flat, gently sloping platform 36 m long N.W. to S.E. by up to 18 m wide. Its surface is separated from the rampart on all sides except the S.E. by a depression between 0.6 m and 1.2 m deep. Although some material may have been added to the platform it is probably a largely natural surface made more prominent by excavation around its edges, which was the probable source of material for the earth and stone

13 Clawdd British (HF 2)

14 Clawdd British (HF 2): the defences from the south-east

(HF 3) Cefn Trybedd Gwilym (Fig. 15)

A small, univallate enclosure stood at 415 m above O.D. towards the E. end of the ridge of Cefn Trybedd Gwilym on ground falling steeply to the S.E., 1.5 km W. of Llanwrtyd. It had a flattened-oval shape about 70 m long E. to W. by 50 m wide. The bank on the uphill side appeared to be more substantial than that on the downhill side. It is now inaccessible in dense forest.

Llanwrtyd (E), Llanwrtyd Without (C)
SN 84 N.W. (8486 4783)   5 i 83

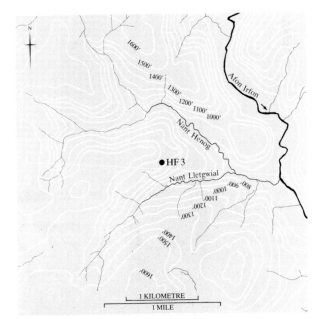

15 Cefn Trybedd Gwilym (HF 3): physical setting

(HF 4) Craig y Ddinas (Figs. 16-19)

This long, narrow, limestone promontory, which rises to about 152 m above O.D. at the confluence of Afon Mellte and Afon Sychryd, about 1 km E. of Pont-neddfechan, is defended for the most part by sheer cliffs. Its original W. end has been quarried away but was probably a very steep bluff. The artificial defences which cut off the neck of the ridge occupy the crests of steep slopes and crags forming the N. edge of a narrow, dry hanging valley. The easiest approach is from the higher ground of Foel Penderyn to the E.

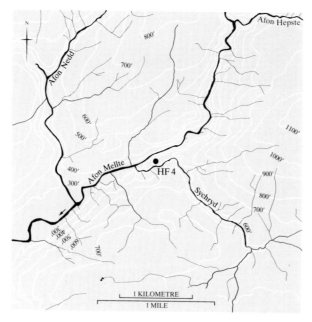

16 Craig y Ddinas (HF 4): physical setting

Over the last two hundred years the Craig y Ddinas area has been the scene of intensive industrial activity, especially quarrying for silica.[1] The W. end and parts of the N. edge of the ridge have been quarried away. Part of the old road that linked Penderyn with the Neath valley crosses the site and it is possible to trace the remains of two tramways of different dates which connected the workings beyond the S.E. side of the hill-fort with the quarry at its W. end.

There are two defensive lines which, commencing from the W., are as follows:

(i) A tree-covered bank of limestone rubble runs W. to E. along the crest of a steep natural scarp before curving across the neck of the ridge to stop just short of its N. edge. A modern, dilapidated field-wall follows the top of the bank. The rampart is between 1 m and 2.5 m high, being at its strongest where it changes direction. There is some shallow hollowing of the rock in the gap between this bank and the W. end of the eastern rampart, which suggests that an attempt may have been made to construct a ditch across the ridge. A length of low crag in the interior, parallel to the S. branch of the rampart, may be the edge of a quarry ditch from which material for the bank was obtained. The part of the promontory defended by the first rampart was at least 542 m long with a maximum width of 77 m, an area of at least 2.52 ha.

(ii) The outer bank is sited and constructed in a similar fashion to the inner but it is in a more denuded condition. At its most eroded point it is only 0.5 m high but it increases in height eastwards to attain a maximum of 2.2 m internally and 3 m externally at its slightly curved end. A modern, vertical-sided mining cut occupies the presumed position of any original ditch, which could not have been more than 5 m wide or 2 m deep. The zone defended by the outer rampart is 103 m long and a maximum of 16 m wide, an area of about 0.15 ha.

The track to Penderyn passes through an oblique breach near the W. end of the inner bank which may be the site of an original entrance. A tramway has destroyed the junction of this rampart with the cliffs of the S. side of the ridge. There are also narrow gaps between the ends of both ramparts and the N. slopes of the promontory where small gates may have been sited. There are no structures visible in the interior other than those resulting from recent industrial activity. It is not possible to ascertain the chronological relationship of the two ramparts from the surface remains.

[1]*Glamorgan Historian*, 5, p. 91 ff.

Penderyn
SN 90 N.W. (9150 0805)   9 v 78

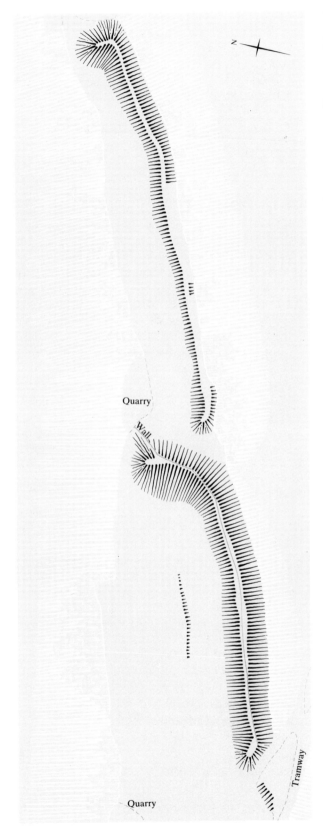

Quarry

Wall

Quarry

Tramway

Quarry

17 *(left)* Craig y Ddinas (HF 4)

18 *(below)* Craig y Ddinas (HF 4)

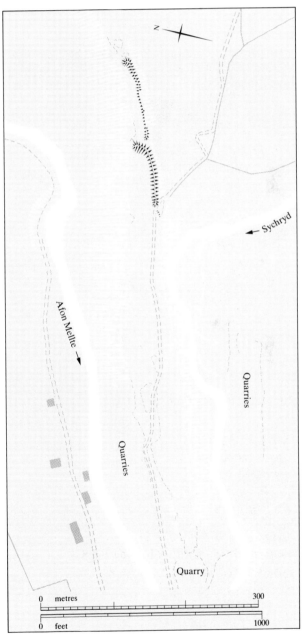

Sychryd

Afon Mellte

Quarries

Quarries

Quarry

19 Craig y Ddinas (HF 4): the outer enclosure viewed from its eastern end

(HF 5) Gelli-nedd (Figs. 20-22)

A small, oval, univallate enclosure stands at about 365 m above O.D. on the summit of a limestone ridge, 1.4 km N.W. of Ystradfellte. The W. side of the site is defended by precipitous natural cliffs overlooking the valley of the River Neath. On the E., a narrow, steep-sided valley separates the fortified knoll from neighbouring ridges. The approaches from the N. and S. have poor natural defences. The interior of the enclosure which slopes upwards moderately E. to W. measures 60 m N.W. to S.E. by 45 m, an area of about 0.41 ha. The rampart consists of a partly grass-grown bank of limestone rubble which may have formed

originally a roughly coursed wall. In its present denuded state the bank is strongest on the N. where its outer scarp, in combination with the natural slope, is up to 3 m high. The inner face of the rampart nowhere exceeds 0.9 m high. A vertical-sided, rock-cut ditch up to 1.3 m deep provides additional defence on the N. and there are shallow, discontinuous traces

20 *(opposite)* Gelli-nedd (HF 5): the defences viewed from the limestone outcrop about 70 metres to the north

of an attempt to dig a similar feature elsewhere. The
entrance is a simple gap on the N.E., 3 m wide and
the vague outline of a quarry scoop behind the rampart
can be traced just to the N. of it. In 1976 the Ordnance
Survey[1] identified two small, circular hut scoops in
the W. part of the largely grass-covered rock interior
but no convincing traces of such features can be seen
now among the slight hollows and shelving of the area.

[1]O.S. Record Card SN 91 SW 14.

Ystradfellte
SN 91 S.W. (9174 1399)   23 iv 80

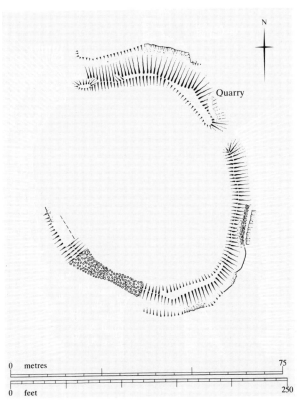

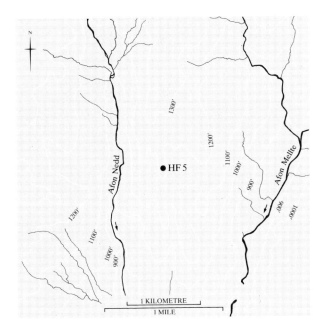

22 *(above)* Gelli-nedd (HF 5)

21 *(left)* Gelli-nedd (HF 5): physical setting

(HF 6) Rhyd Uchaf (Figs. 23-25)

A very small, roughly triangular, trivallate enclosure
stands on a moderate, east-facing slope at about 440 m
above O.D., 2.6 km S. of Storey Arms. The site lies
in the angle formed by the deeply incised Nant yr Eira
stream to the N. and a scarp above a terraced track
to the E.[1] There is no natural protection to the W.
and S., and it is against approach from the moorlands
in these directions that the earthworks are directed.
The grass-covered interior measures only 10.7 m by
9.9 m, an area of just under 0.01 ha, but the curving
defences occupy a zone of up to 22 m wide, which
suggests that the site may have been larger originally
although the present topography would support little
further extension. The earthworks consist of three low,
grass-covered banks, built of earth and stone and
fronted by shallow ditches. Severe erosion has masked
the distinctions in the original profile of the defences
and the banks have been reduced to maximum heights

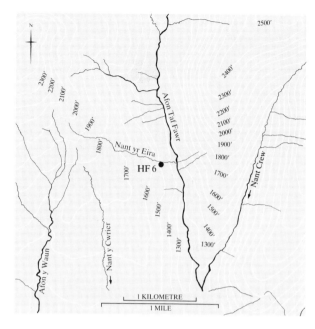

23 Rhyd Uchaf (HF 6): physical setting

of: inner 1 m, middle 0.4 m, outer 0.8 m. The outer lip of the outer ditch is only 0.1 m deep. The most likely position for an entrance is at the E. end of the banks by way of a narrow passage along the top of the scarp. There are no internal features visible.

Arch. in Wales, 9 (1969), p. 17
[1] For this track see p. 164.

Llansbyddyd (E), Modrydd (C)
SN 91 N.E. (9874 1776)   1978

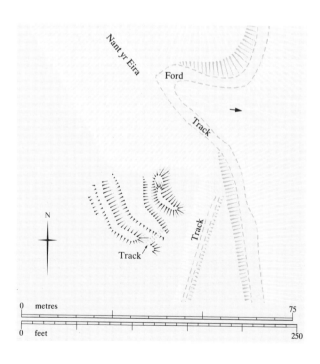

24 Rhyd Uchaf (HF 6)

25 Rhyd Uchaf (HF 6), looking east across Taf Fawr from the west slopes of Gwaun Crew

(HF 7) Llwyncelyn-fawr (Figs. 26, 27)

About 1 km S. of Libanus the S.E. side of Glyn Tarell is dissected into a series of short, narrow spurs and ravines by streams originating on the slopes of Pen Milan. Bivallate defences, which are strengthened on the S.E. by an additional, more widely spaced rampart, run across the common neck of two of these spurs at about 244 m above O.D., cutting them off from rising ground to the S. The edges of the spurs become increasingly precipitous to the N.W. making artificial defences unnecessary elsewhere. The irregular interior slopes down moderately to the N.W. and has an area of about 0.36 ha. Deciduous woodland covers the whole of the enclosure but the surviving earthworks are well preserved generally. A later, but old, track from a ford of Afon Tarell to the modern lane above the site crosses the enclosure N.W. to S.E.

There are three defensive lines which, commencing from the N., are as follows:

(i) A stony bank whose crest is up to 1 m above the interior and up to 2.5 m above the base of the fronting ditch on the S.E. This bank decreases westwards until at the S.W. corner it is a single scarp coalescing with the natural slope.

(ii) Another stony bank, up to 2.5 m above the base of the inner ditch, which also decreases westwards taking advantage of steepening natural slopes. Its outer face is only 1.8 m above the base of the fronting ditch, which stops short of the marshy ground at the S.W. corner.

There is a narrow gap between both banks and the ravine on the S.E., which is the probable site of the entrance. The curving, level platform which continues the line of the second bank here may have been the site of a gatehouse.[1]

(iii) On the S.E., about 12 m in front of the second ditch is a shorter, curving bank with no accompanying ditch. Its inner scarp is a maximum of 1.6 m high and its outer 1.2 m. This was built probably to strengthen the defence of the entrance. The breach at the turn in the bank is recent.

A short ditch up to 2 m deep crosses the E. spur of the enclosure but had no apparent useful function. There are no recognisable ancient features in the interior.

[1] O.S. Record Card SN 92 SE 6.

Llansbyddyd (E), Modrydd (C)
SN 92 S.E. (9930 2463)   20 iii 80

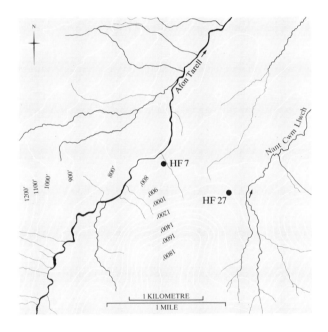

26 Llwyncelyn-fawr (HF 7): physical setting

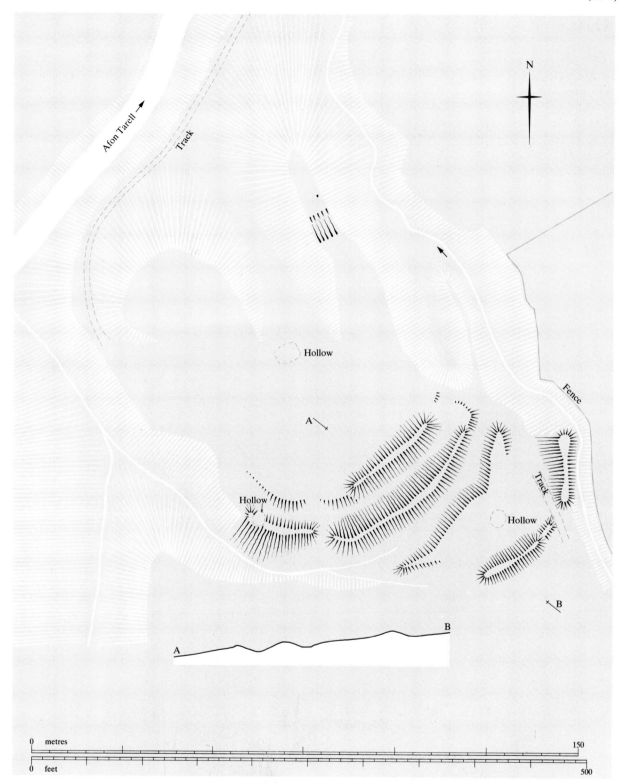

27 Llwyncelyn-fawr (HF 7)

(HF 8) St. Illtyd's Churchyard (Fig. 28)

The enclosure which contains the nineteenth century chapel of St. Illtyd and its associated graveyard stands in a conspicuous but uncommanding position on the W. part of a low hillock at 345 m above O.D., about 2.3 km W. of Libanus. It is a roughly oval, univallate structure measuring internally 84 m E. to W. by 77 m, an area of 0.57 ha. In the S.W. corner there is an oval subdivision measuring internally 43 m N.E. to S.W. by 34 m. The turf- and tree-covered bank of the main enclosure is between 2 m and 7 m wide, composed of earth and stone rubble, and stands between 0.25 m and 1 m high above the graveyard interior. A relatively modern drystone wall revets its outer face which stands between 0.9 m and 1.5 m high above the surrounding ground, being most prominent on the S.E. There is no trace of either an associated ditch or the original entrance which may have been where the E. gate of the graveyard now stands. The main enclosure shares a common perimeter with a smaller internal enclosure on the W. and S.W. The distortion in the outline of the larger enclosure that this entails perhaps suggests that the smaller structure was the earlier. The earth and stone rubble bank of the inner earthwork is best preserved on the S.E. where it is about 4 m wide with an inner scarp up to 0.8 m high and outer face up to 1.4 m. The elevated platform on which the chapel stands is superimposed on the bank on the E. and to the N. of the chapel the bank has been severely mutilated and spread by grave-digging. Immediately in front of the bank on the S.E. is a hollow about 3 m wide and 0.3 m deep, possibly a surviving fragment of a ditch. A modern breach in the earthwork S. of the chapel may be on the site of the original entrance. Apart from the chapel and graveyard the only recognisable feature in the interior is a low linear bank 3 m to 4.7 m wide and up to 0.6 m high running from the S. side of the E. gate of the churchyard towards the S.E. corner of the inner earthwork. As it conjoins neither, its relationship to the two enclosures is uncertain, as is its function. About 9 m beyond the S. and S.W. sides of the main enclosure are the remains of a bank concentric with it and originally a constituent of a partially defunct field system developed around the structure in relatively recent times.

A late eighteenth century map does not show the enclosure around the church.[1]

[1] *Tredegar Mapbook*, Map VIII (1781), N.L.W.

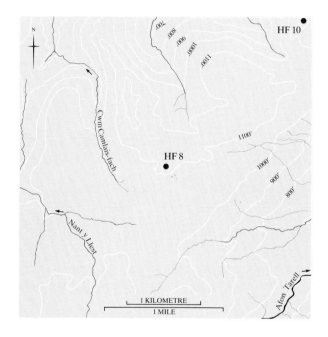

28 St. Illtyd's Churchyard (HF 8): physical setting

Defynnog (E), Glyn (C)
SN 92 N.E. (9712 2611)   28 ii 79

(HF 9) Y Gaer, Defynnog (Figs. 29-31)

About 1.5 km S. of Defynnog is a small, oval, univallate enclosure with a sub-rectangular annexe. The site stands at about 340 m above O.D. towards the N. end of a ridge bounded by Cwm Treweren on the W. and Afon Senni on the E. The defences of the main enclosure take advantage of the natural scarps of the ridge summit which is divided into a higher, small, fairly flat-topped knoll on the S. and a lower, more extensive, gently undulating area to the N. Linear quarrying has left exposed crags along the break of slope between the two areas. The annexe occupies the fairly steep slopes immediately S. of the summit. Beyond the site, the ground falls away on the E. and W. while to the N. there is a short stretch of gently sloping land before the steep drop at the end of the ridge. The easiest approach is from the S. along the crest of the ridge. The denuded, grass-covered main enclosure measures internally 113 m N.N.E. to S.S.W. by 80 m, an area of about 0.7 ha. The annexe is better preserved and its bracken-infested interior measures 71.5 m N.N.E. to S.S.W. by 70 m, an area of about 0.35 ha.

The rampart of the larger enclosure has been reduced mostly to a single scarp but in a few places the inner face survives up to 0.5 m high. The outer scarp stands between 1.1 m and 2 m high above the fronting ditch or shelf, being most prominent on the N.E. and S.W. The toe of the rampart is fronted on the N. by a ditch up to 0.4 m deep and, elsewhere, by a shelf continuing the line of the latter except on the S.E. and S.W. where it appears to be absent. A curving hollow up to 0.5 m deep connected to the N. end of the enclosure is perhaps the remains of either an unfinished ancillary enclosure or an entrance approach although there is no indication of a significant break in the rampart here. The entrance was probably at the S.E. corner.

The annexe bank is best preserved on the S., its inner scarp standing up to 0.6 m high and outer scarp up to the 2.5 m above the bottom of the fronting ditch. The ditch is about 0.8 m deep and has traces of a counterscarp bank along its outer lip. It is not present on the W. where the rampart has been reduced to a single scarp up to 1 m high. The N.E. corner of the annexe is approached from the S.E. by an embanked track which is probably contemporary with it. The track is between 3 m and 7 m wide. Its N. bank runs along the edge of a natural change of slope and is reasonably well preserved although the precise nature of its junction with the main enclosure is obscure and the linear quarrying here gives the false impression that it continued right across the S. end of the latter. Its outer scarp is up to 0.9 m high and its inner scarp up to 1.1 m above the hollowed track. The less well preserved S. bank is roughly parallel to the N. bank and adjoins the toe of the N.E. end of the annexe bank. Its inner scarp is up to 1.5 m high above the track but its outer scarp is preserved only to a maximum of 0.3 m. It is probable that the annexe and its approach are later than the main enclosure. The old ridgeway, Heol Cefn-y-gaer, appears to cross and post-date the track which can be traced as a hollow-way for at least 40 m S.E. beyond it. There are no recognisable ancient features in the interior of either enclosure.

S 1950 b. 7.

Defynnog (E), Crai (C)
SN 92 N.W. (9225 2630)   October 1977

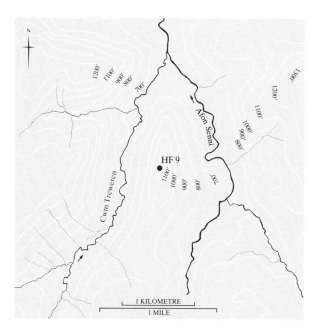

29 Y Gaer, Defynnog (HF 9): physical setting

30 *(opposite)* Y Gaer, Defynnog (HF 9)

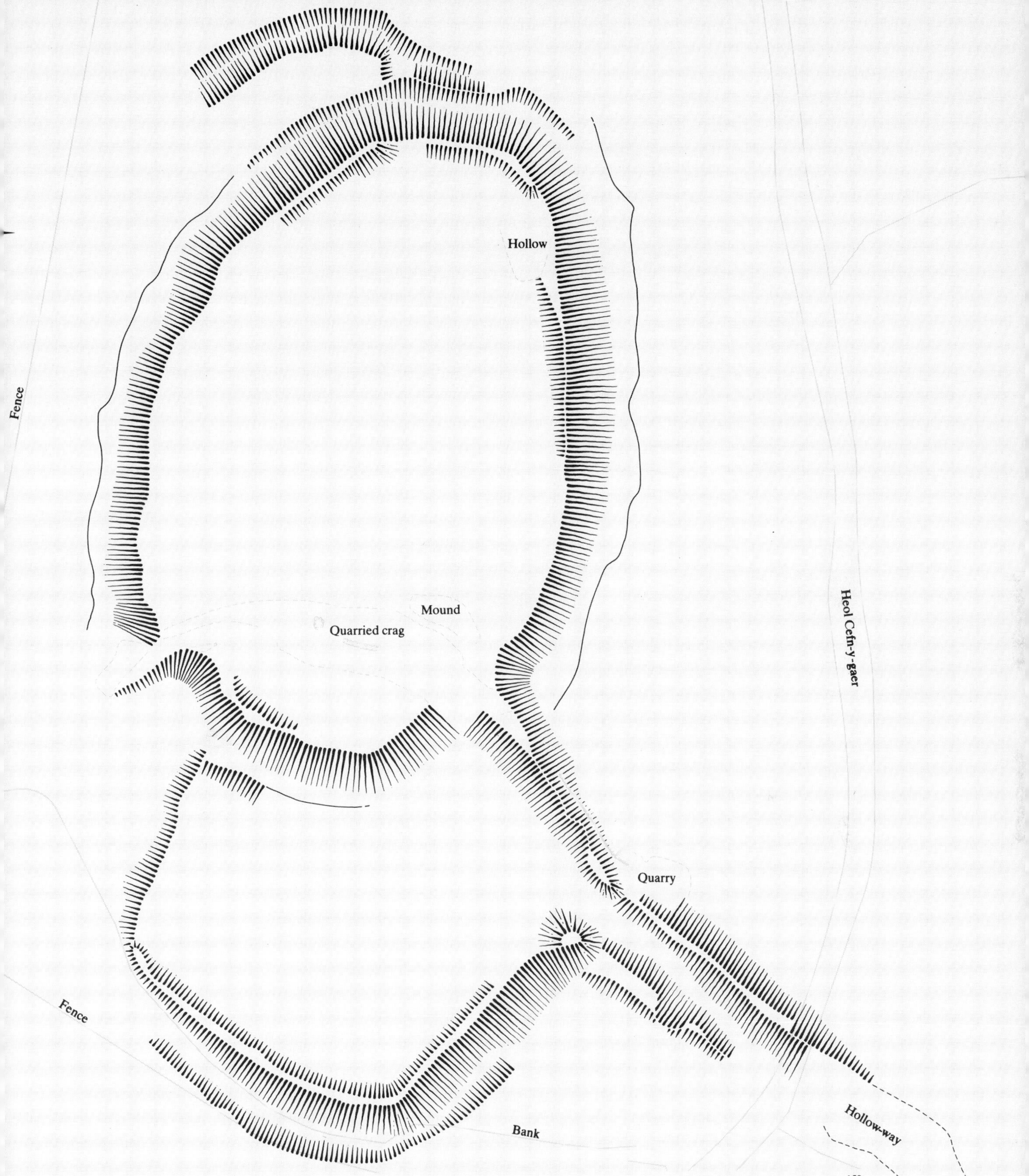

Fence

Hollow

Mound

Quarried crag

Heol Cefn-y-gaer

Quarry

Fence

Hollow-way

Bank

0   metres   150

0   feet   500

31 Y Gaer, Defynnog (HF 9) from the north

(HF 10) Twyn y Gaer (Figs. 32-35)

About 1.8 km E. of Pen-pont church a small, oval, univallate enclosure occupies the upper slopes of a rounded hilltop whose summit is 367 m above O.D. The hill is at the N.E. end of the ridge of Mynydd Illtyd. To the N. the ground falls away steeply to the River Usk 1.25 km away and W. to Nant Rheon, a tributary of the Usk, 0.5 km away at its nearest. The slopes on the E. are less formidable but still relatively steep while to the S. there is a saddle leading to rising, though less elevated, land.

The site measures internally 112 m E. to W. by 85 m, an area of 0.7 ha. The earth and stone rampart stands on the lower of two concentric natural scarps which seems to have been terraced to receive it. The bank is best-preserved at the entrance where

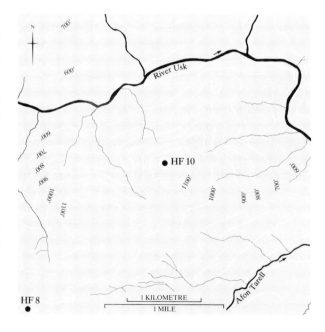

32 Twyn y Gaer (HF 10): physical setting

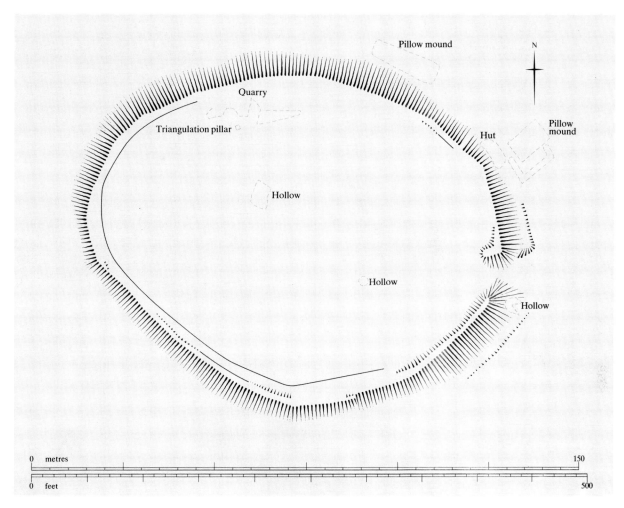

33 Twyn y Gaer (HF 10)

immediately S. of the gap its outer scarp is 3.5 m high and inner scarp 0.8 m high. Elsewhere it consists of a denuded, grass-grown outer scarp that is nowhere higher than 2 m, being generally slighter on the S. than N. The inner face of the bank is preserved only sporadically and is nowhere more than 0.2 m high. On the N.W. the rampart is difficult to define giving rise to doubts as to whether it actually was constructed here. The only sign of a ditch is at the E. end, either side of the entrance, where to the S. of the gap there is a short length 3 m wide and 0.2 m deep, and to the N. 5 m wide and 0.4 m deep. The greater degree of preservation of the bank and the restricted extent of the ditch at the entrance may represent an unfinished

reconstruction of the site[1] or the less damaged remains of stronger original defences at the entrance. The entrance gap is 2.5 m wide at its narrowest and the rampart on the N. side is inturned at a right angle for 3.5 m.

There are no definitely ancient features in the grass-grown interior although the linear quarrying of the upper natural scarp along the N. side appears to be of some antiquity. The two small hollows in the interior are probably recent.

On the land surrounding the enclosure are one circular and several linear earthworks. Two of these which are clearly pillow mounds, and the remains of an enclosure lie adjacent to the rampart on the N.E.

34 *(opposite, upper)* Twyn y Gaer (HF 10): the defences from the north-east. In the foreground are pillow mounds (not on plan, fig. 33)

35 *(opposite, lower)* Twyn y Gaer (HF 10) from the north-east

Also, dug into the base of the rampart here is a sub-rectangular hut, possibly of medieval date.

S 1950 b. 5.
[1] O.S. Record card SN 92 NE 5.

Llansbyddyd (E), Pen-pont (C)
SN 92 N.E. (9900 2805)   12 v 78

(HF 11) Twyn-y-gaer (Figs. 36-39)

About 1.1 km N. of Trallwng church a small, roughly oval, univallate enclosure occupies the highest part of a small, south-projecting spur which has a maximum altitude of 350 m above O.D. The ground to the E. falls away steeply to the narrow valley of Nant Brân and to the N. a saddle connects the hill with somewhat higher moorland to the N.W. Near the W. side of the enclosure is the source of Nant Sefin which descends rapidly to join the Usk 1.7 km due S. The enclosure commands broad views of the valleys of the Usk and Nant Brân.

The earthworks have been reduced considerably by agricultural activity and erosion. The grass-grown interior of the enclosure slopes gently down from W. to E. and measures about 92 m N. to S. by 67 m, an area of approximately 0.45 ha. The earth and stone bank appears to have been laid out in short, straight stretches to take full advantage of the crest of the natural hillslope except at the S.W. corner where a small, projecting knoll was excluded from the enclosure. Its outer scarp has a maximum height of 2 m on the N.E. while its inner scarp is best preserved to a height of 1.2 m on the N.W. For a 10 m length around the N. corner of the site the ditch survives as a depression 0.2 m deep and up to 2 m wide. In 1968 it appeared to be a series of irregular, conjoined hollows pecked into the rock.[1]

The probable site of the entrance is indicated by an interruption of the bank just S. of the centre of the W. side. Movement along a modern path has caused breaches in the rampart on the N. and S.W.

A vague linear bank between 3 m and 5 m wide and only a few cms high with faint traces of a ditch on its S. side bisects the interior of the enclosure and is probably an ancient structure. A gap in both features towards their W. ends is probably the site of a gateway between the two halves of the interior. Another low bank, 2.7 m wide, crosses the interior N.E. to S.W. but, from its alignment, it is clearly associated with the better preserved, recent field boundaries extant to the N.E. of the site.

Formerly it was possible to discern clearly a complex of earthworks on the slopes adjacent to the W. side of the site but recent ploughing has rendered them

36 Twyn-y-gaer (HF 11): physical setting

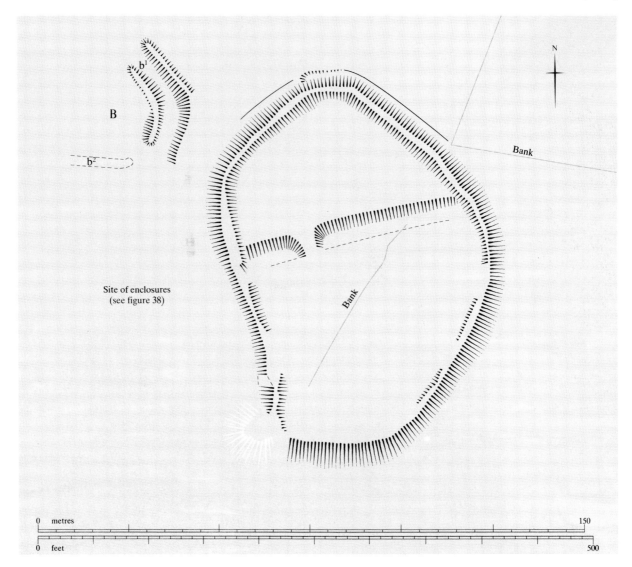

B

b¹

b²

Bank

Site of enclosures
(see figure 38)

Bank

N

| 0 | metres | | | | | | | | | | | | | | | 150 |
| 0 | feet | | | | | | | | | | | | | | 500 |

37 Twyn-y-gaer (HF 11)

indistinct.[2] A series of hollow-ways and terraced tracks subdivided the ground into irregular plots. The following major features were observed (fig. 38): A. A sub-rectangular plot measuring 40 m by 38 m. This was bordered on the N.W. by a hollow-way (a1) about 6 m wide approaching the entrance of the hill-fort. The fort forms the boundary on the N.E. while the S.W. and S. sides are limited by a partially embanked terraced track (a2), 14 m wide overall, connecting the hollow-way, a1, with the foot of the natural knoll at the S.W. corner of the main enclosure. The track peters out 16 m S.E. of the knoll. It is continued for

26 m N.W. of the junction with track a1 as a partial hollow-way. B. To the N. of A two hollow-ways approach the N.W. corner of the hill-fort. The more northerly (b1) runs for 54 m and is embanked on both sides as it ascends the hill with an overall width of 12 m and surviving depth of 0.3 m. As it turns S. to run parallel to the hillslope it is scarped on the uphill side and embanked on the downhill. It is joined by a shorter track (b2) which is 20 m long W. to E. and only embanked on its N. edge. From this junction a terraced track (b3) 22 m long and 4 m wide connects them with the hollow way a1.

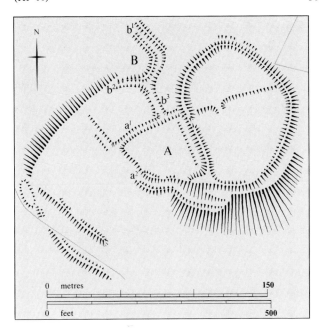

A series of lynchets between 80 m and 100 m S. and S.W. of the main enclosure may represent ancient features but are more probably accumulations over geological scarps.

S 1950 b. 6.
[1] R. E. Kay, Notebooks, pp. 1110-13. Copy in N.M.R. Further ploughing since this date has obscured this feature.
[2] O.S. Record card SN 93 SE 1.

Trallwng
SN 93 S.E. (9699 3061)   23 v 78

38 *(left)* Twyn-y-gaer (HF 11): external enclosures formerly visible as earthworks (based on an O.S. plan)

39 *(below)* Twyn-y-gaer (HF 11) from the north-west

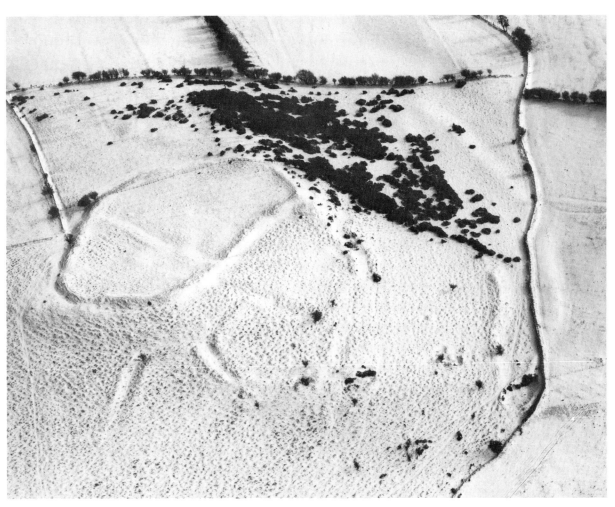

(HF 12) Enclosure N.E. of Ffinnant Isaf (Figs. 40, 41)

3 km N.W. of Aberysgir is a small, oval, univallate enclosure at 335 m above O.D. on a moderate S.E.-facing hillslope. The site has been damaged considerably by ploughing, particularly on the downhill (S.E.) side. Its overall dimensions are 73 m N.E. to S.W. by 63 m and the area enclosed is approximately 0.24 ha.

The earthwork is best preserved in its western half where the main bank rises to a maximum height of 1 m above the interior on the N.W. and 0.9 m above the exterior on the S.W. Further to the S. the bank fades into a single scarp before disappearing completely. On the N.E. the bank is only 0.2 m high above the interior and 0.3 m above the ditch. On the S.E. it has been ploughed out completely. Around the uphill (N.) side is a shallow ditch which may have served as a drainage hood.[1] Around the N.W. side only, there is a short

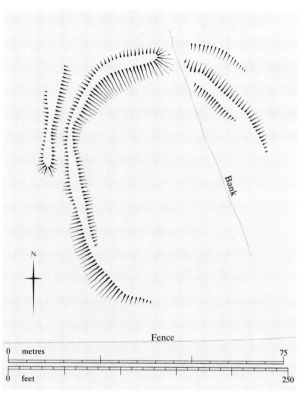

41 Enclosure north-east of Ffinnant Isaf (HF 12)

length of counterscarp bank standing to a maximum height of 0.6 m above the base of the ditch.

A modern field boundary bisects the enclosure on the E. The site of the entrance is uncertain and there are no recognisable ancient features in the interior.

[1] O.S. Record Card SN 93 SE 3.

Aberysgir
SN 93 S.E. (9819 3195)   11 xi 80

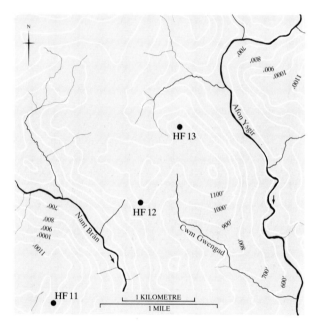

40 Ffinnant Isaf (HF 12) and Coed Gaer (HF 13): physical setting

(HF 13) Coed Gaer[1] (Fig. 40)

A small, roughly rectangular, univallate enclosure stands at about 351 m above O.D., 1.5 km S.W. of Pont-faen. The site occupies the upper end of a ridge which extends N.W. from the slightly more elevated summit of Mynydd Aberysgir (367 m above O.D.) overlooking the narrow valley of Afon Ysgir. The ground falls away steeply on the N.W. and N.E. but there are relatively gentle slopes to the S.

The site has been damaged by former cultivation and is now under pasture. The enclosed area measures about 75 m N.W. to S.E. by 60 m, an area of 0.45 ha, and comprises two summits separated by a shallow, natural depression running S.W. to N.E. The plan, following the shape of the ground, is roughly rectangular with rounded corners.

The rampart is best preserved on the S.W. where it is a simple, grass-grown bank with external ditch, about 13 m wide by 1.5 m high overall. No trace of it appears on the N.E. and the other two sides are worn down. The entrance was a simple gap, now about 8 m wide, through the S.W. side near the W. corner and the adjacent rampart to the S.E. appears to be slightly thickened and curving outwards. No features are visible in the interior. It is possible that the enclosure is an unfinished structure.[2]

About 100 m S.W. of the fort is a broad, low bank, almost levelled, which can be traced for about 200 m N.W. to S.E. Its function and age are uncertain, but it does not seem to have been defensive and was probably a field boundary.

Arch. in Wales, 8, 1968, p. 6.

[1] Field name no. 10, Tithe Award Schedule.
[2] O.S. Record card SN 93 SE 4.

Llanfihangel Nant Brân (E), Aberysgir (C)
SN 93 S.E. (9873 3294)   15 v 68

(HF 14) Corn y Fan (Figs. 42-45)

The fort consists of a triple system of banks and ditches defending the summit of a prominent knoll which stands 350 m above O.D., 2 km S. of Merthyr Cynog. The area enclosed is small and irregularly oval in shape, measuring about 50 m N.E. to S.W. by between 16 m and 20 m, an area of 0.09 ha. The S. edge of the site is formed by sheer cliffs, and elsewhere the ground slopes down steeply from the summit. The site would have been very difficult to approach except from the N. and N.E. against which the defences are set. The fort has commanding views of the middle reaches of the Afon Ysgir valley.

The earthworks are well preserved for the most part. Ploughing has obscured the outermost ditch which is only faintly discernible, and quarrying of uncertain date has destroyed some details of the entrance approach on the E. There are three, close-set, curving ramparts of earth and stone, now grass- and tree-covered. The spacing between the centres of the bank crests averages just over 10 m between the inner and middle and just under 10 m between middle and outer. The broadest spacing, over 11 m, occurs at the E., entrance, end. All three banks are inturned at their W. ends, the inner particularly sharply. The E. end of the

42 Corn y Fan (HF 14): physical setting

outer bank is inturned also. The maximum surviving heights of the inner and outer scarps of the banks, taken in succession outwards, are respectively 0.2 m, 4.2 m, 0.3 m, 3 m, 0.3 m and 3.9 m. The ramparts were probably built according to the technique termed *downward construction*,[1] whereby the material for the rampart was heaped downwards on the hillslope from a quarry ditch above, and the process repeated for the other two banks by excavating the inner and middle ditches. The outer ditch may have been relatively shallow, providing some upcast for the outer bank and possibly some for a low counterscarp bank which, if it existed, is no longer visible. An irregular ditch up to 1.2 m deep can be traced behind the inner rampart. There is no convincing evidence of a suggested fourth, more widely spaced, rampart on the W.[2]

The entrance approach is from the N.E. up a V-shaped stretch of sloping ground between the ends of the earthworks and the sheer slopes and crags of the S.E. side. In its present form this approach seems more

44 Corn y Fan (HF 14) from the north-east

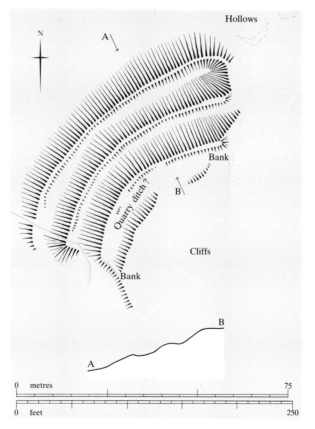

43 Corn y Fan (HF 14)

poorly defended than is consistent with the strength of the main defence. It is possible that the change of slope at the edge of the most easterly of the more recent quarries in this area is the severely damaged remains of some additional protection and that other works have been destroyed. A narrow passage is formed between the end of the main inner rampart and a short length of bank along the cliff edge, and here there was probably a gate.

The surface of the interior is very irregular, the main features being two rock bosses separated by a hollow. The least exposed and most habitable area is the base of the quarry ditch behind the inner rampart.

S 1950 b. 2.

[1] D. Harding (ed.), *Hillforts* (London, 1976), p. 363.
[2] R. E. Kay, Notebooks, p. 1023. Copy in N.M.R.

Merthyr Cynog
SN 93 N.E. (9851 3539)   24 v 78

45 Corn y Fan (HF 14): view of the defences from rising ground on the west

(HF 15) Merthyr Cynog Churchyard (Fig. 46)

The small, oval, univallate enclosure which contains the church and graveyard of Merthyr Cynog stands at about 320 m above O.D. on the crest of a small ridge in the saddle between Cefn Merthyr Cynog and Mynydd Bach. The site is set back from the steeply sloping S. scarp of the ridge and has poor command of the approach from this direction. Beyond the sharp scarp of the E. side of the enclosure the ground falls away gently, but to the W. the fall is more marked, though not particularly steep. On the N. and N.W. there is a very gentle incline towards the foot of Cefn Merthyr Cynog.

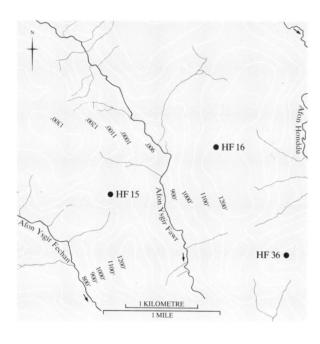

46 Merthyr Cynog Churchyard (HF 15) and the enclosure north-east of Llwyn-llwyd (HF 16): physical setting

The site measures internally 98.5 m N.E. to S.W. by 78.5 m, an area of 0.66 ha. The enclosure bank is grass-grown with planted trees and bushes growing on its crest and inner scarp. It has been suggested[1] that the bank is a product of tree growth and the heaping of earth during the renovation of the church and graveyard in 1860 but, while this may be a contributory factor to its present appearance, it is clear from an early source[2] that the outline of the enclosure pre-dates this activity and on the S. side the trees do not coincide with the main part of the bank, but instead are associated with a very low bank running inside its line.

The bank is constructed of tightly-packed clayey earth and small stones. For most of its circuit, except the E. side, it has a recognisable inner scarp between 0.3 m (W.) and 1.5 m (N.) above the interior of the churchyard. The outer scarp is between 1.4 m (N.) and 2.1 m (S.E.) above present ground levels. It appears to be most pronounced on the E., above the modern road, but the greater part of this scarp is probably natural. The bank is fronted by a drystone wall which probably dates to the time of the reconstruction of the churchyard. More recently it has been strengthened in places with mortar. Around the N. side this wall rises onto and cuts across the toe of the bank which projects up to 1.75 m beyond the front of the wall. The toe also projects between 0.75 m and 2 m beyond the face of the wall on the W. and S. On the S. the bank may have been truncated by the present road. There are breaks in the bank on the N., S. and W. corresponding to gateways in the churchyard wall. On the N., the wall and part of the bank were removed during the construction of the S. gable-end of a later, nineteenth century house. The cutting was backfilled with clayey earth and stone and domestic rubbish, including pottery.[3] There is no trace of any ditch.[4] The site of the original entrance is uncertain but the most likely position is on the N. side.

The church is set on the highest point of the interior. The surrounding surface of the graveyard is relatively flat to the N. but falls away elsewhere. Pathways from the gates cross the churchyard which is grass-covered and planted with trees. Immediately S. of the church is a small knoll 22 m E. to W. by 13 m and about 2 m high which is planted with trees and has graves dug into its top and sides. This is probably a feature created when the graveyard was landscaped as there are slighter mounds also associated with trees elsewhere. There are no other features visible apart from those associated with the graveyard.

[1] O.S. Record card SN 93 NE 4.

[2] O.S. Map, 1-in Series, 1st edition, Sheet 141 (1832).

[3] This filling was observed in an open slit-trench dug against the gable end of the house to allow its footings to be damp-coursed.

[4] Stated to exist by Downman, E. A., *The earthworks of Breconshire,* No. 21.

Merthyr Cynog
SN 93 N.E. (9847 3753)

26 ii 79

(HF 16) Enclosure N.E. of Llwyn-llwyd (Fig. 46)

1.9 km N.E. of Merthyr Cynog are the severely damaged remains of a small, oval, univallate enclosure which stands at 358 m above O.D. on gently sloping land overlooked on the E. by the N. summit of Cefn Bach (389 m above O.D.). To the W. of the site the ground falls away fairly steeply but there are relatively easy approaches along the hillside from the N. and S.

The site seems to have been of oval shape, measuring about 70 m N.E. to S.W. by 44 m. The only reasonably well preserved part is a 20 m length of W.S.W-facing bank and ditch, 13 m wide overall, which is partly encroached upon by later boundaries. The bank is constructed of earth with a few stones and stands 2.5 m high above the ditch and 1 m high above the interior. The outer lip of the ditch is masked by a recent field bank but is at least 0.4 m deep. The earthwork can be traced for some distance to the N.W. in an adjacent field as a single, ploughed-down scarp with a vague hollow in front. The best preserved length of bank is truncated on the S. by a trackway which passes through the interior of the enclosure, now subdivided by recent field boundaries. During ploughing the course of the earthwork on the E. is indicated by a linear spread of stones but otherwise all surface traces have been removed completely.

Merthyr Cynog
SN 93 N.E. (9996 3869)   23 v 78

(HF 17) Enclosure N.W. of Tŷ-mawr (Fig. 47)

A small, sub-rectangular, univallate enclosure stands at about 274 m above O.D. on the fairly steep S.E.-facing slope of a hill between Estyn Brook and Hirnant, 3 km W. of Newbridge-on-Wye. The site which is under pasture at present has been severely damaged by ploughing so that only its general character is apparent now. A reliable assessment of the original shape and dimensions of the interior is not possible but overall it measures 59 m N. to S. by 50.5 m.

The bank was constructed of earth and stone. On the N. it is represented by a levelled spread of material 23 m wide with an inner scarp 1.3 m high, which suggests that the uphill side of the site was the most substantial part of the circuit, possibly even bivallate. The W. side is poorly defined with an outer scarp up to 0.2 m high. The E. side is better preserved, the outer scarp being up to 0.5 m high and the inner up to 0.6 m. On the S. the bank has been reduced to a single outward-facing scarp up to 1 m high. The ditch can be traced on all sides except the E. On the N. it has been reduced to a terrace 4 m wide with an uphill scarp 0.2 m deep. The distinction between its inner lip and the outer scarp of the N. bank has been obliterated almost totally. There is a more definite hollow on the W. side about 4 m wide and up to 0.2 m deep. On the S. the ditch is represented by a slight depression and shelf. The position of any entrance is no longer clear but an aerial photograph taken in 1974[2] suggests that there was one in the lower, S.W., side.

[1] C.U.A.P. BLJ 48.

Llanafan Fawr (E), Llysdinam (C)
SN 95 N.E. (9884 5755)   6 i 83

47 Enclosure north-west of Tŷ-mawr (HF 17): physical setting

(HF 18) Enclosure on Cefn Cilsanws (Figs. 48-50)

A small, quadrilateral, univallate enclosure stands at 410 m above O.D., 1.9 km N. of Cefncoedycymer. The site lies towards the end and on the E. side of an undulating ridge in rolling limestone upland. Within the enclosure the surface rises gently to the N. and W. while outside the ground falls away on all sides except the N. Although the banks have been subject to natural erosion and interference from grazing animals they are well defined throughout. The site measures 79 m N.W. to S.E. by 59 m overall, and the area enclosed is 0.16 ha. Three sides of the enclosure are formed by a bank of loose stones and boulders. The fourth side is defined by the irregular scarp of a fairly steep natural slope. The interior which is covered by short, cropped grass displays no visible ancient features.

The N. half of the W. side of the site consists of rubble piled against the outer face of a band of outcrop and stands 2.5 m high above the exterior and 1.8 m above the interior. Further S. the outcrop diminishes in height and it is here enhanced by rubble added to both faces forming a bank which is carried round

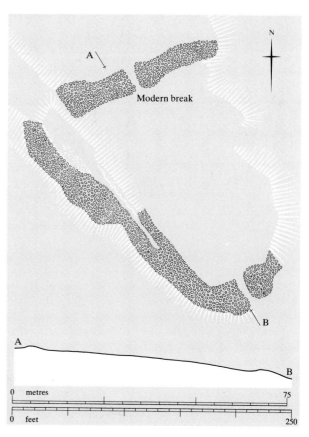

49 Enclosure on Cefn Cilsanws (HF 18)

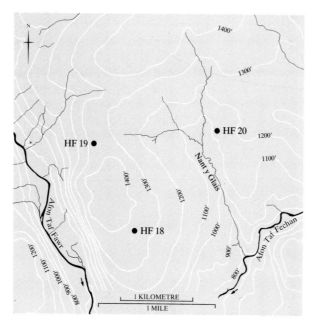

48 Enclosure on Cefn Cilsanws (HF 18), enclosure on Coedcae'r Ychain (HF 19) and enclosure east of Nant Cwm Moel (HF 20): physical setting

eastwards to form the S., and shortest, side of the enclosure, 1.25 m high above the exterior and 0.75 m above the interior. The latter bank diminishes in height and fades as the natural scarp of the E. side is approached. Halfway along its length is a simple entrance gap, 2 m wide. The N. bank, up to 1.1 m high, runs between the outcrop band on the W. and the natural scarp of the E. side where part of it has slipped downhill. Halfway along the N. side there is a partial breach in the bank which is probably recent.

Vaynor

SO 00 N.W. (0283 0998) 14 vii 81

50 Enclosure on Cefn Cilsanws (HF 18): the defences viewed from limestone outcrop on the south-west

(HF 19) Enclosure on Coedcae'r Ychain (Figs. 48, 51, 52)

A small, D-shaped, univallate enclosure stands at about 400 m above O.D. on the moderately steep, S.-facing slope of a saddle in a limestone ridge, 3.2 km N. of Cefncoedycymer. The poor state of preservation of the grass-covered earthwork is due to natural erosion and, probably, robbing to provide stone for more recent boundaries in its immediate vicinity. The surface of the interior is uneven where there are outcrops of bare rock, particularly towards the N. end of the site.

The enclosure measures 51 m N.W. to S.E. by 52 m overall, the area of the interior being 0.18 ha. The downhill, S.E., side of the site is undefended. The other sides are formed by a curving bank of earth and stone which is best preserved on the W. to a maximum height of 0.5 m above the interior and 0.4 m above the base of a well defined external ditch. The ditch is fronted on the W. only by a counterscarp bank up to 0.25 m high. The S. end of the counterscarp bank is

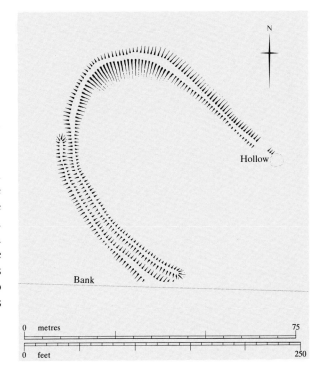

51 Enclosure on Coedcae'r Ychain (HF 19)

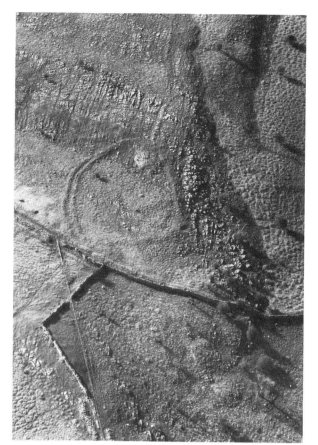

52 Enclosure on Coedcae'r Ychain (HF 19) from the south-west

truncated by a later field bank running E. to W. The uphill, N., part of the main bank is very poorly preserved, but for a short stretch on the N.E. it stands up to 0.7 m high above the exterior and 0.4 m above the interior. From here it becomes increasingly indistinct as it approaches the open side of the site. There is a shallow scoop immediately beyond the end of the bank here which may be a hut site.[1]

Aerial photographs suggest that this enclosure may be associated with a more extensive system of linear banks. One of these which crosses a cairn at SO 0229 1142 can be traced S.E. running towards the enclosure. Immediately to the N. of the site the bank becomes difficult to define among bands of eroded limestone and although aerial photographs suggest that the two are linked it is not readily apparent on the ground. Beyond the recent field wall to the S. of the enclosure another bank can be traced running S. which is joined by cross-banks from the E. and W.

[1] O.S. Record card SO 01 SW 22.

Vaynor
SO 01 s.w. (0238 1125) 16 vi 82

(HF 20) Enclosure E. of Nant Cwm Moel (Figs. 48, 53)

A small, univallate enclosure stands at 340 m above O.D., 1.4 km N.W. of Vaynor church, on a gently sloping shelf in the upper slopes of the E. side of the broad, shallow valley of Nant Cwm Moel. The poor state of preservation of the site is due to natural erosion and, probably, robbing of stone to provide material for more recent field walls in the vicinity. The site is covered at present by grass, bracken and a few small trees. The surface of the interior is uneven with frequent outcrops of bare limestone rock.

The enclosure measures 48 m N. to S. by 38 m overall, the internal area being about 0.12 ha. A bank or scarp of stone and earth survives on all sides except the W. where the crest of a fairly steep, natural scarp forms the boundary. The bank is best preserved on the S.E. where it is up to 0.7 m high above the interior. On the N. and N.E. it has been reduced to only an inward-facing scarp up to 0.75 m high. At the N. limit of the site is a short length of outer scarp which is up to 0.25 m high and another short stretch occurs at the

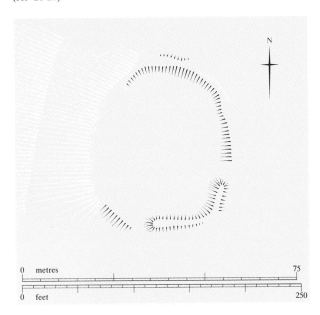

S.W. which is up to 1.2 m high. There are no apparent traces of a ditch. Breaks in the bank occur on the S.W. and S.E. which may represent the sites of entrances.

Vaynor
SO 01 S.W. (0396 1131)   1 x 80

53 Enclosure east of Nant Cwm Moel (HF 20)

(HF 21) Y Gaer (Figs. 54-56)

A small, D-shaped, univallate enclosure stands at 427 m above O.D. on the S. edge of a ridge between the Taf Fechan and its small tributary Nant Callan, 3.6 km N. of Pontsticill. The ground to the W., S. and S.E. of the site drops sharply to the rivers but that to the N. and N.E. rises gradually to the twin ridge-summits, Pant y Creigiau and Cefn Tareni-cochion.

Where it has not been disturbed by later activity the earthwork is well preserved and covered predominantly by moorland grass and bracken. The centre of the W. side has been obliterated by quarrying for a length of about 40 m and, elsewhere, there has been sporadic damage by the same activity leaving hollows and spoil heaps. The remains of a kiln dug into the outer scarp of the bank are visible on the N.E. There is a gap about 30 m wide between the N.E. end of the earthworks and the natural scarp forming the S.E. side of the enclosure where either the construction of the defences was not completed or any remains have been completely ploughed out. The site is crossed by modern field walls, including a sheepfold in the N.E. part of the interior.

The enclosure measures internally 143 m N.E. to S.W. by 89 m, an area of about 0.75 ha. The S.E. side is formed by a steep, natural scarp with no artificial defences. The other sides are defended by a curving bank of earth and stone with an external ditch. The bank is most prominent on the N. where its inner face stands up to 1 m above the interior and its outer face

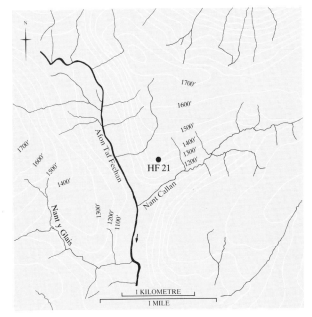

54 Y Gaer (HF 21): physical setting

is up to 2.2 m high above the base of the partially infilled ditch. The visible ditch is of variable depth with a maximum 0.8 m. The entrance was probably on the S.W. where there is a simple gap between the end of the rampart and ditch and the natural scarp. There are no ancient features visible in the relatively level interior. It is recorded[1] that an excavation took place at the site but no details have been published.

S 1950 b. 4.
[1]O.S. Record card SO 01 SE 1.

Llanddeti
SO 01 S.E. (0595 1480)   22 ii 77

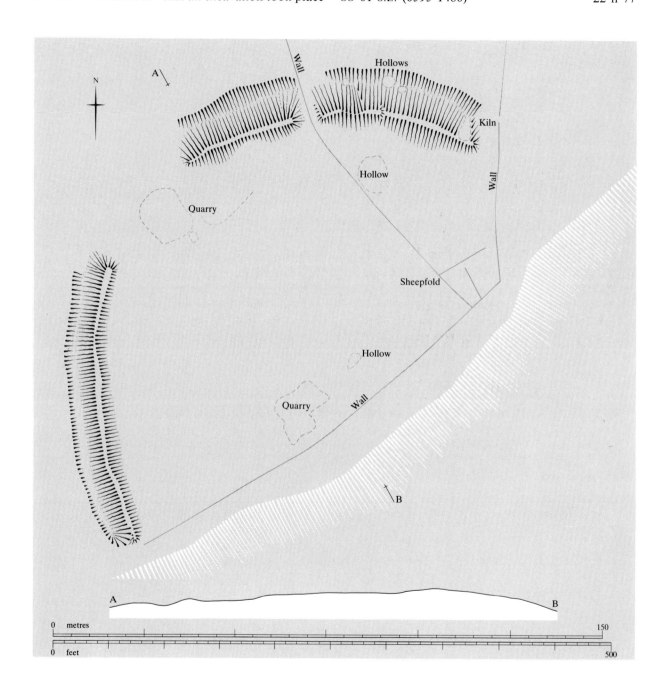

55 Y Gaer (HF 21)

56 Y Gaer (HF 21): view of the defences from rising ground on the north

(HF 22) Enclosure S. of Nant Tarthwynni (I) (Figs. 57, 58)

A small, sub-rectangular, univallate enclosure stands between 395 m and 420 m above O.D. on a moderately sloping, E.-facing hillside, 4.1 km S.W. of Tal-y-bont ar Wysg. A short distance to the N. is the narrow, steep-sided valley of Nant Tarthwynni. The N.W. corner of the enclosure lies in open moorland but the majority of the site is in forestry, the planting of which has damaged and obscured parts of the structure.

The enclosure measures internally 60 m N. to S. by 62 m, an area of about 0.26 ha. The bank is built of earth and stone and survives for the most part as a single outward-facing scarp about 1.1 m high, but on the W. and S.W. part of the inner face of the bank is preserved to a height of 0.7 m. Part of the external ditch, 0.5 m deep, survives on the W. and S.W. and either side of the simple entrance gap on the E. Aerial

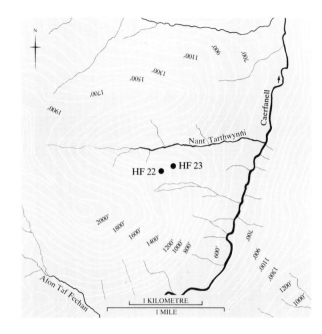

57 Enclosures south of Nant Tarthwynni (HFs 22, 23): physical setting

photographs[1] show a ditch on the N. side of the site which is no longer visible. They also show what appears to be a hut circle in the interior but this is no longer identifiable in the forestry.

A small, multivallate site with wide-spaced ramparts (HF 23) lies 60 m to the E. of the site and the two may have formed (part of) a single settlement complex.

S 1953 d. 5.
Brycheiniog, I (1955), p. 120. Fig. 58 redrawn from O.S. Record card SO 01 NE 1. Survey date 14 vii 76.
[1] 106 G/UK 1652, Nos. 4105-6; F22/58 3609, Nos. 0114-5.

Llanfigan
SO 01 N.E. (0895 1944)   30 iv 80

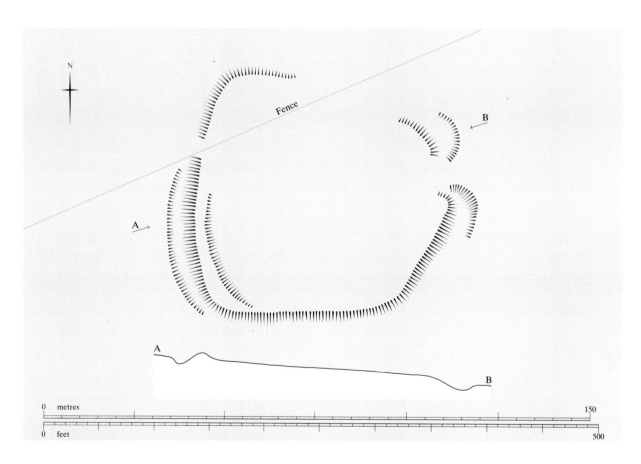

58 Enclosure south of Nant Tarthwynni (I) (HF 22): based on an O.S. plan

(HF 23) Enclosure S. of Nant Tarthwynni (II) (Figs. 57, 59)

The site stands between 370 m and 390 m above O.D. on a moderately sloping, E.-facing hillside, 3.9 km S.W. of Tal-y-bont ar Wysg. A short distance to the N. is the narrow, steep-sided valley of Nant Tarthwynni. Part of the N. side of the enclosure lies in open moorland but the majority of the site is within forestry, the planting of which has damaged and obscured parts of it. A section of a post-medieval field system impinges on the W. side of the outer bank and ditch.

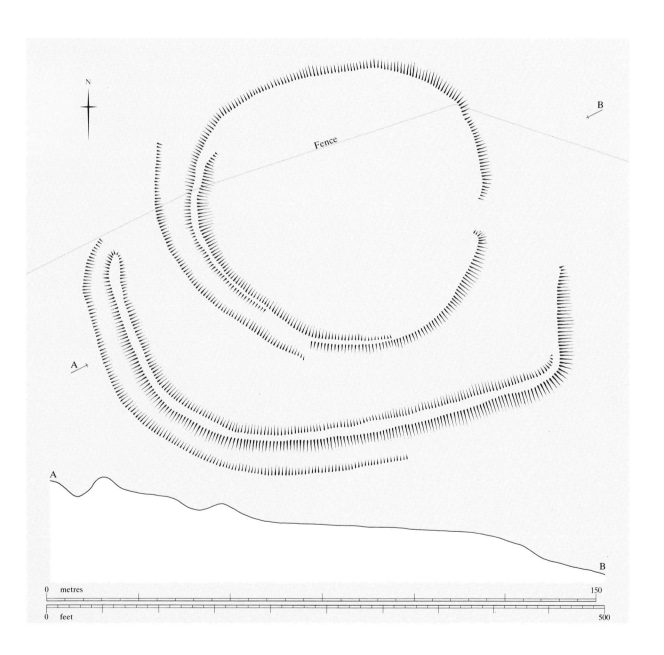

59 Enclosure south of Nant Tarthwynni (II) (HF 23): based on an O.S. plan

The oval, inner enclosure measures internally 69 m N. to S. by 70 m, an area of about 0.38 ha. An outer earthwork, roughly concentric with the S. half of this enclosure, is spaced between 12 m and 26 m (average 18.6 m) beyond it. Aerial photographs[1] show a further bank between 60 m and 70 m to the S., apparently conforming to the alignment of the S. side of this complex but it could not be identified within the dense forestry.

For most of its circuit the earth and stone bank of the inner enclosure is reduced to a single, outward-facing scarp 1.6 m high but on the uphill (W. and S.W.) side an inner face is preserved up to 1.2 m high above the interior. An external ditch, 0.4 m deep, is extant only on the uphill side and may not have been a continuous feature. The entrance is a simple gap in the scarp on the E. There are no discernible ancient features in the interior. The outer bank of earth and stone is up to 2 m high on its outward face and 1.5 m high on its inner. The accompanying ditch is up to 0.6 m deep.

This earthwork may be one component of a larger settlement complex which also incorporated the smaller enclosure (HF 22) 60 m upslope to the W.

S 1953 g. 1.
Brycheiniog, I (1955), p. 120. Fig 59 redrawn from O.S. Record card SO 01 NE 1. Survey date 14 vii 76.
[1] 106 G/UK 1652, Nos. 4105-6; F22/58 3609, Nos. 0114-5.

Llanfigan
SO 01 N.E. (0911 1951)   30 iv 80

(HF 24) Enclosure N. of Tyle Clydach (Figs. 60, 61)

The site stands at 320 m above O.D. on the tip of a sloping spur, 1.8 km S.W. of Tal-y-bont ar Wysg. The extant remains are a semicircular length of bank and ditch which probably formed the uphill side of a univallate hillslope enclosure. The site is overlooked by moderately rising ground to the W. but the land falls away steeply in other directions. Despite being engulfed in forestry the surviving earthwork is well preserved in parts. A modern track follows the line of the ditch on the S. and the recent passage of machinery has done further damage here. A ruinous, modern field wall rises across the scarp of the bank on the S. to follow its crest around the S.W. before diverging uphill to the W.

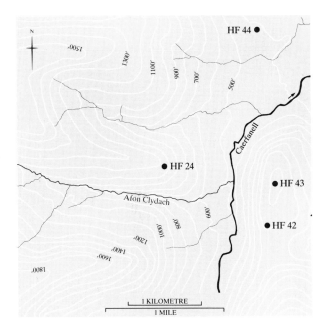

60 Enclosure north of Tyle Clydach (HF 24): physical setting

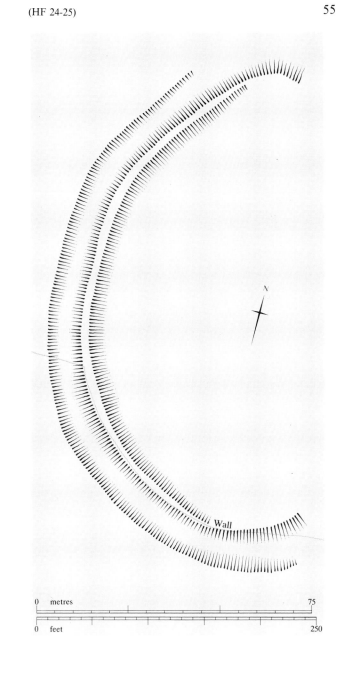

N

The area delineated by the existing bank measures internally 112 m N. to S. by 53 m. There is no surviving surface evidence for a continuation of the earthwork on the E. which, if symmetrically placed, would have created an enclosure of just under 1 ha. Hillslope enclosures of this nature tend to have slighter works on the downhill sides which in this case may have been obliterated by afforestation. Alternatively, either some defence other than embanking was employed originally for the E. side of the enclosure or the site was abandoned in an uncompleted state.

The earth and stone bank has an outward-facing scarp up to 1.7 m high on the W. and an internal scarp up to 1.1 m high. The external ditch is 0.7 m deep on the S. and up to 1.4 m deep on the W. There are no signs of an entrance or internal structures.

Brycheiniog, I (1955), pp. 119, 122. Fig. 61 redrawn from O.S. Record card SO 02 SE 10. Survey date 23 iv 76.

Llanfigan
SO 02 S.E. (0974 2175)   30 iv 80

61 Enclosure north of Tyle Clydach (HF 24): based on an O.S. plan

(HF 25) Enclosure in Coed y Brenin (Figs. 62, 63)

A small, sub-rectangular, univallate enclosure stands at 300 m above O.D., 2 km S.W. of Llanfrynach. The site is on steeply sloping, N.W.-facing land which forms part of the E. side of the valley of Nant Menasgin. Some natural protection is provided by deep stream gullies on the E. and W. but to the S. the enclosure is overlooked by steeply rising ground. The defences are poorly preserved but the sloping interior shows little sign of having been disturbed. Dense bracken covers the majority of the site.

The enclosure measures internally 57 m N.E. to S.W. by 43 m, an area of just over 0.2 ha. The majority of the stony rampart has been reduced to a single outward-facing scarp but on the S.E. and for a short length on the N.E. a slight inner face about 0.15 m high is preserved. The outer scarp is most prominent on the W. where it is up to 1.2 m high but elsewhere it varies in height being as slight as 0.15 m on the S.E. A short length of stone revetment is visible at the S. corner of the bank. The external ditch is up to 1.5 m deep on the uphill side (S.E.) becoming shallower downhill, until on the W. its site is represented by a shelf. The entrance is a featureless gap near the middle of the N.E. side. A hollow trail runs uphill between the N.E. side and a nearby stream gully but there is no indication of a branch from it leading to the enclosure.

In the S.W. half of the interior is an irregular rock

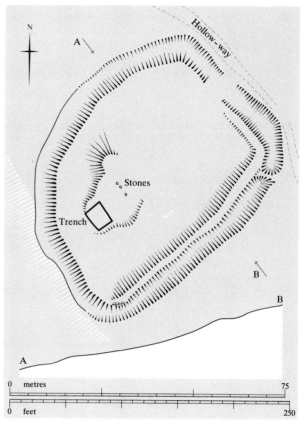

63 Enclosure in Coed y Brenin (HF 25)

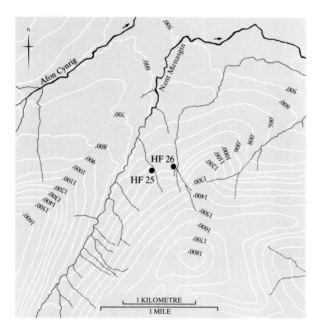

62 Enclosure in Coed y Brenin (HF 25) and Coed y Caerau (HF 26): physical setting

platform which, probably, has been enlarged artificially. On it is a groove about 0.5 m wide but only a few centimetres deep which is probably the wall-trench of a roughly rectangular building about 6 m by 5 m. Further N.E. is a line of three boulders which may have been placed artificially.

Brycheiniog, I (1955), p. 124.

Llanfrynach
SO 02 S.E. (0658 2396)   8 v 69

(HF 26) Coed y Caerau (Figs. 62, 64, 65)

A triangular, univallate enclosure stands at 300 m above O.D. on a fairly steep, N.-facing slope, 1.8 km S.S.W. of Llanfrynach. Natural protection is afforded by ravines on the E. and S.E. but the site is overlooked by ground rising quite steeply to the S.W., against approach from which the most substantial defences are

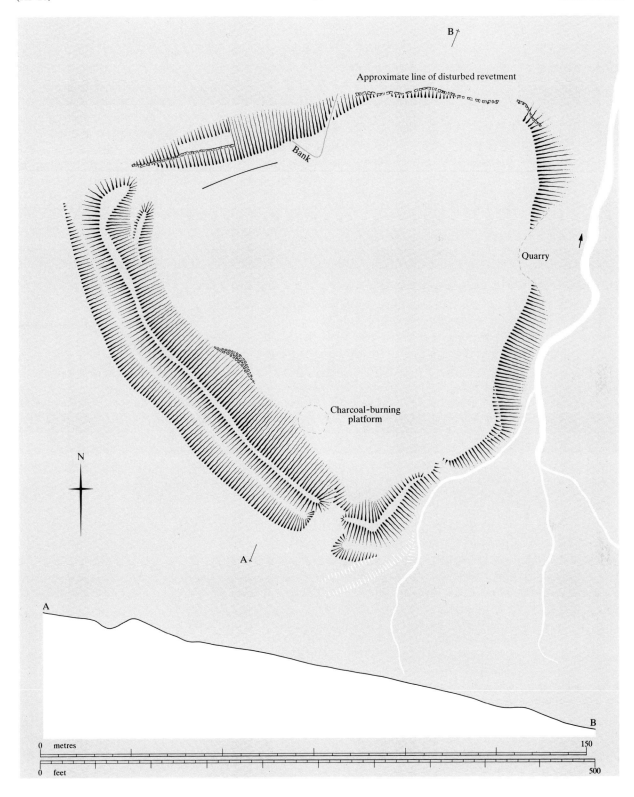

B↑

Approximate line of disturbed revetment

Bank

Quarry

Charcoal-burning
platform

N

A↙

A

B

| 0 | metres | | | | | | | | | 150 |

| 0 | feet | | | | | | | | | 500 |

64 Coed y Caerau (HF 26)

set. These are well preserved under a cover of grass and trees but elsewhere the defences seem to have been relatively slight, perhaps only simple scarping on most of the E. perimeter where the natural side of the ravine provides adequate protection. The earthworks at each corner of the site have been eroded by movement along pathways. The sloping, grass-grown interior has been cultivated.

The site measures internally 102 m N.E. to S.W. by 109 m, an area of 0.86 ha. Beginning as a low barrier at the S. angle of the site, the bank swells rapidly to become a massive rampart with external ditch along the whole of the S.W. side with a maximum overall width of 26 m. The crest of the bank stands up to 3.7 m above the interior and 3 m above the present base of the ditch which is, in places, 3 m deep. The bank is stony here, particularly on its inner slope, but no revetment is visible. The N.W. part of the ditch was created probably by broadening and deepening a natural ravine which can be seen continuing in an attenuated form down the slope beyond the N.W. angle. Along the N. side there is only an outward-facing scarp which is fronted for much of its length by the remains of a drystone revetment wall standing almost 1 m high near the W. end. The position of any entrance is uncertain, though it is likely to have been at one of the angles, all of which have been subject to modern disturbance. A bank of stones 0.3 m high near the middle of the N. side could conceivably be an entrance work but is probably more recent.

The only visible feature in the interior is a level, oval platform about 7 m by 5 m near the S.W. rampart. Charcoal debris is visible on its surface and there are similar platforms in the adjacent wood which were certainly the sites of charcoal-burning hearths.

S 1950 c. 3.

Llanfrynach
SO 02 S.E. (0692 2400)   5 v 69

65 Coed y Caerau (HF 26), looking east: the stone revetment at the west end of the north scarp of the defences

(HF 27) Enclosure W. of Nant Cwm Llwch (Figs. 66, 67)

A small, multivallate enclosure with wide-spaced ramparts stands at 305 m above O.D. on the N.E.-facing lower slopes of Pen Milan, 5.4 km S.W. of Llan-faes church. The site is defensively poor for, although the land falls away fairly abruptly to Nant Cwm Llwch on the E., the approach uphill from the N. is relatively easy and to the S. the land rises gradually for 450 m to the foot of the main, steep-sided N. scarp of Pen Milan.

Coarse grass, bracken and gorse cover the poorly preserved earthworks which are dissected by later trails and lesser tracks. The overall shape and area of the enclosure cannot be determined accurately as the W. side of the outer earthworks has disappeared and there are only faint and dubious traces on the E. The surviving plan consists of a roughly oval, univallate inner enclosure with two banks and ditches to the N. and a single bank and ditch uphill to the S. The inner

enclosure measures internally 54 m N.N.W. to S.S.E.
by 27 m, an area of just under 0.1 ha. The overall
dimensions of the site were at least 128 m N. to S. by
65 m.

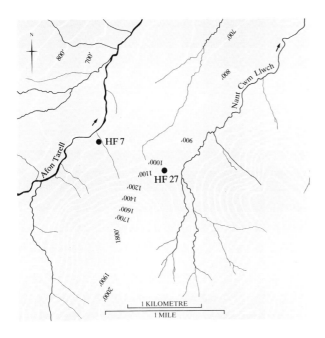

66 Enclosure west of Nant Cwm Llwch (HF 27): physical
setting

The hillslope seems to have been terraced artificially
for the erection of the inner enclosure whose earth and
stone bank has been reduced to a single outward-facing
scarp 1.5 m high on the downhill, N. and E., sides.
On the uphill side an inner scarp is preserved up to
0.6 m high and the outer scarp is up to 0.9 m high.
On the S. and S.W. the external ditch is a shallow
depression 0.15 m deep but elsewhere it has become
thoroughly obscured or was never excavated. The
enclosure is bisected by a trail which may pass through
the site of the original entrance. Two short banks
immediately W. of the gap through the earthwork may
be the remains of an entrance outwork. Two stretches
of vague scarp E. of the enclosure may be the remains
of an outer bank but could equally well reflect a
natural change of slope.

Overlooking the inner enclosure from the S., about
10 m away, is a bank up to 2.1 m high at its present
W. end with an external ditch 0.3 m deep. Curving
away N.E. from near the N. end of the inner enclosure

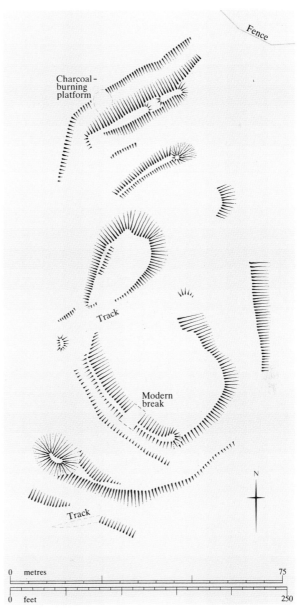

67 Enclosure west of Nant Cwm Llwch (HF 27)

is a low bank 0.3 m high with a hump at its E. end
up to 1.2 m high. North of this is a short, vague scarp,
probably a vestige of an accompanying ditch. A more
substantial stretch of bank and ditch lies 3 m N. of
the latter scarp. The crest of the bank is up to 0.6 m
above the interior of the enclosure and up to 0.9 m
above the present bottom of its accompanying ditch
which is 0.6 m deep. A platform dug into the outer

scarp of the ditch is probably the site of a later charcoal-burning hearth. The S. outer defences and probably the inner works on the N. are associated clearly with the inner enclosure but the outer of the N. works are less closely aligned. It is possible that the latter acted as a droveway approach to the site, although no continuation can be traced N.E.

There are no other visible ancient features within the earthworks.

S 1953 g. 2.

Llansbyddyd (E), Modrydd (C)
SO 02 S.W. (0020 2424)   4 vi 69

(HF 28) Plas-y-gaer (Figs. 68, 69)

The site stands at about 300 m above O.D. on the N.E.-facing lower slopes of Allt Ddu, 3.7 km S. of Llan-faes church. The terrain levels out a short distance to the N. of the sloping ground on which the enclosure stands, but to the S. the site is overlooked by steeply rising moorland.

The surviving earthworks are fairly prominent grass-grown banks of earth and stone covered by trees and scrub vegetation. Small streams have dissected the outer ditch on the S. and exaggerated its depth on the

E. Recent field walls and fences occupy part of the line of both banks. The interior has been ploughed repeatedly and is at present grazing land.

The existing works form an incomplete oval the main element of which is a substantial rampart and ditch around the whole of the surviving perimeter with a shorter, less-elevated bank inside it. A short spur of bank acts as a counterscarp to the outer ditch on the W. Aerial photographs[1] indicate that slighter works which have been ploughed away completed the circuit on the N. The site measures internally approximately 65 m N. to S. by 115 m, an area of 0.58 ha.

The crest of the inner bank stands up to 1.5 m above the sloping interior and is between 1.4 m and 2.2 m above the base of the ditch in front. A faint scarp on the W. may represent the continuation of this bank or may be the product of quarrying for the main bank. The height of the main rampart varies generally between 2 m and 3.2 m but its inner face is up to 3.6 m high on the S. and its outer face up to 4 m high at the S.W. corner. The outer ditch on the S. is between 1.2 m and 3 m deep. On the E. a stream bed was modified to act as a ditch, and erosion has scoured this to a depth of 2.8 m. On the W. edge of the outer ditch is a damaged spur of bank up to 1.3 m high beyond which is unmodified downward-sloping ground. As there is no sign of an entrance through the existing works, access to the interior must have been gained from the N. No ancient features are visible in the interior.

68 Plas-y-gaer (HF 28) and Coed Mawr (HF 29): physical setting

Brycheiniog, I (1955), pp. 120, 122.
[1] CPE/UK 2472, Nos. 3220-1.

Cantref
SO 02 S.W. (0329 2462)   13 v 80

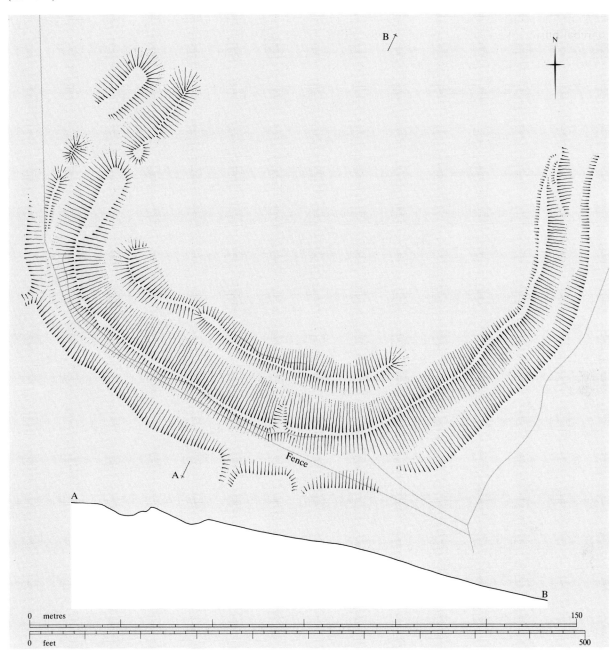

69 Plas-y-gaer (HF 28)

(HF 29) Coed Mawr (Figs. 68, 70)

A small, sub-oval, univallate enclosure stands at 260 m above O.D. on a gentle E.-facing slope, 3.2 km S. of Llan-faes church. The structure is sited poorly for defence as it is easily approachable from all sides. A few large trees of the woodland formerly covering the site stand on the perimeter bank which has been

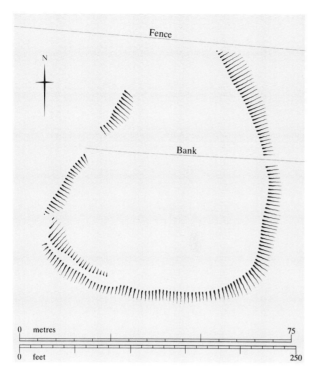

ploughed out on the N. and reduced considerably elsewhere. The enclosure is bisected by a field boundary and truncated by another at its N. end.

Overall, the site measures 68 m N. to S. by 65 m, the area enclosed being about 0.33 ha. At the S.W. corner both faces of the turf-covered, rubble bank survive, the inner 0.3 m high and the outer 0.25 m high. On the W. only an inward-facing scarp is intact to a maximum height of 0.35 m. Elsewhere the bank has been reduced to an outward-facing scarp up to 0.5 m high. A gap on the S.W. between the full bank and the inward-facing scarp may represent an entrance. No ancient features are visible in the interior.

Cantref
SO 02 N.W. (0410 2512)   11 iii 81

70 Coed Mawr (HF 29)

(HF 30) Slwch Tump (Figs. 71, 72)

A large, sub-oval, univallate enclosure incorporates the upper slopes of a prominent hill rising to 246 m above O.D., 1.3 km E. of the confluence of the rivers Usk and Honddu. The ground beyond the fort falls away steeply to the S. and W. but less markedly on the other sides. The highest part of the hill is towards the N.W. corner of the enclosure and the interior slopes upwards to this area from the rampart on the S. and E.

The main perimeter bank has been reduced for the most part to a single substantial scarp, the crest of which is now occupied in several places by lines of trees and bushes. Recent field banks and fences cross the earthwork and run around the circuit of the defences, set back from the crest of the scarp except on part of the W. side where they coincide. There are derelict quarry hollows within the S.E. part of the interior and

71 Slwch Tump (HF 30): physical setting

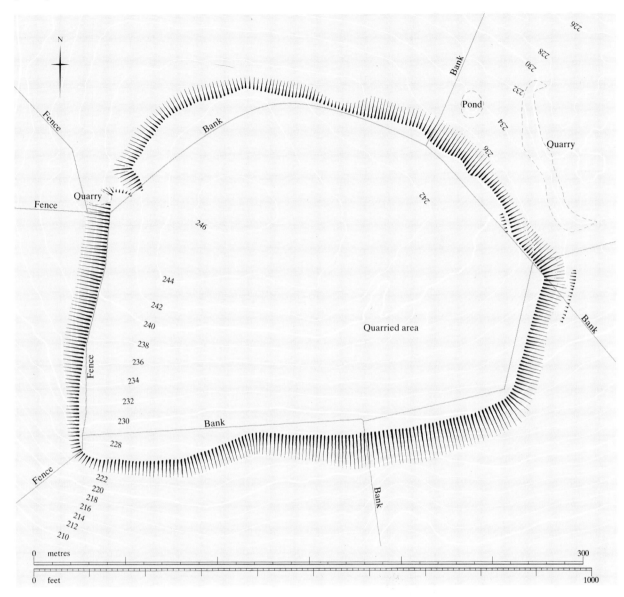

72 Slwch Tump (HF 30)

beyond the defences on the N.W. and N.E. The rampart scarp immediately S. of the entrance has been dug away. The interior has been ploughed and is at present grazing land.

Generally, the defences follow the natural contours of the hill and consist of a single bank and traces of a fronting ditch. Theophilus Jones[1] mentions that the site had "a double foss, in some places nearly destroyed" but there is no trace of a further bank or ditch. The site measures internally 187 m N. to S. by 242 m, an area of 3.8 ha. The greater part of the rampart survives as a single, outward-facing scarp of earth and stone between 3 m and 4.6 m high. A ten-metre length of the inner face of the bank, 0.6 m high, is extant on the N.E. On the N. the site of the ditch is represented by a terrace up to 10 m wide. On the E. a 28 m length of ditch, 0.9 m deep, separates the foot of the rampart scarp from a small knoll and there is a vague hint of a low counterscarp bank at this point. There are no visible traces of the ditch on the S. and W., where it was probably unnecessary because of the steep fall of the ground. The entrance is on the N.E. where the rampart seems to have been inturned either side of a sloping approach. No ancient features are visible in the interior.

An estate map of 1780-81[2] records that the fort lay in a field named 'Ginger Wall'.

S 1950 a. 2.
[1] T. Jones, *Hist. of Brecknock*, I (1898 ed.), p. 43.
[2] N.L.W., Tredegar documents, vol. 2 (a).

St. John the Evangelist Brecon/St. Mary Brecon
SO 02 N.E. (0562 2840)   25 vii 78

(HF 31) Twyn Llechfaen (Figs. 73, 74)

A small, triangular, univallate fort encloses the summit of a prominent hillock rising to 317 m above O.D., 0.7 km N.N.E. of Llechfaen village. The slopes of the hill immediately adjacent to the defences fall away steeply but after a short distance the surrounding land takes on a much gentler gradient. The ploughed interior is dominated by a largely grass-grown rock ridge trending approximately E. to W. from which the defensive perimeter is overlooked. The rampart has been reduced to an outward-facing talus scarp partially masked by trees and undergrowth and incorporated in a later field system. The ditch located by excavation on the S.W. side is not visible as a surface feature.

The site measures 89.5 m by 63 m, an area of about 0.37 ha. Limited excavations by Dr. H. N. Savory in 1959[1,2] revealed detailed evidence of the construction of the defences, showing that the scarp visible now gives only an indirect indication of the original form of the enclosure bank. The present scarp is between 3 m and 4 m high on the N., up to 3.5 m high on the S.W. and a maximum of 2.6 m high on the S.E.

Excavation at the S.W. corner of the enclosure showed that the lower part of the original bank was just over 3 m wide and built of dumps of clay and clay with pebbles derived from the ditch in front which had been dug through sandstone into underlying marl. Sandstone blocks from the same source may have been used for revetting and capping the front of the bank, though few were found *in situ*. Short lengths of partly displaced wall-facing formed of courses of sandstone

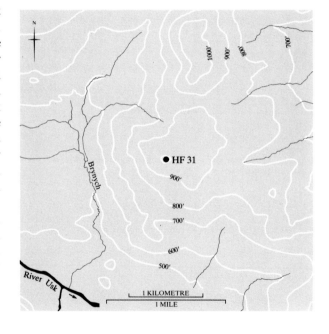

73 Twyn Llechfaen (HF 31): physical setting

slates are visible on the S.E. side near the E. corner. The ditch at the S.W. corner was flat-bottomed, 4.57 m (15 ft) wide by 0.91 m (3 ft) deep. At the junction of the S.W. and S.E. ramparts a simple

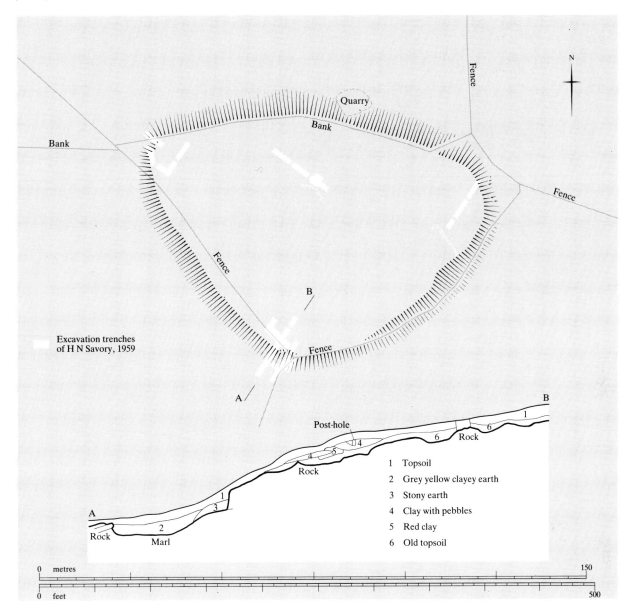

74 Twyn Llechfaen (HF 31)

entrance gap was identified but not thoroughly examined. A hollow was found on the W. side of the gap which may have held an upright timber belonging to a gate structure. At the E. corner there is an embayment in the line of the scarp which may represent the site of another entrance.

Trenches in the N.W. and E. parts of the site failed to locate any evidence of occupation. However,

overlapping the tail of the rampart just W. of the entrance was an oval occupation deposit 5.79 m (19 ft) long associated with a posthole at its E. end. The excavator considered this to be connected with a lean-to hut. The deposit contained coarse, hand-made pottery, slingstones and animal bones. Near the centre of the enclosure a small, sub-rectangular hut floor paved with small flags was excavated which yielded a few coarse potsherds, slingstones and a corroded iron object.

The bones from the hut by the entrance represented at least three oxen, nine sheep and four pigs, a ratio which Savory considered gave a rough indication of the relative importance of these species in the local Iron Age diet.

The pottery assemblage contains fragments of jars of Iron Age 'A' character and probably a sherd of Malvernian stamped ware. A fourth or third century B.C. date is assigned to this material.[3]

S 1950 b. 9.
[1] *B.B.C.S.*, XIX (1961), pp. 174-176.
[2] *Brycheiniog*, XV (1971), pp. 18-22.
[3] *Guide Cat. Early I.A. Colln.* N.M.W. (Cardiff, 1976), p. 76.

Llanhamlach
SO 02 N.E. (0821 2911) 26 v 78

(HF 32) Coed Fenni-fach Camp (Figs. 75, 76)

A fairly large, oval univallate fort encloses the summit of a prominent hill rising to 289 m above O.D., 2.5 km W. of Brecon. Beyond the defences the hillslope falls away steeply on all sides, the least arduous approach being from the S.

Dense conifer forest encroaches on the S. and N.E. perimeter but elsewhere recent felling has opened up the margins of the site. A less closely planted stand of fir with a dense undergrowth of bracken and bramble covers the interior S.E. of the fieldbank that bisects the enclosure. The N.W. half of the interior is more open with a cover of larch, bracken and bramble undergrowth and areas of grass. A fieldbank crossing the site, with an associated quarry ditch and derelict fence, is part of a long boundary which runs from the Roman road (RR 3) at the N.E. foot of the hill, across its crest, to the River Usk on the S.W. The construction of this feature and traffic along its line have breached the earthwork on the N.E. and S.W. and other modern breaks occur in the N. and S. perimeter. There are traces of relatively recent quarry hollows in the S.W. of the interior.

The site measures internally 131 m N.E. to S.W. by 87 m, an area of 0.88 ha. The rampart on much of the N. and W. sides has been reduced to a single, outward-facing earth and stone scarp whose crest stands up to 2.8 m above the terrace or faint depression of a ditch which lies in front of it. The bank is better preserved on the N.E. where its inner face is up to 0.9 m high and the crest of its outer face between 2.7 and 3.4 m above the base of the ditch which is a well-defined hollow, about 0.2 m deep, immediately in front of it. A low counterscarp bank may have stood on the outer lip of the ditch but there are no unambiguous traces of it. The entrance was probably on the S.W. where a simple gap in the rampart is approached by a shallow hollow trail. No ancient features are visible in the interior.

S 1950 a. 6.

St. John the Evangelist Brecon (E), Fenni-fach (C)
SO 02 N.W. (0140 2945) 24 iv 80

75 Coed Fenni-fach camp (HF 32): physical setting

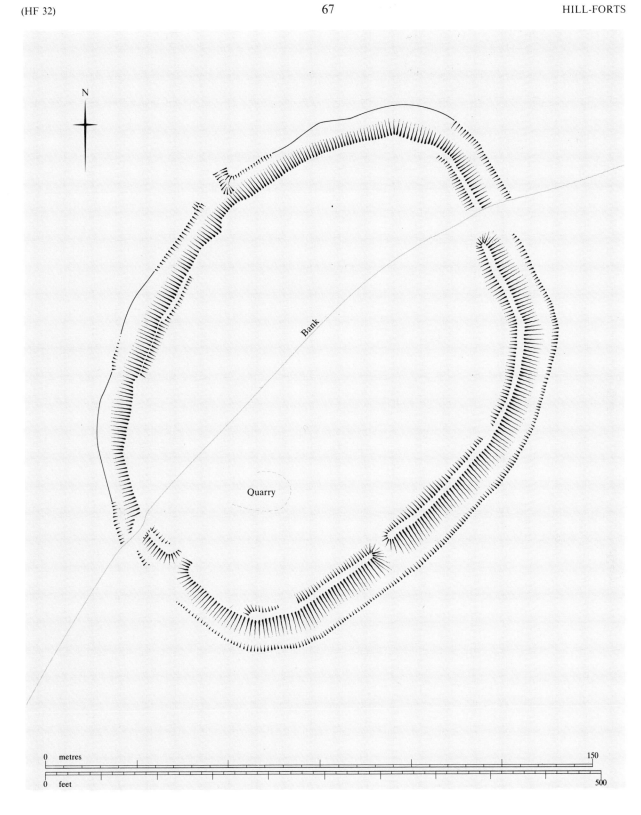

N

Bank

Quarry

0   metres   150

0   feet   500

76 Coed Fenni-fach Camp (HF 32)

(HF 33) Pen-y-crug (Figs. 77-80)

A large, oval, multivallate fort encloses the summit of a prominent, isolated hill about 2 km N.W. of the confluence of the rivers Usk and Honddu at Brecon. The undulating interior of the site rises from E. to W. with a peak towards the W. side 330.3 m above O.D., and another on the S. 331.62 m above O.D. The position is a conspicuous and commanding one, the ground beyond the defences falling away fairly steeply in all directions.

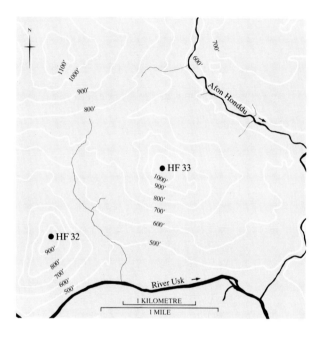

77 Pen-y-crug (HF 33): physical setting

Although denuded, the surviving earthworks are still prominent features. Quarrying has damaged the outer perimeter defences on the N., S. and E. and parts of the site have been eroded by movement along the paths and tracks crossing it. The defences are covered by grass, bracken and patches of gorse and the ploughed interior is grazing land at present.

The series of ramparts follows closely the contours of the upper part of the hill. For most of the circuit there are four ramparts and a counterscarp bank, reduced to three on the W. where the slope is steeper. The banks were constructed of earth and stone, probably by the method termed 'downward construc-

tion'[1] (cf. HF 14). Traces of a quarry ditch are visible behind the innermost rampart. The enclosure measures internally 182.5 m N. to S. by 134 m, an area of about 1.86 ha.

The innermost rampart is the most substantial with an inward-facing scarp up to 0.6 m high on the N. and E. and an outer scarp between 4 m high on the S.E. and 5.2 m high on the N.E. On the S.E., the inner scarp of the second rampart is up to 1.9 m high and the outer scarp just under 4 m high but elsewhere it is less substantial. The inner face of the third bank is up to 0.7 m high and the outer face varies between 0.9 m high on the S.E. and 2 m on the S.W. The fourth rampart which coalesces into the third on the N.E. and S.W. appears as either a bank or terrace. The outer scarp is up to 1.5 m high and where an inner face exists it is about 0.5 m high. The fifth rampart or counterscarp bank has an inner face a maximum of 0.9 m high on the S. and an outer scarp which varies between 1 m and 3 m high, being especially prominent on the N.W. Attached to the counterscarp bank on the S., to the W. of the entrance, is a mutilated stretch of bank and ditch forming a triangular annexe measuring internally 65 m E. to W. by 22 m. The bank has been reduced to a single outward-facing scarp at its W. end, 2.4 m high, and the ditch is extant only on the E. side where it is a shallow hollow. The earthworks are discontinuous at the S.E. corner, terminating either side of a sloping track approaching the interior at a slight angle to the main trend of the defences. The third and fourth banks are inturned both sides of the entranceway which narrows as it ascends to the restricted gap between the sharply inturned ends of the innermost rampart.

In the S.W. corner of the interior, overlooked by the highest point of the hill, is an L-shaped scarp up to 1.7 m high on the W. and 0.5 m high on the S. At the foot of the W.-facing side is a vague irregular hollow. It has been suggested[2] that this is the remains of an earlier hillslope enclosure but it could be equally well a structure contemporary with the occupation of the fort. Its alignment does not suggest a connection with the annexe on the S. side of the fort which is probably a later addition. Apart from the latter, the

78 (opposite) Pen-y-crug (HF 33)

79 Pen-y-crug (HF 33) from the south-east

80 Pen-y-crug (HF 33): the defences, looking towards the south-west corner from mid-way along the uppermost west rampart

only other internal feature is a semicircular hollow cut into the N.E. slope of the S. summit of the site. Its purpose is obscure, possibly a quarry or hut site.

S 1950 a. 4.
[1] D. Harding (ed.), *Hillforts* (London, 1976), p. 363.

[2] A. H. A. Hogg, *Early Iron Age Wales* in I.Ll. Foster and G. E. Daniel (eds.), *Prehistoric and Early Wales* (London, 1965), p. 145, fig. 22 and pl. 17.

St. John the Evangelist Brecon (E), Fenni-fach (C)
SO 03 S.W. (0293 3037)   9 iii 83

(HF 34) Fort S.W. of Pwll-y-cwrw (Fig. 81)

Early authorities[1,2] record the existence of a fort on Pwll-y-cwrw farm which is probably that identified by R.C.A.M. in 1968.[3] The earthworks enclose the upper slopes of the S. end of a small ridge which rises to 290 m above O.D., 1.5 km W.S.W. of Llandyfalle. The easiest approach to the site is from the N.W. where the ground beyond the defences slopes away less steeply than elsewhere.

Surface indications of the supposed fort are meagre and difficult to interpret as the field in which they

occur has been, and continues to be, intensively cultivated. When re-identified in 1968, the fort appeared to be of roughly circular plan, about 160 m in diameter overall and possibly 100 m internally, an area of about 0.8 ha. A strong scarp up to 2.5 m high, below the existing field boundary on the S.E., and a less prominent curving scarp, up to 1.5 m high, coinciding with the field boundary on the N.W., were taken to form the outer defences of the site, and concentric changes of slope within the field to represent

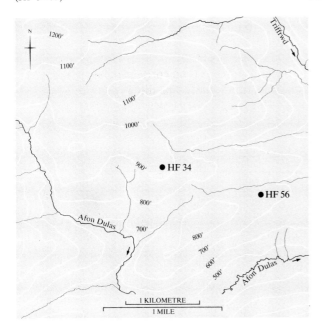

81 Fort south-west of Pwll-y-cwrw (HF 34): physical setting

at least one inner rampart.

In 1973 these general details were confirmed by an O.S. investigator[4] who identified within the outer works three poorly defined scarps on the E., reducing to two on the S. and one on the W. forming with the N.W. boundary a roughly circular plan. However, there was considerable uncertainty about the degree to which these reflected fortifications or erosion features.

Since then further damage has been done to the site and in 1982 there remained only vague traces of the lines identified by the O.S.

A depression in the scarps on the S.E. may indicate the position of an entrance.

The site requires confirmation by excavation.

S 1950 e. 2.
[1] T. Jones, *Hist. of Brecknock* (Glanusk Edition), iii, p. 25.
[2] Lewis, Top. Dict., s.v. Llandevalley.
[3] *Arch. in Wales*, 8 (1968), p. 5.
[4] O.S. Record card SO 03 NE 2.

Llandyfalle
SO 03 NE (0930 3510)   14 v 68/23 xi 82

(HF 35) Twyn-y-gaer (Figs. 82-84)

A small, oval, univallate fort encloses a rounded hilltop rising to 370 m above O.D., 4.4 km N. of Llanddew. Natural defences are provided by ground falling steeply to a small, marshy valley on the N. but, from other directions, the site is approached easily across land falling gently away from the defences on the S. and W. and almost level ground on the E.

The grass- and bracken-covered earthworks are well preserved generally although the main rampart has been reduced for the most part to an outward-facing scarp. Modern ploughing has damaged the mound projecting from the entrance and the passage of tractors has churned up the ditch on the S.W. The interior appears to be undisturbed.

The site measures internally 80 m N.E. to S.W. by

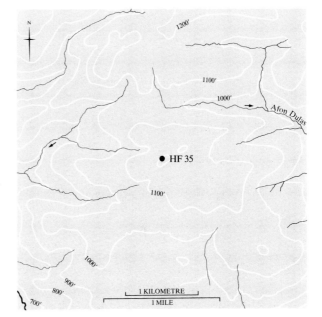

82 Twyn-y-gaer (HF 35): physical setting

60 m, an area of 0.38 ha. The rounded summit of the interior overlooks the main rampart whose outer scarp, between 1.5 m and 3 m high, is most prominent above the ditch either side of the entrance. The inner face of the bank survives in intermittent lengths up to 0.6 m high. Concentric with the main rampart and composed similarly of earth and stones is a continuous counterscarp bank standing between 0.9 m and 1.2 m high above the surrounding ground. On the N. side of the entrance the counterscarp bank is heightened to 1.5 m, but there is no corresponding strengthening of the main rampart. The ditch is an infilled hollow on all sides except the N. where it is reduced to a shelf and the inner face of the counterscarp bank is absent.

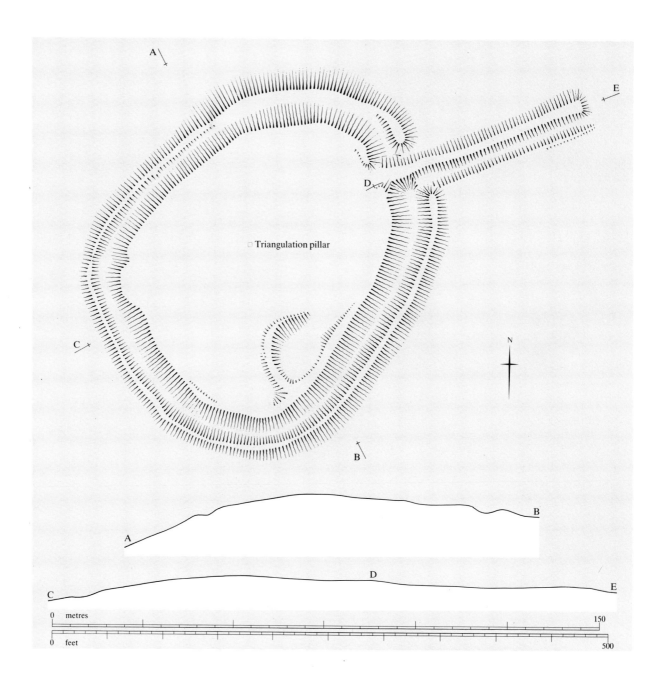

83 Twyn-y-gaer (HF 35)

84 Twyn-y-gaer (HF 35): the defences from the north-west

The ditch bottom is deepest on the S. side of the entranceway being up to 1.8 m below the crest of the counterscarp bank.

A long mound of earth and sandstone rubble, flanked by ditches, projected E. from the entrance gap for about 50 m. Recent ploughing has shortened the mound and obliterated the ditch on the N. side. Originally the feature was about 14 m wide overall by 0.6 m high, the top of the mound being between 2 m and 3 m wide. The mound is placed symmetrically relative to the entrance. It is not possible to be sure of its relationship with the enclosure without excavation. The probability is that it is a later feature functionally unrelated to the fort. The mound bears a superficial resemblance to pillow mounds found in the vicinity (cf. HF 10).

The only feature visible in the interior is a levelled platform with a slight, curving bank on its upper side attached to the S.E. rampart. This may be the site of a contemporary hut about 10 m in diameter or the remains of a later fold.

A post-Roman date for the enclosure cannot be ruled out.

Dr. C. B. Crampton, from a study of enlarged aerial photographs, records[1] an extensive system of very small fields surrounding the fort. These were not identified during ground inspections in 1968 and 1978 and part of his map seems incompatible with the visible remains: e.g. the tongue extending the line of the long mound across the fort. However, on the steep slopes N.E. of the enclosure there were remains of what appeared to be very irregular, probably hand-dug, ridge-and-furrow or lazy-bed cultivation. The lines of this were not parallel but converged and butted-up against each other, the average width being about 2 m by up to 0.3 m high. The whole area of these "fields" was ploughed in 1981.

S 1950 e. 1.
[1] Arch. Camb., CXVI (1967), p. 64, fig. 5.

Llanfihangel Fechan
SO 03 N.E. (0544 3526)　　　　　　14 v 68/3 viii 81

(HF 36) Gaer Fach (Figs. 85-87)

A small, bivallate fort stands in a commanding position on the summit of a ridge rising to 413 m above O.D., 2.5 km E.S.E. of Merthyr Cynog church. The ground beyond the defences falls away steeply in all directions especially on the S.E. where there is a sharp drop between 15 m and 25 m deep. The site has been eroded severely by ploughing and is at present grazing land with sporadic bracken cover.

The elongated-oval plan is formed by natural defences on the S.E. and a single-curved rampart following the contours of the ridge on the other sides.

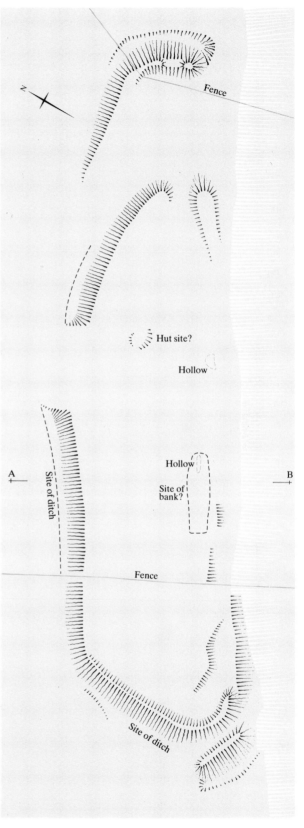

85 *(above)* Gaer Fach (HF 36) and Gaer Fawr (HF 37): physical setting

86 *(right)* Gaer Fach (HF 36)

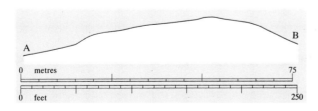

The site measures internally 140 m N.E. to S.W. by 44 m, an area of 0.48 ha. The N.E. side is strengthened by an additional widely-spaced rampart and the S.W. end by a closely-spaced short length of bank.

Most of the main rampart has been reduced to a single outward-facing scarp up to 1.8 m high, but at the S.W. end it survives as a low bank about 5 m wide by 1.2 m high externally. For a distance of 23 m on the N. the line of the rampart is interrupted by an expanse of bare rock which would have been cut away had the bank been constructed.

On the S.W. the site of the ditch is indicated by a lusher growth of grass at the toe of the rampart scarp, and further N. by a vague hollow. At the foot of the scarp around the N. is a shelf up to 3 m wide.

Immediately outside the main rampart on the S.W. is a bank 20 m long standing 2.3 m high above the shallow ditch in front of it. There is no sign that this rampart was originally longer. The outer rampart on the N.E is separated by about 30 m from the inner. It stands up to 1.8 m high above its fronting ditch which is 0.9 m deep. The N. arm of the rampart is an outward-facing scarp tapering westwards into the natural slope. The indications are that efforts to strengthen the original enclosure were curtailed before the works were completed. The ditches and the lower parts of the rampart scarps are rock-cut and the main body of the banks constructed of earth and stone rubble. A quarry-ditch, 0.9 m deep, is visible behind the bank on the S.W., which suggests that much of the material for the inner rampart may have been obtained from the interior. There are no discernible traces of the denuded scarp claimed[1] to stand 16 m in front of the main bank and represent further works around the N. side.

The only entrance seems to have been at the N.E. end through a gap between the outer rampart and the edge of the natural scarp and through a gap in the inner rampart a short distance from its N.E. termination. In the N.E. half of the interior a possible hut site is represented by a levelled platform about 5 m

87 Gaer Fach (HF 36) from the north

across which has been damaged considerably by ploughing. Elsewhere there are several modern pits, one of which may have been a beacon.

S 1950 b. 3.
[1]O.S. Record card SO 03 NW 3.

Merthyr Cynog
SO 03 N.W. (0090 3664)   15 v 68

(HF 37) Gaer Fawr (Figs. 85, 88)

A small, bivallate fort encloses the summit of the terminal spur of the Allt Arnog ridge, 3.5 km E. of Merthyr Cynog. The elongated-oval plan of the site is formed by precipitous natural defences on the S. and curving, bivallate fortifications on the other sides, enclosing an area sloping downwards from S. to N.

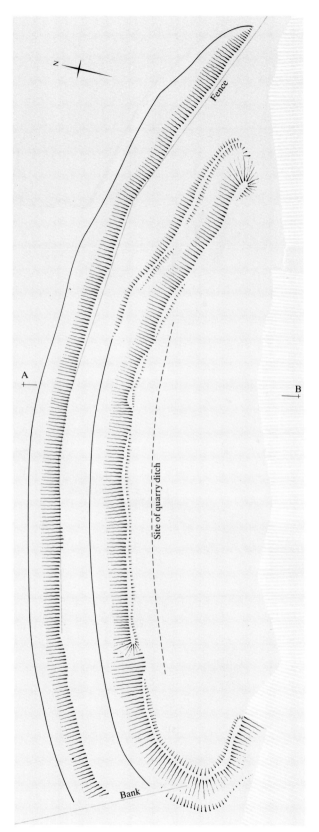

from a maximum altitude of 388 m above O.D. The ground beyond the defences falls away steeply on the N. and S.W. and the least arduous approach to the site is from the N.E. where a low saddle separates it from the main ridge.

Lying in improved grassland, the fortifications are well preserved despite some damage by ploughing especially to the outer ditch. A modern field bank and ditch impinge on the W. end of the earthworks and a modern fence occupies the crest of the outer rampart.

The enclosure measures internally 155 m E. to W. by 40 m, an area of 0.48 ha. The inner rampart is curved back on the W. to join the natural slope but on the E. stops short of the precipice to allow access to the interior. The inner face of the bank is preserved best on the W. where it is 0.9 m high. The outer scarp is up to 3 m high. The earth and rubble comprising the bank were obtained probably from the fronting ditch and an internal quarry ditch of which there are slight indications along the N. side. Most of the inner ditch has been reduced to a shelf at the toe of the rampart but a shallow depression at the W. end, and a hollow and slight counterscarp bank 0.6 m high on the E. are still visible. Between 5 m and 10 m in front of the inner ditch is the outer rampart which has been reduced to a stony, outward-facing scarp up to 2.75 m high. Ploughing has obscured the full extent of the W. end of the bank which does not seem to have been continued round to correspond to the inner rampart since there is no trace of it on the uncultivated ground above the natural S. slope. A shelf running the length of the rampart toe probably represents the site of the outer ditch. There is no trace of the counterscarp bank noted by R. E. Kay.[1]

The entrance is on the E. through simple gaps between the ends of the ramparts and the natural slope.

88 Gaer Fawr (HF 37)

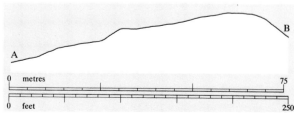

The inner rampart appears to have been strengthened here but there is no trace of the inturn indicated by Kay.[1] Traffic crossing towards a wet hollow about 50 m outside the enclosure has eroded both ramparts in corresponding positions towards the W. end of the N. side for a length of about 10 m. The use of this route rather than a more direct one suggest there may have been narrow gaps in the original works. There are no ancient features visible in the interior except the quarry ditch.

S 1950 b. 1.

[1] R. E. Kay, Notebooks, p. 1004 f. Copy in the N.M.R.

Merthyr Cynog
SO 03 N.W. (0206 3802) 17 v 68

(HF 38) Garth (Fig. 89)

Garth is a steep-sided hill rising to 280 m above O.D. about 1 km E.S.E. of Builth castle. To the E.N.E. it overlooks the confluence of Afon Dunhonw and the River Wye. The easiest approach to the summit is from the S. along the main axis of the hill crossing a moderately sloping saddle which connects Garth with a less elevated eminence just N. of Maescwm farm.

Dr. C. B. Crampton[1] has identified a "camp" just to the S. of the summit on the basis of evidence from aerial photographs and ground inspection. A trial excavation at an unspecified point across the bank of the postulated enclosure revealed that turf had been stripped from the area prior to the construction of the earthwork. R.C.A.M. investigations have not confirmed the "camp" as shown by Crampton but have identified transverse to the long axis of the hill two lengths of bank and ditch which may represent an unfinished attempt to fortify the hilltop. Lying 124 m S.S.W. of the O.S. triangulation station on the summit is a S.-facing, grassed scarp, 23 m long by 8 m wide and up to 2.5 m high, at the toe of which is a shallow ditch or shelf 2 m wide. 55 m further S. is another S.-facing, grassed scarp, 48 m long by 4.5 m wide and 0.6 m high, at the toe of which is a shelf between 2.5 m and 3.5 m wide. Both features are artificial and of defensive character but they are not continued around the rest of the hilltop and no other features likely to be related to them were discovered.

[1] Arch. Camb., CXVI (1967), pp. 65-6.

Llanddewi'r-cwm
SO 05 S.E. (0528 5055) 6 iii 81

89 Garth (HF 38): physical setting

(HF 39) Coed Pen-twyn (Figs. 90-93)

A large, oval, bivallate enclosure stands about 305 m above O.D. at the S.E. end of a small, gently undulating ridge separated by the small valley of Cwm Onneu fach from the imposing cliffs of Craig y Cilau to the S. The E. and S. sides have steep natural defences but the N. perimeter is easily approached and it is here that the strongest fortifications are found.

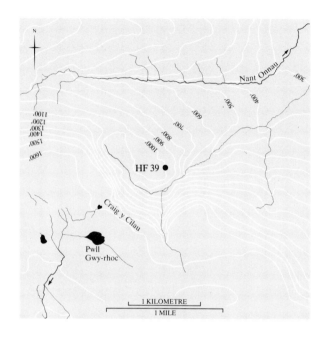

90 Coed Pen-twyn (HF 39): physical setting

The defences survive as substantial earthworks although they are denuded and covered with grass, bracken and trees. Ploughing has damaged the gently S.E.-sloping interior and has spread badly the W. counterscarp bank. The W. outer bank seems to have been slighted and levelled deliberately. In several places drystone walls of a later field system cross and utilise part of the line of the banks. Traffic along a later trackway has made breaches in the defences on the N.W. and S. South of the break in the N.W. are the ruinous remains of a sub-rectangular drystone structure built into the inner rampart and ditch. The lower walls of a derelict cottage built into the outer scarp of the N.E. rampart are better preserved. Rubble mounds against the inner scarp of the outer rampart

on the S. are probably the remains of a building. The inner end of the original entrance has been blocked deliberately with piles of stone, probably when the later field system was constructed. Other dumps and spreads of rubble unrelated to the structure are scattered about the enclosure.

The site measures internally at least 140 m N.W. to S.E. by 103 m, an area of 0.89 ha. Steep natural slopes form the only visible defence on the S.E. but it is probable that some artificial work, perhaps a fence, completed the fortified perimeter. The main rampart, constructed largely of stone, is most prominent around the N. where its inner and outer scarps are respectively up to 1.7 m and 4.2 m high. Around the S. it has been reduced to a single outward-facing scarp. No revetment is visible. The outer bank is concentric with the inner teminating on the N. opposite where the latter inturns sharply to form the N.W. side of the entrance and increasing therefore the length of the covered approach on this side. Around the N. the rampart is up to 3.3 m high externally, becoming less prominent westwards. On the W. it appears as a broad, level-topped embankment, apparently slighted, its inner and outer faces respectively 1.5 m and 1.3 m high. The outer rampart is accompanied, on the W. side only, by a short length of outer ditch and counterscarp bank, the latter badly spread by ploughing but still up to 0.8 m high. It is uncertain whether or not the inner and outer defences were constructed at the same time but it appears that an attempt to strengthen the fortifications on the W. was left unfinished.

The entrance was formed by inturning sharply the main rampart on the N.E. creating a passage sloping upwards to a gap at the ends of the inturned banks where the gate presumably stood. The passageway is now blocked and partially infilled with tumbled stone. The bank forming its E. side is up to 1.7 m high. The bank on the W. side is 4.2 m high at the outer end reducing to 1.3 m at the inner. A faint depression indicating the continuation of the passageway can be traced for about 2 m S.W. of the later blocking of the

91 *(opposite)* Photograph taken in winter snow from the cliffs of Craig y Cilau, looking north-east. The fort of Coed Pen-twyn (HF 39) is in the centre and beyond are the Usk valley and the Sugar Loaf

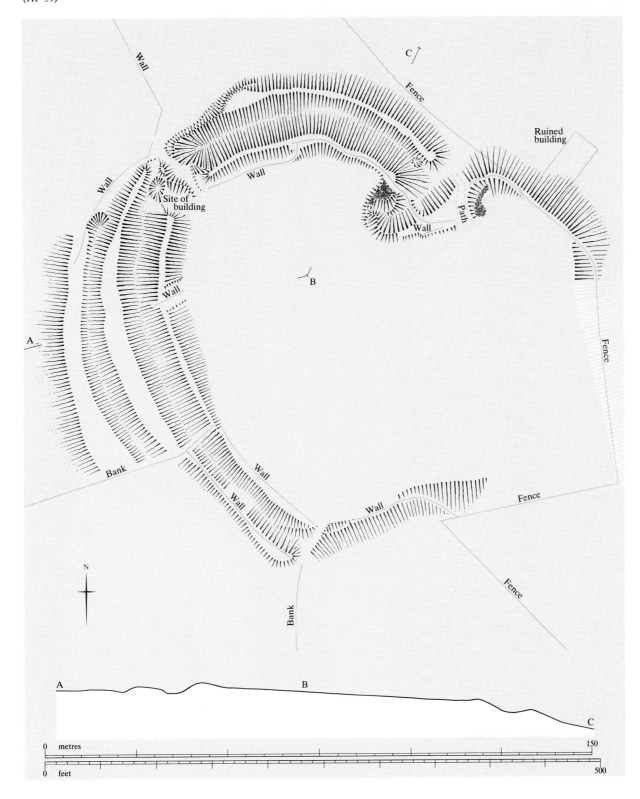

92 Coed Pen-twyn (HF 39)

93 Coed Pen-twyn (HF 39): the inturned entrance seen from its north-east corner

gateway. A possible hut-site is represented by a round hollow 9 m in diameter by 0.4 m deep lying in the angle formed by the natural scarps on the S.E., but the feature may be geological.

S 1955 p. 119 and pl. VIiI.

Llangatwg
SO 11 N.E. (1935 1622)   18 ii 77

(HF 40) Penffawyddog (Figs. 94-96)

A small, oval, univallate enclosure stands at 214 m above O.D. on a N.-facing hillslope, 1.5 km W.N.W. of Llangatwg. Overlooked by gently rising ground to the S., the earthwork is sited poorly for defence although beyond its N. side the ground is marshy and slopes away fairly steeply.

The S. half of the defences is well-preserved under grass and trees but the N. side has been reduced to a single, outward-facing scarp. A badly ruined, recent stone building impinges on the ditch in the S.W. corner where the earthworks are breached also by a modern trackway. Much of the interior is covered by a dense mat of bracken. Circular hollows, which under grass

94 *(right)* Penffawyddog (HF 40): physical setting

95 *(below)* Penffawyddog (HF 40): the defences viewed from the charcoal-burning platform

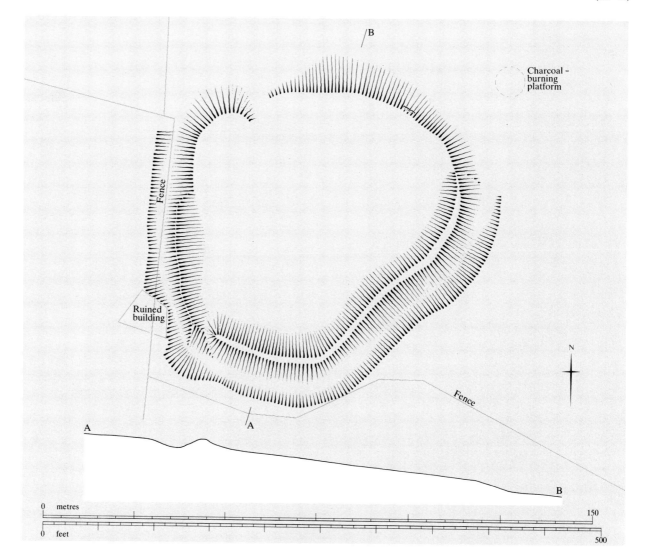

96 Penffawyddog (HF 40)

appear to represent hut sites, have been created by the movement of cattle around feeding troughs.

The site measures internally 83 m N.E. to S.W. by 67 m, an area of 0.4 ha. On the S. and S.E. the rampart is a substantial earth and stone bank whose inner and outer faces are respectively up to 2.5 m and 2.7 m high. Around the N. side the rampart is reduced to a single, outward-facing scarp from which a roughly-coursed stone revetment protrudes for a length of 3 m. The ditch is well preserved on the S. where it is up to 2.5 m deep but fades as a discernible feature

downhill and is absent apparently around the N. side. A depression in the scarp on the N.N.W. probably represents the site of the entrance. No ancient features are visible in the interior. About 15 m N.E. of the site is a circular hollow 8 m in diameter, probably a charcoal-burning platform.

S 1950 d. 2.

Llangatwg
SO 11 N.E. (1957 1845)   10 iii 77

(HF 41) Myarth (Fig. 97)

Myarth is a prominent, steep-sided hill rising to just over 297 m above O.D., 5 km N.W. of Crickhowell. It dominates a narrow stretch of the middle Usk valley to the S. and the lower reaches of the Rhiangoll valley to the N.E.

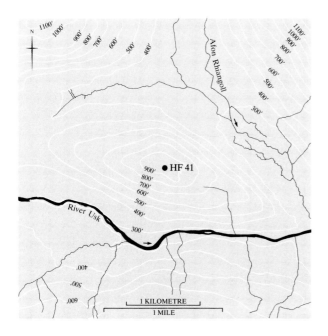

97 Myarth (HF 41): physical setting

Early antiquaries[1] mention that the hilltop was fortified with a slight stone-built defence. The 1st edition of the 1-in O.S. map[2] published in 1832 and based on a survey made in 1828[3] clearly indicates in the style used for other undoubted antiquities a mainly univallate, oval enclosure situated in the E. half of that area of the hilltop delineated by the 900 ft (274 m) contour on later 6-in maps.[4] The site measures about 354 m W.N.W. to E.S.E. by 210 m. On the E.S.E. side is a centrally-placed entrance formed by a deep inturn of the rampart and in front of this are two short lengths of bank either side of the entrance approach. The indicated position of this entrance is SO 1741 2061 approximately. Two mounds or small enclosures are shown in the interior, one abutting the N.W. corner of the rampart, the other adjacent to its S. side.

The first large-scale O.S. map of the area[5] omits these details indicating "Site of Camp" by a general antiquities symbol, a convention maintained in subsequent editions of the large-scale series until the 6-in Provisional Edition of 1964 which omits any mention of the site.[6]

In 1947 Dr. H. N. Savory[7] observed on the E. tip of the hilltop traces of a partially bivallate system of drystone rampart which appeared to end at the precipitous face on the S. but possibly continued around the N. side. On the E., Savory located a well-preserved, inturned entrance with a rectangular chamber of drystone walling about 1.5 m square built into the internal face of the N. rampart return.

The aforementioned evidence suggests strongly that a partly bivallate fortification once occupied the E. part of the hilltop, but on several visits between 1973 and 1982 O.S. and R.C.A.M. surveyors failed to locate the remains or find any unequivocal traces of ancient construction. Myarth is now heavily afforested and scattered about the hilltop are linear quarries with their associated spoil dumps which were last worked during the First World War.[8] These activities may account for the disappearance of most of the defences since 1828 but it is difficult to explain the absence of the entrance-way noted by Savory unless it was destroyed by the re-afforestation which has taken place in the general area of the feature between 1948 and 1973. At 1729 2061 a turf-covered stone mound about 10 m in diameter by 1.5 m high occupies the crest of a narrow ridge. The N.W. end of the ridge has been quarried extensively and built into one of the spoil heaps at about 1718 2061 is a ruined drystone-walled shelter. This is not to be confused (*contra* ref. 8) with Savory's "guardchamber" which was apparently further E.

A plausible line of defence can be postulated by following a sequence of scarps, crags and breaks of slope around the hilltop just within the 900 ft contour but at no point, e.g. between 1695 2083 and 1690 2080, can the observed scarp be attributed conclusively to artificial agencies. A defensive circuit based on this line would entail a fort about 630 m long by up to 260 m wide which is larger than the enclosure indicated by the 1-in O.S. map, 1st edition, but better adapted to the local topography.

Despite the complete absence of positive traces of a defensive work at the present day, the evidence of the early O.S. surveyors and Dr. Savory's observations seem to point to the former existence of a hill-fort on Myarth which would have been the largest in the county.

S 1950 a. 1.

[1] T. Jones, *Hist. of Brecknock* (Glanusk Edition), iii, p. 172; Lewis, *Top. Dict.*, s.v. Llanfihangel Cwmdu.
[2] O.S. 1-in Series, 1st edition, sheet 42, 1832.
[3] O.S. Hill Sketches (B.L. shelf-mark Maps 176, Sheet 42 SE) drawn up at a scale of 2 in to 1 mile, surveyed and sketched March 1828.
[4] 1st Edition 1891, surveyed 1885-86.

[5] O.S. 25-in Series, Brecknockshire Sheet XXXV. 14, published 1887, surveyed 1886.
[6] Sheet SO 12 SE.
[7] *B.B.C.S.*, XIV (1950-52), pp. 69-71.
[8] O.S. Record card SO 12 SE 7.

Llanfihangel Cwm Du
SO 12 S.E. (1730 2070)   9 vi 82

(HF 42) Enclosure N.W. of Pantywenallt (Figs. 98, 99)

A small, sub-rectangular, univallate enclosure stands at 310 m above O.D. on a relatively gentle, S.-facing hillslope, 1.8 km S. of Tal-y-bont ar Wysg. About 60 m to the W. the ground falls away steeply to the floor of the Clydach valley 150 m below. To the N. the land rises gradually to the hilltop occupied by Tump Wood fort (HF 43), about 0.5 km away. About 1970 the site was levelled extensively by bulldozer and is now a low earthwork covered by grass and bracken. A recent fieldbank encroaches on the S.E. corner.

The site measures internally 53.5 m N. to S. by 41 m, an area of about 0.18 ha. On the N. side the slighted stone bank has an outer and inner scarp respectively 0.2 m and 0.6 m high but elsewhere it has been reduced to a very low, stony platform. The ditch

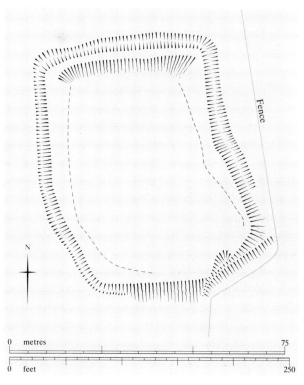

0 metres 75
0 feet 250

99 Enclosure north-west of Pantywenallt (HF 42)

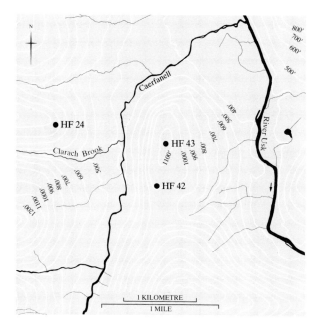

1 KILOMETRE
1 MILE

98 Enclosure north-west of Pantywenallt (HF 42) and Tump Wood (HF 43): physical setting

is a shallow depression up to 0.4 m deep, apparently absent on the S. side where it is probably masked by talus and the encroachment of a modern field bank. A depression in the rampart on the S.E. may indicate the position of the entrance. No internal features are visible.

Llanddeti
SO 12 S.W. (1117 2095)   19 xi 75

(HF 43) Tump Wood (Figs. 98, 100-102)

A small, oval, bivallate fort stands on the summit of a prominent hill rising to 356 m above O.D., 1.2 km S. of Tal-y-bont ar Wysg. The enclosure is set diagonally across the long axis of the hilltop and has steep natural defences beyond it on all sides except the S. where the slopes of the saddle connecting Tump Wood and Tor y Foel are more moderate. The fort is approached from the S.E. by a probably ancient trackway guarded by outworks.

The defences are well preserved despite some damage by erosion and afforestation. The interior is subdivided by a modern fence which has replaced an earlier boundary bank. To the N. of the fence is partially felled woodland and to the S. the land has been ploughed and is under grass. A modern track breaches the N.E. side.

The site measures internally 120 m N. to S. by 69 m, an area of 0.63 ha. The banks are constructed of stone and earth probably derived largely from ditch-digging. In the early part of this century Lt.-Col. Ll. Morgan noted[1] that "The inner face of the inner rampart is a rough stone wall" but such positive signs of construction are no longer visible. The inner bank is most prominent on the S. where its inner and outer

101 Tump Wood (HF 43) from the south

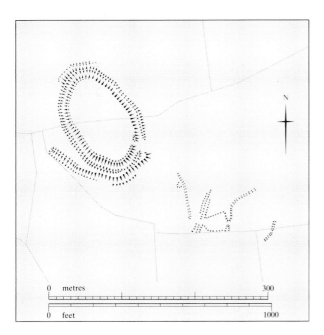

100 Tump Wood (HF 43) and outworks

scarps are respectively up to 0.6 m and 3.3 m high. Elsewhere, it is a less impressive feature. The inner scarp of the outer bank varies between 0.3 m and 1.6 m high and the outer face between 0.6 m and 1.9 m high. The only trace of a ditch in front of the outer bank is a short stretch up to 0.9 m deep around the N. end with the remains of a stony counterscarp bank up to 0.55 m high occupying its outer lip. A third rampart and ditch make use of the side of a large, natural hollow to the S. of the site to enhance its defensive capability. Constructed from the S. side of the entrance, the bank is concentric with the inner works for just over half its length, but then diverges heading N.W. before coming to an abrupt end. It would appear to represent an unfinished attempt to add a wider-spaced extra defence around the S.W. side of the site where it was most vulnerable to attack. The

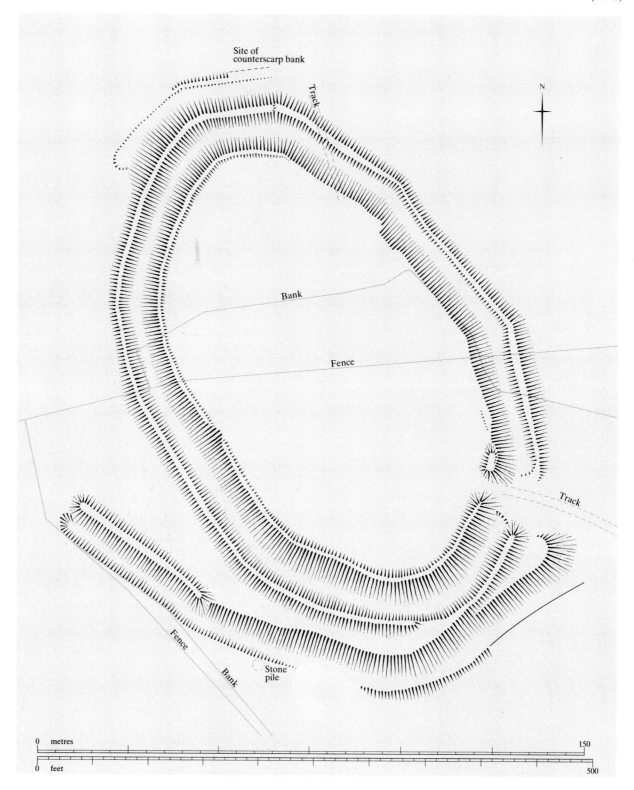

Site of
counterscarp bank

Track

N

Bank

Fence

Track

Fence

Bank

Stone
pile

| 0 | metres | | | 150 |
| 0 | feet | | | 500 |

102 Tump Wood (HF 43)

inner and outer scarps of the bank are respectively up to 1 m and 2.7 m high. The ditch continues the line of the natural hollow N.W. and is up to 1 m deep. The entrance is a simple gap in the ramparts on the S.E. No ancient features are visible in the interior.

S 1950 a. 8.

[1] Notes by Lt.-Col. Ll. Morgan in N.M.R. (Wales).

Llanddeti
SO 12 S.W. (1127 2149)   6 xii 69

(HF 44) Cross Oak Fort (Figs. 103, 104)

A small, nearly circular, univallate enclosure occupies a small knoll rising to almost 140 m above O.D. on the W. edge of the flood plain of the Usk, 0.7 km N. of Tal-y-bont ar Wysg. The position is slightly elevated but of no particular strength and is overlooked by rapidly rising ground to the W. Periodic flooding of the river valley would have provided additional natural defence on the N. and E. where the site is now skirted by the Brecknock and Abergavenny Canal.

The enclosure has been denuded severely by ploughing which has filled in the ditch and left the bank only just traceable above the general surface of the knoll. The form is discernible most readily from the air.[1] The fort measures internally 105 m N.E. to

104 Cross Oak Fort (HF 44) from the east

S.W. by 95 m, an area of 0.8 ha. The overall width of the defences seems to have been about 20 m originally. A group of four field names to the S.E. include the *gaer* element.[2]

[1] Discovered by Dr. J. K. St. Joseph. C.U.A.P. ARF 81, ASA 99.
[2] Llanfigan Tithe Award Schedule, Nos. 425-6, 466-7.

Llanfigan
SO 12 S.W. (1105 2355)   6 v 69

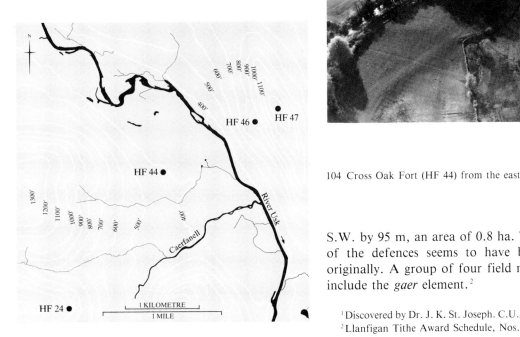

103 Cross Oak Fort (HF 44): physical setting

(HF 45) Coed y Gaer (Figs. 105-107)

A small, triangular, univallate enclosure stands at about 229 m above O.D. on a steep, S.-facing hillslope, 0.4 km N.W. of Cwm-du. Beyond the defences on the N. the site is overlooked by rapidly rising ground while in other directions the land falls away steeply to the Clarach Brook and the Rhiangoll.

The N. and W. sides of the earthworks are preserved reasonably well under a cover of grass and trees. Ploughing has damaged the interior, now under grass, and reduced the defences on the S. and E. to outward-facing scarps. Breaches in the earthworks occur on the N. and S.E., the latter apparently associated with a

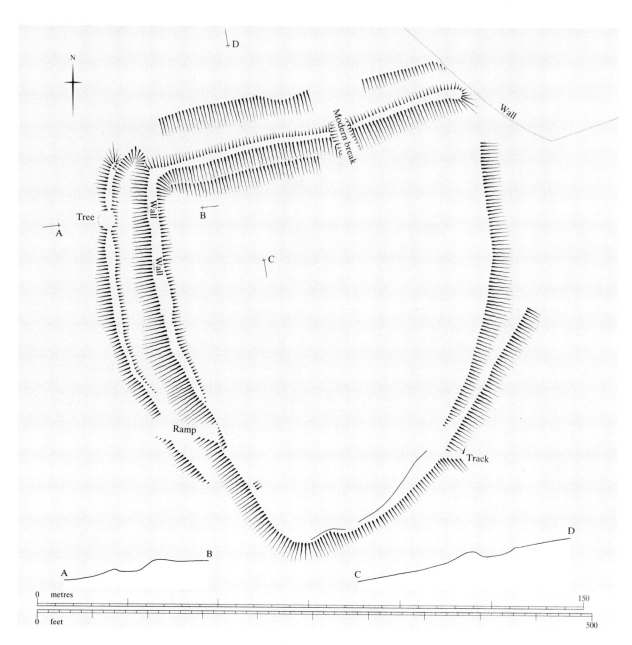

105 Coed y Gaer (HF 45)

track approaching a quarry.

The site measures internally 97 m N. to S. by 88 m, an area of 0.57 ha. On the N. the main rampart is a substantial earth and stone bank whose inner and outer faces are up to 3.2 m and 2 m high respectively. On the W. the bank is much slighter on its inner face, up to 0.2 m high only, but the outer face is between 2.5 m and 3 m high and along the outer crest are the remains of a drystone wall between 0.8 m and 1 m wide. Elsewhere the rampart has been reduced to a single, outward-facing scarp between 1.1 m and 1.7 m high on the S. and 0.3 m to 1.5 m high on the E. A ditch is present only on the N. and W. where its maximum depth is respectively 2.2 m and 1.5 m. It fades as a discernible feature at the S.W. corner and is absent on the S. and E. sides where it was probably never

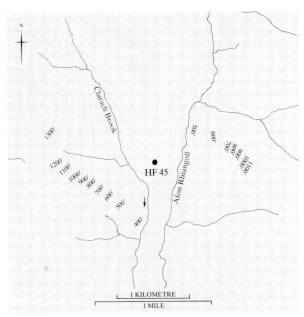

106 *(right)* Coed y Gaer (HF 45): physical setting

107 Coed y Gaer (HF 45): view of the defences from rising ground to the north

built. At the N.W. corner and at the point corresponding to the later breach in the N. rampart the ditch has been partly infilled. A counterscarp bank between 1.3 m and 2 m high stands on the lip of the W. ditch. The breaches in the N. and S.E. were made probably later than the period of occupation of the enclosure and the most likely site for an original entrance is on the W. side where there is an angled ramp-like approach across the defences.

A vague hollow in the N.W. corner at 1758 2404 may be a hut platform,[1] but otherwise there are no visible ancient features in the interior.

S 1950 c. 2.

[1] O.S. Record card SO 12 SE 3.

Llanfihangel Cwm Du
SO 12 S.E. (1762 2402)   18 iii 76

(HF 46) Enclosure W. of Allt yr Esgair (Figs. 108-110)

A small, oval, univallate enclosure stands at about 244 m above O.D. on the edge of a narrow natural terrace in the steep S.W.-facing slope of the ridge Allt

yr Esgair, 0.7 km N. of Llansanffraid. To the E. the site is overlooked by steeply rising ground while to the S. and W. the land falls rapidly to the flood plain of the Usk.

Recent cultivation activities have denuded the earthworks which are largely grass-grown with sporadic patches of bracken and other vegetation. In places, particularly the W. side, piles of stones from field clearance have been added to the bank.

The site measures internally 44 m N.W. to S.E. by 25.5 m, an area of 0.085 ha. The defences seem to be weaker on the uphill side but this impression may have been created by the later damage to the site. On the W. the stony bank takes advantage of the natural change of slope and in its present spread form the outer scarp is up to 3.1 m high while the inner scarp is only 0.25 m high. In contrast, on the E. the inner scarp is up to 1.1 m high while the outer is only 0.2 m high. There are no signs of an external ditch. The entrance is a simple gap in the bank on the N.W.

108 Enclosure west of Allt yr Esgair (HF 46) and Allt yr Esgair (HF 47): physical setting

109 (opposite) Enclosure west of Allt yr Esgair (HF 46): the site seen from rising ground on the north-east. Beyond are the Usk valley and the eastern escarpment of the Brecon Beacons

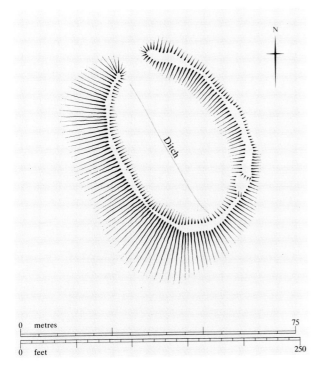

0 metres   75

0 feet   250

110 Enclosure west of Allt yr Esgair (HF 46)

The interior is subdivided by a shallow ditch up to 2.2 m wide by 0.25 m deep which runs from the toe of the inner scarp of the bank on the S.E. to a point just short of the toe of the W. butt-end of the entrance, the gap here being possibly the site of a gate. The relationship of the interior ditch to the main bank is unclear.

Llansanffraid
SO 12 S.W. (1231 2420)   24 v 79

(HF 47) Allt yr Esgair (Figs. 108, 111-113)

A very large, multivallate fort occupies the upper part of a prominent ridge rising to 393 m above O.D. between the Usk and Afon Llynfi, 3 km N.W. of Bwlch. Beyond the enclosure are steep natural defences on all sides, the least arduous approach being from the S. along the main axis of the hill.

Interpretation of the remains is rendered difficult by the afforestation of most of the E. half of the site and the very extensive pit and linear quarrying that has been carried out, particularly in the area of the summit. The unwooded parts of the enclosure are covered by moorland grass and often dense bracken. Field walls and banks of various later dates also dissect the site.

At its S. end the main enclosure takes in the summit of the ridge which is marked by prominent cliffs along its W. edge. The rest of the perimeter follows mostly the line of a major break of slope around the ridge-top to the N., and on the N.E. stands about 60 m below the summit. It is very difficult to distinguish genuine defensive earthworks from linear quarrying around the summit but it is possible that the main enclosure incorporates an earlier fort confined to the highest part of the ridge. To the S. of the main defences a smaller enclosure takes in less sharply sloping ground, about 30 m below the summit at its S. end.

The principal enclosure measures internally 566 m N.N.W. to S.S.E. by 114 m, an area of 5.45 ha. In most places the rampart is represented by a single, substantial, outward-facing scarp continuous except where later narrow breaches have occurred or, as near the S. end of the W. side, it was dispensed with because adequate natural defences were available. The scarp varies in height between 2 m and 8 m, being particularly prominent along the N. part of the W. side. At the S.E. corner the main scarp on the E. seems to have merged into the outer scarp of the counterscarp

111 *(above)* Allt yr Esgair (HF 47) from the south-east   112 (*opposite*) Allt yr Esgair (HF 47)

113 Allt yr Esgair (HF 47): the north entrances viewed from the east side of the approaching hollow-way

bank around the S. end while the main bank around the S. fades into the natural slope of the interior. A stone revetment 28 m long was visible near the centre of the E. side, but recently part of it has been destroyed. Near the middle of the W. side are discontinuous traces of a low inner scarp up to 0.7 m high. In several places within the line of the rampart are irregular depressions, probably the sites of quarries providing stone for the bank. A ditch and counterscarp bank lie in front of the main bank on the N. and S. sides, and at the S. end of the W. side. The inner face of the counterscarp bank is up to 0.3 m high, while the outer scarp is up to 3 m high in its present eroded form. On the E. the ditch has been reduced to a terrace and along part of the W. side it was dispensed with where the ground is particularly steep.

The main entrance is a simple gap in the defences at the N. end. A hollow-way, undoubtedly deepened by later traffic, leads N.N.W. down the hill. A lesser entrance may have existed near the centre of the W. side where the ditch and counterscarp bank give out and a terrace approaching at an angle breaks the line of the main scarp. Another minor entrance may have existed in the corresponding position on the E. side but the details have been obscured by recent bulldozing.

The smaller enclosure appears to be annexed to the larger although the details of the N. junction are uncertain. The main defence is a robbed stone wall above outcrop on the W., continued round the S. and E. as an outward-facing scarp up to 3 m high which appears to fade into the natural hillside. Between the apparent end of this scarp and the E. edge of the hill is a small, curved length of rubble bank, now partly destroyed, which appears to represent one side of a funnel-shaped entrance-passage. It is possible that a bank or fence once connected the latter to the S.E. corner of the main fort making an enclosure of just under 0.8 ha. Alternatively, the curved bank is unrelated and the annexe either unfinished or destroyed along its N.E. side. Later building activity at the S.E. corner of the main enclosure has obscured the surface details further. The surviving defences are accompanied by a ditch up to 1 m deep and a counterscarp bank up to 1 m high.

No definitely ancient features are visible in the interior of either enclosure.

S 1953 a. 9 supersedes S 1950 e. 3.

Llansanffraid/Llangasty Tal-y-llyn
SO 12 S.W. (1270 2430)   1972-75

(HF 48) Enclosure near Caeau (Figs. 114, 115)

A small, oval, univallate enclosure stands at 330 m above O.D. on a fairly steep, E.-facing slope, 3 km E. of Llan-gors. To the W. the site is overshadowed by the cliffs of Mynydd Llan-gors while to the E. the ground falls away rapidly to the small stream in Cwm Sorgwm. The approach to the site from N. and S., parallel to the mountain side, is relatively easy. Covered in tussocky grass and bracken, the enclosure is in a ruinous condition having been used as a stone quarry.

At the N.W. corner there is a discontinuity between the uphill scarp and the beginning of the free-standing bank. The inner crest of the latter is continuous with a stony scarp running S., a short distance in front of the foot of the uphill scarp. As this feature curves S.E. it becomes a ruined, free-standing wall about 0.3 m high with a narrow gap towards its end. There is a corresponding break in the walling of the outer perimeter close to its present termination. The inner scarp and wall may represent a later reduction in the size of the enclosure and either its entrance was placed relative to a pre-existing one or a breach in the outer perimeter walling was made to correspond to the new one.

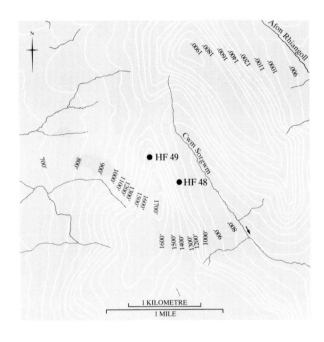

114 Enclosure near Caeau (HF 48) and earthwork on Cockit Hill (HF 49): physical setting

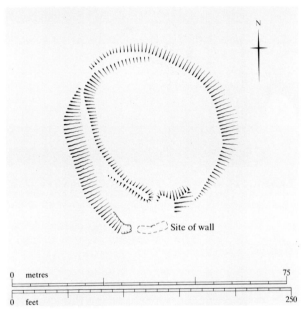

115 Enclosure near Caeau (HF 48)

The site measures 45 m N. to S. by 38 m, an area of 0.13 ha. The hillslope has been terraced to give a more moderate gradient to the interior. The downslope side is bounded by a stony bank up to 2 m high which probably supported originally a stone wall of which badly ruined traces are visible on the S. Upslope the hillside is scarped to a maximum depth of 2.2 m. Material excavated from here was probably used in the construction of the bank. On the S.W. a substantial length of a retaining wall of boulders is visible, and sporadic remains of it occur on the W. side also. There is no trace of a ditch which was probably not required.

Adjacent to the site are later stone quarries and running from it in a general direction a few degrees W. of N. is a broad, stony lynchet about 2 m high falling to the E. The relationship of the lynchet and enclosure is uncertain.

Llan-gors

SO 12 N.E. (1646 2738)25 v 78

(HF 49) Earthwork on Cockit Hill (Figs. 114, 116, 117)

A single bank and ditch at 460 m above O.D. cut off from the rest of the ridge the triangular N. tip of Mynydd Llan-gors, 2.5 km E. of Llan-gors. The edge of the promontory is formed by precipitous cliffs on the N. and E. and very steep, grassed slopes on the W. To the S. the ground faced by the earthwork rises gradually to the summit of the ridge.

The promontory defined by the earthwork is 60.6 m long by 30 m at its broadest, an area of about 0.09 ha. The grass-grown bank consists of two unequal lengths of earth and stone rubble up to 1.2 m high. The E. end curves inwards slightly and there is a narrow gap between it and the natural cliff-edge. The largely infilled ditch in front is up to 0.3 m deep and does not seem to run to either edge of the ridge. A trackway divides the bank into two unequal lengths and seems to have truncated the E. part. The track ascends the N.N.W. side of the ridge, crosses the promontory and continues S. along the crest of the mountain. The breach in the bank is probably the site of an entrance that was orginally narrower.

The site might be interpreted as a promontory fort although in its present form the earthwork is an unimpressive barrier. Alternatively it might be a *cross-ridge dyke* controlling traffic along the ancient ridgeway in the manner of those known from Glamorgan which are assigned to the eighth or ninth century A.D. or earlier.[1]

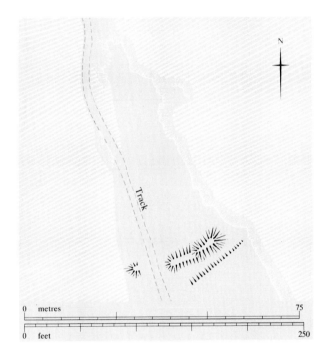

[1] *Inv. Glam.*, I, iii, pp. 5-6.

Llan-gors
SO 12 N.E. (1603 2774)   25 v 78

116 *(left)* Earthwork on Cockit Hill (HF 49)

117 Earthwork on Cockit Hill (HF 49): the south face of the earthwork

(HF 50) Castell Dinas (Figs. 118-121)

A large, irregularly oval, multivallate fort occupies the summit of a prominent, steep-sided hill rising to 450 m above O.D., 4.2 km S.E. of Talgarth. On the N. and W. additional works enclose the more moderate slopes below the crown of the hill. The site commands the saddle between Mynydd Troed and Y Grib which forms a pass through the N.W. edge of the Black Mountains between the Rhiangoll valley and the Afon Llynfi valley, a tributary of the Wye.

118 Castell Dinas (HF 50): physical setting

The site consists of fortifications of at least two periods, a pre-Roman Iron Age hill-fort and a medieval castle. The remains of both are now largely reduced to grassed stony banks and scarps covered in places, particularly on the E. and S.W., by scattered trees and bushes. A small coniferous plantation covers the outworks on the S.W. Post-medieval boundaries cross and follow part of the line of the earthworks. There has been damage by quarrying to part of the W. outworks and at the S. end of the main defences.

The summit of the hill is subdivided into three enclosures (A, B, C, fig. 119). The interior of A is fairly level though it begins to fall away on the E. B

slopes downwards more markedly to the S. and E. while the surface of C stands considerably below B and falls away sharply to the S.E. Enclosure A is divided from B by a wall, a ditch deeply rock-cut on the W., and a counterscarp bank which in their present form represents works of the castle period although they may have been founded on an earlier system. Together the enclosures measure internally 174 m N. to S. by 93 m, an area of about 1.03 ha. The common inner rampart occupying the edge of the hilltop has been modified substantially by being incorporated in the medieval perimeter defences. The latter are described, along with the other remains of the medieval castle, by R. E. Kay.[1] The present outer scarp of the inner rampart is between 5.2 m and 15 m high but this may represent an exaggeration of the original dimensions as Kay (*op. cit.*) has suggested that this scarp was deepened during the building of the castle. The main gate of the castle lies in the S.W. of the rampart and is approached by a ramped track from the N.W. crossing the line of the defences at an angle. It is not possible to say whether or not the gate occupies an original gap in the Iron Age defences. However the N. gate of the castle probably does, for although later building has obscured the details it seems that the original rampart was inturned, at least on the N.W. The approach to this entrance is more complicated as several sloping, terraced tracks converge to the N. at the foot of the second rampart through which there is an inclined passage between somewhat inturned bank terminals which emerges at the toe of the N. corner of the inner rampart and follows it in a curving course to the site of the gate.

The second rampart, considerably below the edge of the hilltop, runs concentric with the inner on the E. and W. On both sides a low inner scarp is present up to 0.8 m high on the E. and 2.3 m high on the W. The outer scarp is up to 6.7 m high on the W. and 11 m high on the E. To the N.E. of the entrance the defence is strengthened in depth by widening this rampart and splitting it into two levels for a short distance. Similar strength in depth is given to the W. of the entrance by the coalescing of the second with the N.E. ends of two other ramparts. Although the details are somewhat obscure it appears that on the S.E. and S.W. the rampart departed from running parallel with the circuit of the inner bank to take in quite steeply sloping ground to the S. forming the irregularly shaped enclosure C. This suggests that the

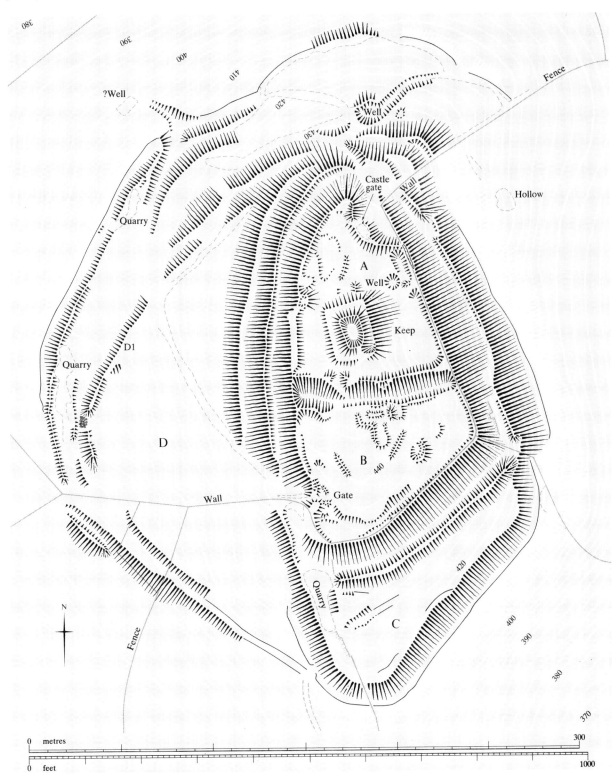

119 Castell Dinas (HF 50)

second rampart system is a later addition to the original plan. The scarp forming the S.W. and S.E. perimeter of enclosure C is between 6 m and 8.5 m high. The N.W. side is formed by the outer scarp of the inner rampart, up to 10 m high, with a rock-cut ditch up to 4 m deep in front on whose S. lip is a massive counterscarp bank up to 3.5 m high. The ditch is almost certainly an original feature but its depth was probably increased, and the counterscarp created or heightened, during construction of the castle. Kay (*op. cit.*) considers that the quarry hollow extending S. from between the W. end of the counterscarp bank and the W. perimeter scarp is an unfinished dry moat

120 Castell Dinas (HF 50) from the south

intended to continue that of the middle bailey (enclosure B) of the castle. In the interior, N.E. of a length of outcrop within and parallel to part of the S.W. side, is a shallow cut of uncertain purpose or date. Around the foot of the perimeter scarp is a narrow shelf below which it is uncertain whether or not any further artificial scarping has occurred. Although the junction and relationship of enclosure

C and the outworks on the W. is indistinct, the latter are probably later.

The evidence for a consistent third rampart system is ambiguous. Along the toe of the second rampart on the E. side of the main enclosure is a shelf below which it is also uncertain whether there has been further artificial scarping. However, N.W. of the modern field wall crossing the N.E. corner of the ramparts the slope definitely has been modified below a short length of ditch to further strengthen the area in front of the entrance. Along the W. side and concentric with the inner two is a third rampart between 4.3 m and 6 m high originating from the lower part of the outer scarp of the second rampart just W. of the entrance and perhaps re-coalescing with it in the area obscured now by the ramp leading to the S.W. gate of the castle.

A series of partly artificial terraces in the N. and N.E. slopes below the main entrance comprise approach tracks and possibly additional defences of uncertain date. Among these, just outside the entrance, is Dinas Well, a hollow containing a brackish pool from which a boggy channel leads downslope.

To the W. of the hill-fort ploughing, quarrying and tree-planting have combined to render the system of outworks on the lower slopes of the hill indistinct and fragmentary. Whatever the nature of these structures, they are unlikely to have been defensive and their dating is uncertain. A crescentic area of land about 210 m N. to S. by 75 m seems to be enclosed by a discontinuous curving earthwork (D 1) whose N. end branches from the outer scarp of the third rampart 55 m S.W. of the entrance. Where an inner scarp is present, on the W., it is up to 0.6 m high while the denuded outer scarp is between 0.8 m and 3.2 m high. Immediately in front of the N.W. side of this structure, below a shelf, is another scarp up to 4 m high concentric with it, which has its origin at the point where the second and third main ramparts join at the entrance. On the W. also are fragmentary traces of banks and scarps in front, but it is not possible to be sure that these belong to a consistent system. However, running in front of and concentric with the S.W. side of the crescentic enclosure is a distinctive scarp up to 2.5 m high with a short length of counterscarp bank in front. Its line is continued N. by a low bank and scarp partly disturbed by quarrying which diverges

121 *(opposite)* Castell Dinas (HF 50): view of the eastern defences from the lower slopes of Y Grib

slightly W. from a line truly concentric with the enclosure upslope. The earthwork runs N. to the S.W. side of a hollow trail from the N.W. which leads towards the ramp ascending the hill to the S.W. gate of the castle. The earthworks to the N.E. of the trail are ill-defined scarps.

The whole complex of earthworks at Castell Dinas covers a zone 363 m N. to S. by 280 m E. to W., an area of 6.58 ha.

A late prehistoric flint flake was found in 1981 on the second rampart at the S.E. corner (SO 1797 3006).[2]

S 1950 a. 5.
[1] *Brycheiniog*, X (1964), pp. 15-27.
[2] Now in the N.M.W.

Talgarth
SO 13 S.E. (1789 3008)   25 v 83

(HF 51) Drostre Bank (Figs. 122, 123)

A small, oval, univallate fort encloses the top of a small, steep-sided hill rising to 284 m above O.D., 2.5 km S.W. of Llanfilo. The W. part of the enclosure has been denuded severely by ploughing and is at present under sown grass while the E. side is wooded and in parts pitted with quarry hollows and masked by spoil tips. A hollow-way, probably associated with the quarrying, runs through the N.E. corner.

The site measures internally 133 m E.N.E. to W.S.W. by 72 m, an estimated area of 0.65 ha. On the N. and W. the rampart has been reduced to a single outward-facing scarp up to 2 m high. On the S. and S.E. it appears as a discontinuous scarp between areas of quarrying. On the E. a bank of earth with a few stones survives whose inner and outer scarps are respectively up to 0.5 m and 1.2 m high. A linear depression to the rear of this bank may be the remains of an internal quarry ditch. Around the W. and N.W. sides the outer ditch is represented by a shelf at the foot of the rampart scarp. There is no clear evidence that the ditch was present on the other sides. A short stretch of counterscarp bank, 0.3 m high, survives on the N.

A possible position for an entrance lies on the S.W. where the line of the rampart scarp is broken by a terrace at an angle to it. The later hollow-way at the N.E. corner may pass through an original gap. No ancient features are visible in the interior.

S 1950 b. 10.

Llanfilo
SO 13 S.W. (1017 3133)   8 iii 77

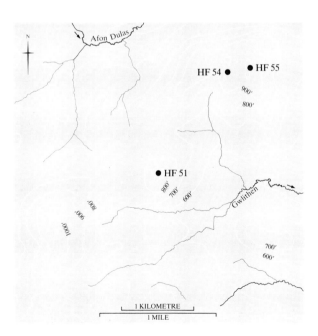

122 Drostre Bank (HF 51): physical setting

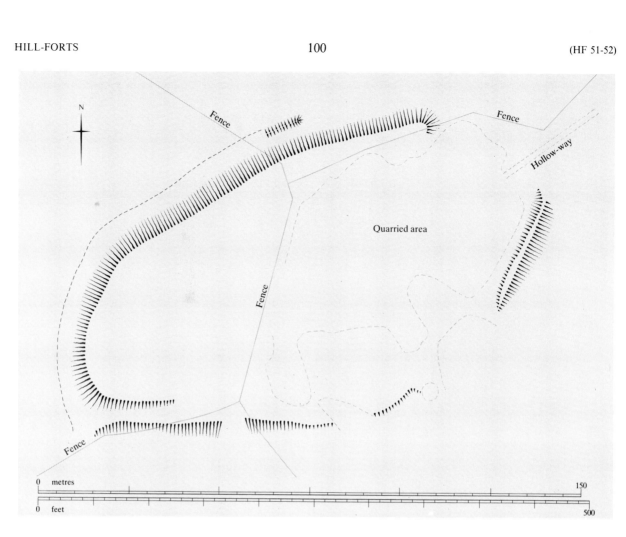

123 Drostre Bank (HF 51)

(HF 52) Enclosure N.W. of Llwyfen (Figs. 124, 125)

A small, oval, univallate enclosure stands at 200 m above O.D. on a fairly steep, E.-facing slope, 2 km S.E. of Llanfilo. The uprooting of the copse formerly covering the site and subsequent ploughing have denuded the enclosure severely. The defences consist of a low, spread earth bank about 9 m wide enclosing an area 38.5 m N. to S. by 25.5 m. The external ditch survives as a barely discernible depression. The most likely position for an entrance is on the S.W. to judge from aerial photographs.[1] No internal features are visible.

[1]C.U.A.P. ABI 91.

Talgarth
SO 13 S.W. (1313 3169)   14 iv 70

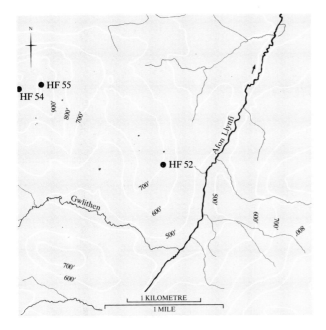

125 Enclosure north-west of Llwyfen (HF 52) from the east

124 Enclosure north-west of Llwyfen (HF 52): physical setting

(HF 53) Pendre (Figs. 126-128)

Curving, bivallate fortifications and steep natural defences define a pentagonal promontory enclosure between 168 m and 183 m above O.D., 1 km S. of Talgarth. The defences cross the broad neck of the promontory protecting it against an easy approach from the E. and N.E. On the other sides there are steep natural falls to a tributary stream of the River Enig.

The E. part of the defensive circuit is well preserved but ploughing has denuded the N.E. side and all but obliterated the surface remains of the outer ditch. Previously both banks were covered by trees and dense undergrowth but this has been removed from the outer. Modern fences cross and in places make use of the line of the defences. Beyond the N. end of the banks are traces of a field bank system pre-dating the modern boundaries but later than the fort. A ploughed-out track is visible crossing the grass-grown interior.

The site measures internally 161 m N. to S. by 154 m, an area of 1.57 ha. The earth and stone banks seem to become less prominent as they run N. but this impression may have been created by plough damage. There is no definite evidence of ancient artificial works

126 Pendre (HF 53): physical setting

around the W. or S. sides where a relatively modern trackway has been terraced into the natural scarp. The inner scarp of the main bank stands up to 3.1 m high, and near its S. end a short line of sandstone blocks is exposed which may belong to a revetment. The outer scarp of the inner bank is up to 5.6 m high towards its S. end. The inner scarp of the outer bank is up to 3.6 m high towards its S. end while the outer scarp is up to 1.7 m high near the N. end. For about 90 m along the E. side are vague traces of the ploughed-out outer ditch. Both banks seem to stop short of the natural scarp edges at either end suggesting that there were two entrances to the site. The N.E. terminations of both banks seem to be very slightly inturned. There are no ancient features visible in the gently undulating interior.

S 1950 c. 1.

Talgarth
SO 13 S.E. (1558 3263)   5 iii 81

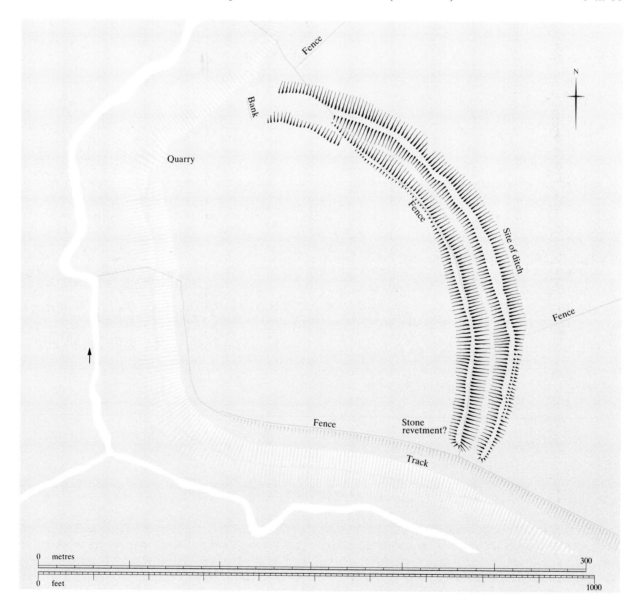

127 Pendre (HF 53)

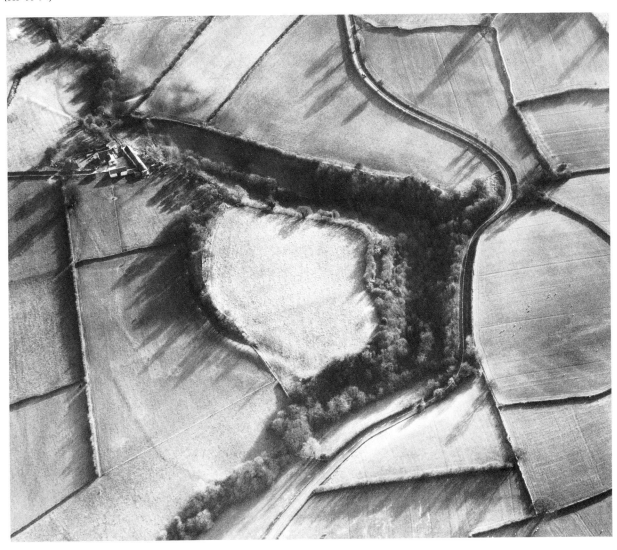

128 Pendre (HF 53) from the north

(HF 54) Enclosure E. of Pen-yr-allt (Figs. 129, 130)

A small, oval, univallate enclosure stands at 300 m above O.D. on the edge of a low, steep, W.-facing escarpment, 1 km S.W. of Llanfilo. To the E. of the site the ground rises gently towards the large fort of Hillis (HF 55) 200 m away. To the S. there is a narrow stretch of level land before the fairly steep fall towards Pengoyffordd. The W. side of the enclosure is formed by a natural escarpment up to 2.5 m deep whose slope may have been enhanced artificially. The latter is now grass-grown and wooded, and in places there are lengths of outcropping rock which have been quarried slightly. The S. and S.E. defences have been denuded by ploughing and are overlain by later field boundaries. The N.E. part of the rampart is grass-grown and tree-covered. Movement along pathways has eroded the W. escarpment and a modern trackway truncates the bank on the N. The interior slopes gently from E. to W. and has been ploughed.

The site measures internally 60 m N. to S. by 47.5 m, an area of 0.23 ha. The rampart is best preserved on the N.E. where it is a grass-grown earth and stone bank whose inner and outer scarps are respectively up to 1.3 m and 2 m high. On the S.E. the bank is reduced to a single outward-facing scarp up to 1.4 m high and on the S. is represented probably by a very low, plough-spread mound. The ditch on the S. is up to 0.7 m deep while that around the E. and N. is between 0.3 m and 0.8 m deep. A likely position for the entrance is the gap between the end of the bank and the natural escarpment on the N. but modern damage has obscured the details.

Similarly, plough damage and later boundary construction have obliterated the original form of the

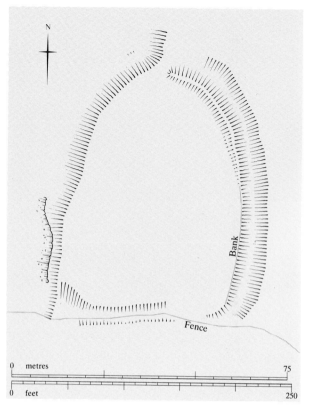

130 Enclosure east of Pen-yr-allt (HF 54)

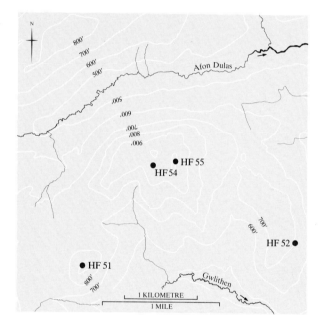

129 Enclosure east of Pen-yr-allt (HF 54) and Hillis (HF 55): physical setting

S.E. corner. A short hollow, partly impinged upon by a field bank, exists at the foot of the natural escarpment beyond the N.W. corner of the enclosure. The nature of any functional relationship between the two features is uncertain. No ancient structures are visible in the interior.

S 1950 d. 3.

Llanfilo
SO 13 S.W. (1108 3269)   1 iii 79

(HF 55) Hillis (Figs. 129, 131-133)

A large, oval, multivallate fort encloses ground rising to 310 m above O.D. at the end of a ridge S. of Afon Dulas, 0.6 km S.W. of Llanfilo. Beyond the defences the land falls away fairly steeply on three sides while

131 *(opposite)* Hillis (HF 55): modern boundaries omitted

132 Hillis (HF 55) from the north-east

133 Hillis (HF 55): the inner end of the south entrance

the approach from the W. is easy across the gently undulating crest of the ridge. The interior rises generally to a high point near the middle of the W. side.

For most of the circuit the defences are grass-covered and wooded and a line of trees follows the crest of the scarp subdividing the interior. Ploughing has denuded the interior and inner defences. Part of the N.E. side has been damaged by quarrying of which there are further remains beyond the S.W. corner. Recent field banks and fences cross and partly utilise the lines of the earthworks and movement along paths and tracks has caused erosion.

The site measures internally 340 m N. to S. by 132 m, an area of 3.6 ha. The ramparts consist at present of consolidated banks of stone rubble. For much of its circuit the inner rampart has been reduced to an outward-facing scarp between 0.8 m and 3.1 m high above a terrace on the site of the inner ditch. Around the N.W. side and at the S. entrance traces of the inner face of the bank survive up to 0.9 m and 1.1 m high respectively. The inner bank is the only defence on the N. and there is no surface indication of a ditch in front. Throughout its circuit the second rampart has been reduced to an outward-facing scarp varying between 0.5 and 3.1 m high. A counterscarp bank gives additional strength to the defences on the

W. and S. where the approach is easiest. The inner and outer scarps of the bank attain maximum heights of 1 m and 1.5 m respectively but in places on the W. the feature is of no more than fieldbank proportions and there are no traces of a ditch in front.

There are two entrances. On the S. the inner rampart is deeply inturned forming a passageway about 28 m long, narrowing to 3 m wide at the gate end. This passageway is approached obliquely from the S.E. through simple gaps in the outer defences. The inner rampart is also deeply inturned on the N.E. forming a passageway at least 25 m long which narrows to 2 m wide. The sloping passage to the gate here may have been partly rock-cut. The approach to the entrance is obscured by quarrying but appears to have been via a causeway at an angle to the line of the defences.

The interior is subdivided by a S.-facing scarp up to 3 m high into two enclosures respectively 191 m and 143 m long N. to S. The scarp is probably the eroded remains of a rampart inserted at a later date to reduce the defensible area to the N. half of the site. No other ancient internal features are visible.

S 1950 a. 3.

Llanfilo
SO 13 S.W. (1140 3273)   1969

(HF 56) Enclosure in Tredurn Wood (Figs. 134, 135)

A small, sub-rectangular, univallate enclosure stands at about 230 m above O.D. on the E. tip of a ridge, 0.8 km S. of Llandyfalle. The site can be approached fairly easily from most directions but on the S. the slopes of the spur falling fairly steeply to the upper reaches of Afon Dulas afford some natural protection.

Afforestation has caused extensive damage to the earthworks. Most of the old conifer plantation has been felled and replaced by young trees but remnants survive on the perimeter of the site. Grass, bramble and holly cover the banks and interior and reeds grow in the ditch and waterlogged hollows.

The site measures internally 74 m E. to W. by 45 m, an area of 0.25 ha. The earth and stone rampart is most prominent where it is transverse to the E.N.E. to W.S.W. axis of the ridge and poorly defined parallel

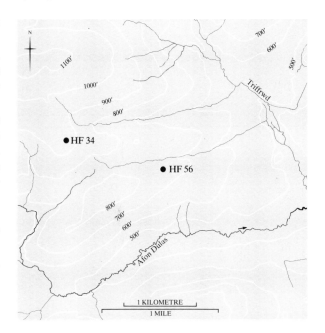

134 *(right)* Enclosure in Tredurn Wood (HF 56): physical setting

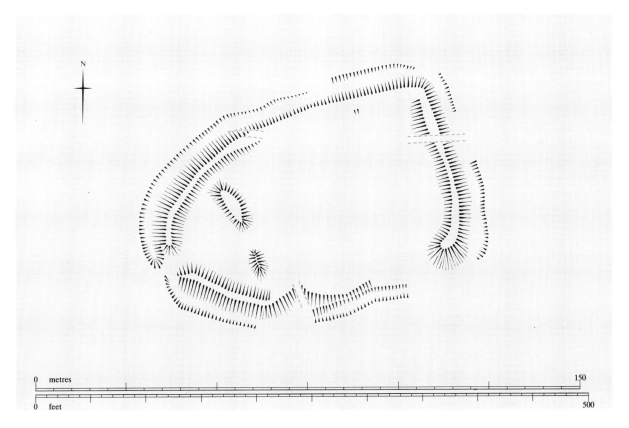

```
0  metres                                                    150
0  feet                                                      500
```

135 Enclosure in Tredurn Wood (HF 56)

to it, particularly on the S.E. On the W. the inner and outer scarps are up to 0.8 m and 2.4 m high respectively and on the E. up to 0.7 m and 1.6 m high. The ditch is a discontinuous feature up to 1.2 m deep on the W. but between 0.2 m and 0.4 m deep elsewhere. The entrance is a simple, narrow gap in the centre of the W. side. A small part of the W. interior is divided from the rest by two lengths of low bank

up to 0.3 m high which may have been accompanied by a very shallow ditch. It is not clear whether or not this is an original feature. No other structures are visible.

Llandyfalle
SO 13 S.W. (1062 3471)   3 iii 81

(HF 57) The Gaer, Aberllynfi (Figs. 136-139)

A small, sub-rectangular, multivallate fort stands up to 115 m above O.D. on a minor plateau overlooking the lower reaches of Afon Llynfi near Three Cocks. The platform is aligned N.N.E. by S.S.W. and bounded on the E. by a small ravine whose stream has its source at a spring close to the S.E. corner of the enclosure. To the N. and W. the ground beyond the defences falls away fairly steeply but the land to the S. is virtually level. As Savory[1] pointed out, the fort is well sited tactically but not in a commanding position being only about 30 m above the valley floor and overlooked by higher ground to the E. of the ravine.

The site is very poorly preserved. Much of it was levelled deliberately just after World War II with the result that the surface remains observed in 1951 bore only a general relationship to the configuration of the defences as revealed by excavation. As an example, the outer scarps of the levelled inner and outer banks E. of the entrance on the N.N.E. were shown to be several metres in front of their presumed original positions. Continual ploughing since 1951 can be expected to have exacerbated the damage.

The main enclosure measures internally 122.5 m N.E. to S.W. by 48 m, an area of about 0.45 ha. The ravine provides natural protection on the E. while the other sides have bivallate defences, the W. being further strengthened with a counterscarp bank. There are inturned entrances on the N.N.E. and S.S.W. The N.N.E. entrance is approached from the N. by a slightly sunken track bounded on its W. side by a low spread bank extending about 55 m downslope. The N. end of this bank is joined by the N. extension of the counterscarp bank on the W. side of the main enclosure. Two short lengths of banking about 0.1 m high lie roughly at right angles to the track on the E.,

136 The Gaer, Aberllynfi (HF 57) and the small 'Gaer' in Gwernyfed Park (HF 58): physical setting

apparently demarcating a small annexe. The present maximum heights of the outer scarps of the three banks on the W., inner to outer, are 2 m, 1 m and 1 m respectively. On the S.S.W. the outer scarp of the inner bank is up to 0.3 m high while the inner and outer faces of the outer bank are up to 0.5 m high.

137 *(opposite)* The Gaer, Aberllynfi (HF 57)

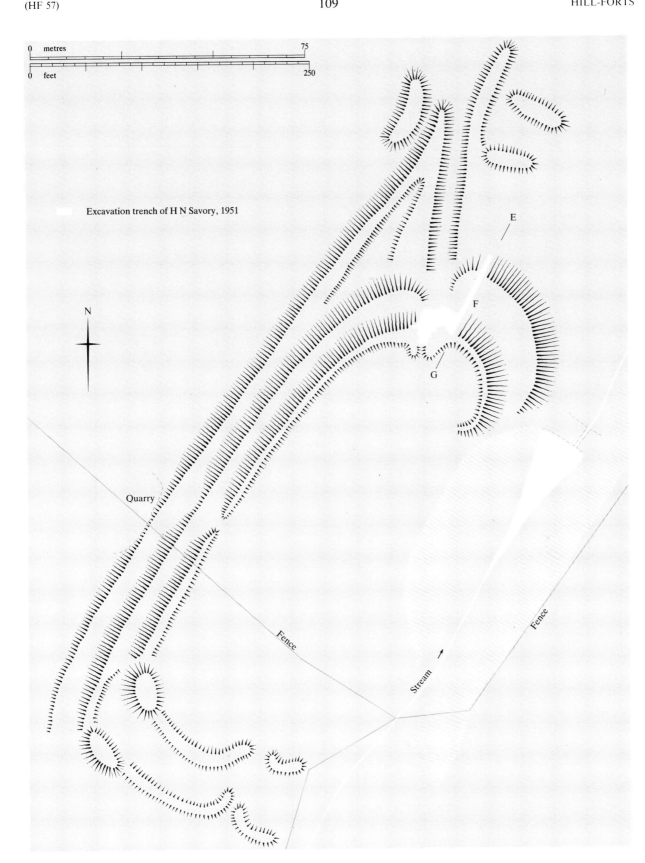

Excavation trench of H N Savory, 1951

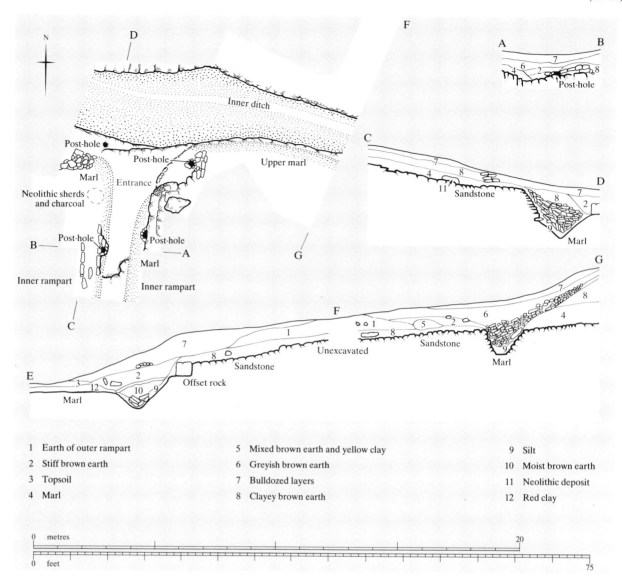

1 Earth of outer rampart
2 Stiff brown earth
3 Topsoil
4 Marl
5 Mixed brown earth and yellow clay
6 Greyish brown earth
7 Bulldozed layers
8 Clayey brown earth
9 Silt
10 Moist brown earth
11 Neolithic deposit
12 Red clay

138 The Gaer, Aberllynfi (HF 57): plan and sections of H.N. Savory's excavations at the north-north-east entrance

The excavations conducted by Dr. H. N. Savory in July 1951 consisted of a trench across the defences just E. of the N.N.E. entrance with a westward extension to include the latter and both ends of the inner rampart on either side of the gap. The inner rampart was not sectioned fully and its structure is inferred from the filling of its associated ditch. The material for both ramparts seems to have been obtained largely from the ditches and varied according to the nature of the subsoil into which they were cut. The inner ditch was dug through an upper layer of marl, a stratum of laminated sandstone and a lower marl deposit. The main trench revealed only the front of the inner rampart consisting of the foot of a sloping-fronted bank of clayey brown earth lying directly on the upper marl. The material was interpreted as the foundation of the rampart, being composed of the old surface soil with the addition of similar material derived from the preliminary stages of ditch-digging. A deposit of small stones rested on the slopes of the brown earth and the marl and was continuous with the main filling of the inner ditch which consisted of a loose accumulation of sandstone blocks and smaller stones with only a slight amount of earth in the interstices. Although the largest slab found lay on the inner slopes of the ditch towards the lower fill, the majority of the larger stones occurred towards the top of the fill near the inner lip. The excavator considered that the deposit derived from the original superstructure of the inner rampart, the outer foot of which stood at a higher level and some distance S. of the end of the main trench. The stones appeared to have accumulated rapidly and Savory favoured the idea that the filling was the result of deliberate slighting of the rampart. The largest block may have been a facing stone which would have been among the first to have been thrown into the ditch, accounting for its lower position. Amongst the stone fill were a few slingstones and, towards its upper part, a small piece of early Romano-British pottery. The bottom filling of the ditch was a sticky clay, up to 0.38 m (15 in) deep in the main trench but decreasing to a very slight deposit as the ditch bottom rose W. to the area opposite the entrance. The clay probably accumulated fairly rapidly and contained redeposited Late Neolithic artefacts, a single Early Iron Age potsherd and a few flecks of charcoal. The profile of the inner ditch as revealed in the main cutting was V-shaped with a flat base, its dimensions being: upper width 1.67 m (5 ft 6 in), base width 0.46 m (18 in), inner lip depth 1.6 m (5 ft 3 in), outer lip depth 1.07 m (3 ft 6 in). A small part of the original superstructure of the inner rampart was extant W. of the entrance consisting of superimposed sandstone blocks revetting an earth core directly over the upper marl.

Between the inner and outer ditches the original brown topsoil was sealed under the lower part of the outer rampart which consisted of clean brown earth containing a few water-worn pebbles. Resting on the inner toe of the bank was a small deposit of mixed brown earth and yellow clay probably derived from cleaning out the inner ditch.

The outer ditch was larger than the inner with a V-shaped profile measuring 3.96 m (13 ft) wide at the mouth, 2.13 m (7 ft) deep at the inner lip and 1.22 m (4 ft) deep at the outer lip. The inner lip was stepped as a result of quarrying through bedded sandstone while the outer slope was cut entirely through the lower marl. Above a shallow primary silt the ditch was filled with sandstone blocks probably derived from the outer revetment of the outer rampart. The upper fills were accumulations after the abandonment of the site.

The excavation of the N.E. entrance gap was not carried to the rear of the inner rampart and therefore it was not established certainly that the latter was inturned as the surface remains suggest. The entrance passage proved to be narrower than expected being only 1.07 m (3 ft 6 in) wide. Two post-holes, one either side of the gap but not directly opposite each other, represented the gate. The sandstone revetment expected at the ends of the inner rampart was absent, presumably removed. In front of the entrance the inner ditch was an unbroken feature widened to 2.74 m (9 ft), its base rising westwards with the natural slope. The continuity of the ditch appeared to be part of the original plan. In front of the main entrance passage and E. of the line of the thoroughfare, a post-hole 0.31 m (1 ft) in diameter and 0.15 m (6 in) deep lay in a mainly natural recess in the bedrock. Opposite it, 3.66 m (12 ft) away on the other side of the entranceway was a smaller post-hole 0.15 m in diameter. Savory suggested that the larger post-hole may have held a support or mooring post of a moveable bridge to span the ditch while the smaller hole held a post to which the bridge was secured at night or at times of attack. The primary fill of the inner

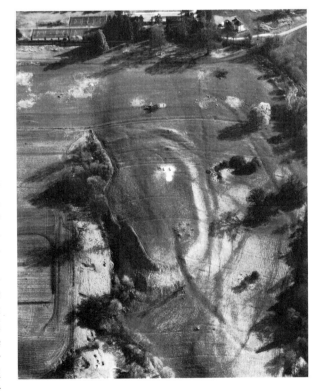

139 The Gaer, Aberllynfi (HF 57) from the north-east

ditch opposite the entrance was a thin deposit of yellow clay containing some charcoal and redeposited Neolithic artefacts. The ditch near the entrance of a hill-fort was a favourite place for dumping rubbish and the sparseness of the deposit here led the excavator to suggest that the ditch had been cleared out only a short time before the demolition of the rampart. However, the N.E. entrance was probably of lesser importance than the S.W. where occupation may have been more concentrated.

Below the rampart core to the W. of the entrance and beneath the old toposil lay a thin spread of dark earth, 0.46 m (18 in) in diameter, associated with charcoal and Neolithic potsherds. The deposit probably filled the base of a hollow of some kind, largely obliterated by agricultural activity a considerable time before the hill-fort was built.

No ancient features are visible in the interior and none were excavated in 1951.

One potsherd of probable pre-Roman Iron Age date was found in the primary silt of the inner ditch but it is of little help for the chronology of the site. A sherd of Romano-British type jar of possible late first century date came from the upper part of the same ditch apparently associated with the rampart debris. Iron smelting at nearby Gwernyfed Park (*cf.* p. 183) attests growing Roman influence in the area towards the end of the first century A.D. and Savory suggested that it it is possibly in the context of this that the slighting of the fort should be seen.

S 1950 b. 8.

[1]*Brycheiniog*, IV (1958), pp. 33-71.

Aberllynfi
SO 13 N.E. (1750 3759)   1951/1983

(HF 58) Small 'Gaer' in Gwernyfed Park (Fig. 136)

The earliest 25-in O.S. map[1] depicts an enclosure named 'Gaer' at about 100 m above O.D. just over 300 m E.N.E. of Three Cocks Inn. Three conjoined straight lengths of bank up to 10 m wide form the W., N.W. and N.E. perimeter while the meander of a small stream forms the S. and S.E. sides. The area enclosed measures 70 m N.E. to S.W. by 40 m. The position is weak defensively as the site is overlooked by higher ground to the S. of the stream and the land beyond the enclosure falls away very gently to the N. and W.

The site was apparently in a ruinous condition at the beginning of this century. In a rather confusing account of the remains,[2] Lt.-Col. Ll. Morgan seemed to regard the extant bank as a counterscarp to a main rampart which had been levelled throughout. A ditch, only intermittently visible, accompanied the bank. The stream had truncated the work on the S.E. Just before a visit by Dr. H. N. Savory in 1950[3] much of the earthwork was bulldozed when the parkland was converted to arable, leaving only part of the W. side upstanding. At present under trees and undergrowth,

the latter is a bank of red-brown clayey earth incorporating angular fragments of local sandstone and waterworn sandstone pebbles. It is perched on the edge of the stream cliff just over 2 m above the present water level and measures about 6 m wide by 2 m high.

The site must be considered doubtfully worthy of inclusion as a defensive earthwork. An alternative interpretation is that it is the remains of an old pond bay at the head of the millrace of the defunct Aberllynfi mill.[4]

S 1953 e. 8 superseding S 1950 e. 8.

[1]O.S. 25-in Series, 1st edition, sheet XXIII. 6, 1887.
[2]Notes on Breconshire hill-forts by Lt.-Col. Ll. Morgan in R.C.A.M. files.
[3]S 1953 e. 8.
[4]O.S. Record card SO 13 NE 21.

Aberllynfi
SO 13 N.E. (1776 3788)   25 v 79

(HF 59) Llys-wen Enclosure (Figs. 140-142)

A large, multivallate enclosure stands between 180 m and 210 m above O.D. on a steep E.S.E.-facing slope

overlooking the Wye valley, 0.5 km W. of Llys-wen church. The land falls away steeply on the N. and E.

while the site is overlooked by rising ground to the W.

Most of the defences lie in deciduous woodland where they have suffered natural denudation which in places has reduced them to single scarps. They have been eroded further by a series of small streams and movement along relatively recent tracks and paths. Stream erosion has made the earthworks appear more prominent than they were originally. Recently, one streamlet has been dammed between the inner and outer scarp at the S.E. corner. The grass- and bracken-covered interior slopes upwards from E. to W. and does not appear to have been ploughed in recent times.

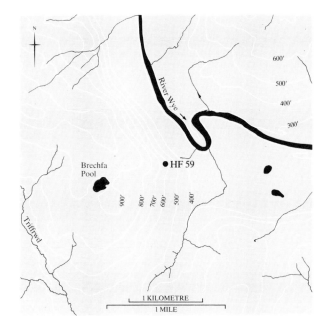

140 Llys-wen Enclosure (HF 59): physical setting

The main enclosure is an irregular pentagon formed by straight lengths of bank and measures internally 97 m N. to S. by 81 m, an area of about 0.7 ha. The annexe is an irregular quadrilateral enclosing about 0.42 ha. The annexe and the outermost rampart on the S. appear to be additions to the main enclosure, probably at the same date.

The inner rampart of the main enclosure is a strong earth and stone bank on the uphill W. and S. sides but around the E. has been reduced to an outward-facing scarp between 1.3 m and 2.5 m high. On the W. the inner scarp of the bank is up to 3 m high. The outer scarp is up to 5 m high at the S.W. corner where

stream erosion has scoured the ditch at its foot but elsewhere it is between 2 m and 4 m high. The outer rampart is slighter than the inner. On the E. it is reduced to an outward-facing scarp between 1.5 m and 2.5 m high. Elsewhere it is a bank whose inner face is about 4 m high at the S.W. corner but between 2 m and 2.7 m high along the S. side. The outer scarp stands up to 3 m high on the S., decreasing to between 0.6 m and 1.2 m on the W. but rising again to 2.5 m on the N.W. The outer ditch is a discontinuous feature, lacking on the N. and E. and poorly preserved on the S. On the W. it is between 1.5 m and 2 m deep with an exaggerated depth of 3.1 m at the S.W. corner where streams have enlarged both ditches into miniature ravines.

There are several breaches in the defences but the simple gap through the two scarps on the E. was probably the only original entrance to the main enclosure. No ancient features are visible in the interior.

The inner scarp of the annexe rampart is up to 2 m high although it is generally lower and partly absent on the S. The outer face is very prominent, about 3.4 m high, near the junction with the S.W. corner of the main enclosure. Around the W. side it is between 0.4 m and 1 m high. It is uncertain whether or not the bank was accompanied by a true ditch. Access to the annexe was obtained through a broad gap at the N. end. A low L-shaped earthwork has divided off from the rest of the interior a small rectangular area at the tip of the enclosure which is entered through a narrow gap in the N.W. corner. This structure may post-date the building of the annexe.

The third rampart on the S. has been damaged considerably but in places the outer crest stands up to 1.7 m above the base of a shallow ditch in front which seems to accompany the earthwork for about half its length.

Llys-wen was an important centre in early medieval times, for legal disputes between Gwynedd and Deheubarth were adjudicated here. It is conceivable that some of the works of the enclosure belong to this period.[1]

S 1950 c. 4.

[1] Suggested by Professor Dewi-Prys Thomas, who also believes that the shape of the enclosure represents a conscious attempt at an architectonic shaping of pentagonal space, setting this site apart from other hillslope enclosures in the county. (Letter to R.C.A.M., 6 ii 85.)

Llys-wen
SO 13 N.W. (1277 3790)   23 iii 79

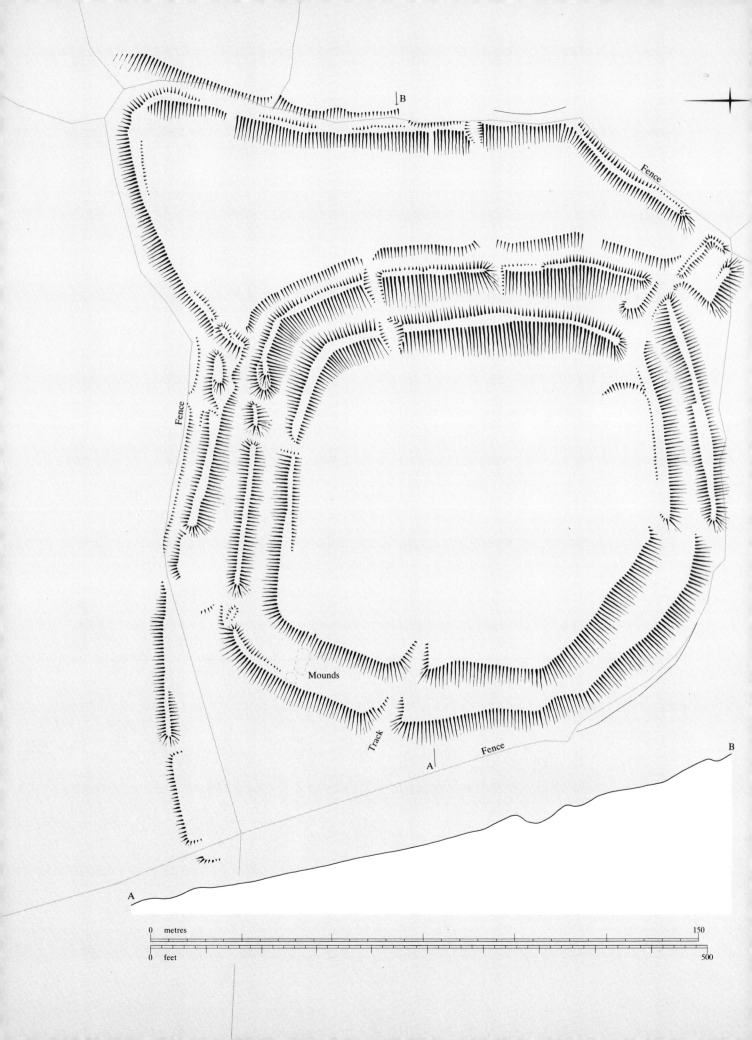

B

Fence

Fence

Fence

Mounds

Track

A

A

B

0 metres 150

0 feet 500

141 *(opposite)* Llys-wen Enclosure (HF 59)

142 *(right)* Llys-wen Enclosure (HF 59): the southern defences of the main enclosure seen from its south-east corner

(HF 60) Trwyn y Ddinas Camp (Fig. 143)

Lt.-Col. Ll. Morgan[1] and the O.S.[2] record the existence of a "camp" here. The site is a prominent limestone spur with strong natural defences. The tip of the spur has been quarried extensively and there are no recognisable traces of any ancient earthwork that may have existed here.

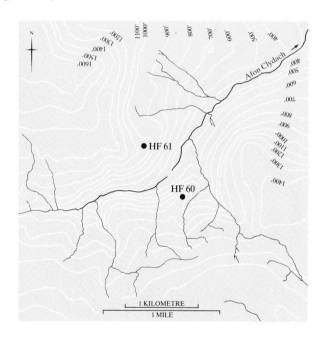

S 1950 e. 5. Dismissed as probably not an earthwork, but not visited.

[1] Notes on Breconshire hill-forts by Lt.-Col. Ll. Morgan in R.C.A.M. files.

[2] O.S. 25-in Series, sheet XLVII. 4, 1904, where it is named Twyn y Dinas.

Llanelli
SO 21 S.W. (2288 1259)   1 v 80

143 Trwyn y Ddinas Camp (HF 60) and Craig y Gaer Camp (HF 61): physical setting

(HF 61) Craig y Gaer Camp (Fig. 143)

The O.S. records a "camp" here.[1] The site has good natural defences on the N. and E. but is weak elsewhere. There are no recognisable remains of ancient earthworks but it is possible that they have been destroyed by quarrying.

S 1950 e. 4. Dismissed as probably not an earthwork, but not visited.

[1] O.S. 25-in Series, sheet XLVII. 4, 1904.

Llanelli
SO 21 S.W. (2234 1326)   1 v 80

(HF 62) Crug-y-gaer (Figs. 144-146)

A small, oval, univallate enclosure stands at 290 m above O.D. on a moderate, E.-facing slope, 0.8 km N.W. of Llanelli church. The position has no particular strength as it is approached easily from all directions. The interior rises from E. to W. and a small, rocky knoll on the N. forms its highest point.

The site is covered in grass and bracken, and trees grow on the line of the defences. The bank has been robbed of its stone in places and part of the interior knoll has been quarried. Several modern tracks breach the rampart and a ruined field wall crosses the W. corner. Around the S. perimeter are dumps of stone from recent field clearance and other modern disturbances.

The site measures internally 79.5 m N.W. to S.E. by 69 m, an area of about 0.43 ha. The single rampart was constructed predominantly of stone to judge from the considerable amount visible in its grassed scarps. Just N. of the entrance a short stretch of front and rear revetment walling is preserved which indicates that the original width of the rampart base was between 6 m and 6.5 m. Four courses of drystone walling composed of superimposed flattish stones is visible. On the N. and N.E. the rampart has been reduced to an outward-facing scarp up to 3 m high. Elsewhere, it survives as a bank of variable dimensions, its inner scarp up to 0.6 m high and its outer scarp as low as 0.3 m high on the N.N.W. A ditch is present in two unconnected lengths on the W. and S.W., a maximum of 0.3 m deep. There are vague hints that it continued further S. but it is uncertain whether or not it surrounded the whole site. The entrance is a simple, sunken gap in the ramparts on the S.E. There are no ancient features in the interior.

S 1950 d. 1.

Llanelli
SO 21 N.W. (2248 1530)   11 iii 77

144 *(above)* Crug-y-gaer (HF 62): the defences from the south-west

145 Crug-y-gaer (HF 62): physical setting

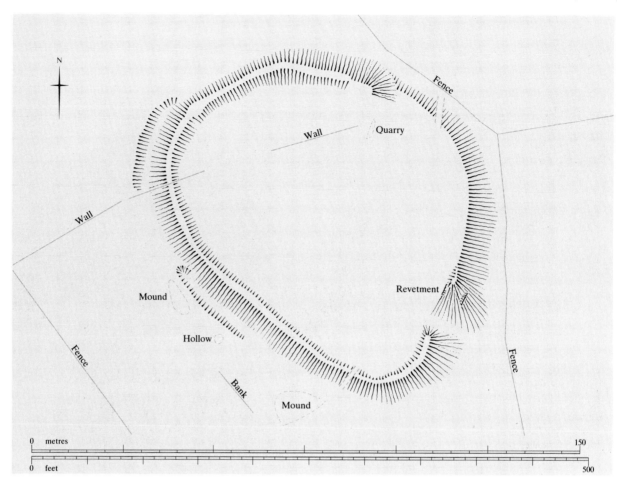

146 Crug-y-gaer (HF 62)

(HF 63) Coed Cefn (Figs. 147, 148)

A small, sub-rectangular, univallate enclosure stands at about 228 m above O.D. on a small hilltop 1 km E. of Crickhowell. Beyond the defences the ground falls away sharply to the S. but more moderately elsewhere. The site is surrounded by woodland and some trees grow on the defences and in the interior which is covered also by areas of dense bracken. The greatest damage to the site has been done by quarrying, especially in the S.W. interior and at the N.W. corner where hollows and tips are in evidence. A modern track breaches the rampart near the centre of the W. side.

The site measures internally 68 m N. to S. by 51 m, an area of about 0.29 ha. On the S.E. the rampart has been reduced to an outward-facing scarp but elsewhere it is an earth and stone bank whose inner scarp is generally between 0.2 and 0.8 m high, though up to 1.1 m at the N.W. corner. The outer scarp is most prominent on the S. where it is up to 1.75 m high. On the N. it is up to 1.25 m high. The remains of a stone wall on the S. were recorded in 1962[1] but these could not be traced in 1977. The site of the ditch is indicated by a shelf at the S.W. corner and along the N.E. side and by two linear depressions, respectively 0.5 m and

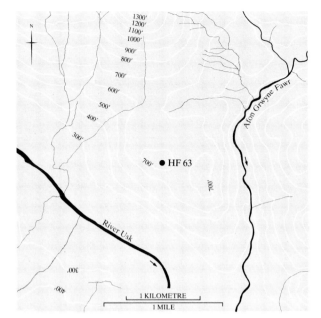

0.7 m deep, along the N. side and at the N.W. corner. A low counterscarp bank may have been present on the N. The original entrance is represented by a simple gap in the rampart just S. of the centre of the E. side. A corresponding gap on the W. side is a relatively modern breach. It is possible that there was another entrance at the N.W. corner but the area is obscured by quarrying. No ancient features are visible in the interior.

S 1950 d. 4.

[1] O.S. Record card SO 21 NW 12.

Llangenni
SO 21 N.W. (2281 1859)   12 i 78   148 Coed Cefn (HF 63)

(HF 64) Crug Hywel (Figs. 1, 149-153)

Crug Hywel is a prominent, small, pear-shaped plateau with steep rock edges and an undulating surface between 437 m and 451 m above O.D., 2.3 km N.N.E. of Crickhowell. The hilltop is a S. spur of Pen Cerrig Calch which rises to 701 m above O.D., 1.7 km to the N.W. In other directions the ground falls away steeply to the Usk and Grwyne Fechan valleys. The site is an ideal temporary refuge, being easily defensible. The

sides of the plateau have been scarped artificially into defences comprising a main upper perimeter and a strong counterscarp.

Because of the differential way in which erosion affects the plateau the remains in the S. and S.E. are better consolidated by moorland turf than those further N. where the scree on the scarps is looser and the crags below are partially exposed. At the pointed

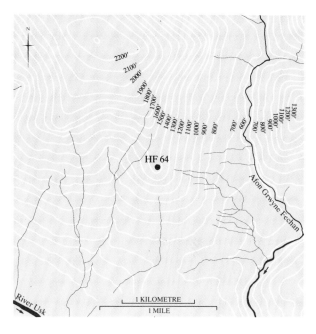

149 Crug Hywel (HF 64): physical setting

N. tip the upper edge consists of low cliffs of bare rock. While natural agencies have done most of the damage to the edges of the defences, the upper part and the interior have been interfered with by humans who have robbed the upper stone defensive wall and built several small stone shelters in the rampart and interior. Disturbance of the interior is still taking place.

The site measures internally 162 m N.W. to S.E. by 59 m, an area of about 0.63 ha. Around the edge of the plateau are the remains of a stone wall. On the S. and S.E. it is a turfed, stone bank, generally low but reaching 1.7 m high S. of the entrance. On the W. and N.E. only the edge of the wall is turf-consolidated, up to 0.6 m high, the crest of the mound consisting of a loose stony area about 1.6 m wide from which boulders have been robbed. In places on the W. there is a suggestion that the base of the core of the wall consisted of stones pitched on edge in a shallow trench. Except at the N. tip of the plateau, there is a steep scree-masked scarp below the wall, generally between 7 m and 8 m high. At its toe are the remains of a rock-cut ditch. This is readily visible as a rock-strewn hollow on the E. but on the S. and W. it is represented mostly by a narrow terrace partly masked by scree. The outer face of the counterscarp is another stony scarp between 4 m high on the N. and 7 m high on the S. There is no ditch beyond it unless the small area of quarrying

below the N. tip is an unfinished attempt.

There is a single entrance on the E. where both the main ramparts and counterscarp are inturned on either side of a steeply inclined passageway which narrows to the site of a gate 1.75 m wide at the terminals of the inner rampart. Immediately W. of this point, inside the fort, there is a distinctively sunken area. Leading N. around and down the hillside from the entrance is a terraced trail, part of a network of tracks of various dates crossing the hillslopes in the vicinity.

In the interior four shallow oval depressions, probably hut sites, are attached to the rear of the defensive wall (Fig. 151, A-D). Their dimensions are: A, 11.5 m by 10.2 m; B, 9 m by 9 m; C, 8 m by 6.5 m; D, 11.5 m by 11 m. There are other vague depressions in the S. half of the interior which may be hut sites. Behind the N. inturn of the inner rampart is a hollow which may be another hut site. Behind the S. inturn of the inner rampart is a sub-rectangular area defined by a low stone bank about 0.3 m high which is probably a later shelter.

On the slopes to the S.W. of the fort are several structures of different periods. Two features appear to be of considerable antiquity (Fig. 150, X and Y). X is a small, semi-circular hillslope enclosure, 19 m N.W. to S.E. by 12 m, open on the uphill side and defined by a sandstone rubble bank up to 0.5 m high.

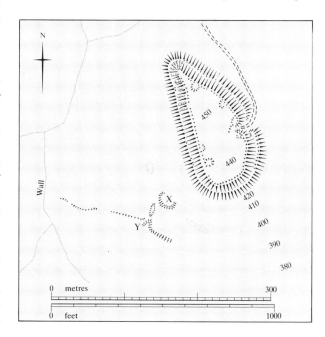

150 Crug Hywel (HF 64): structures on the slopes below the fort

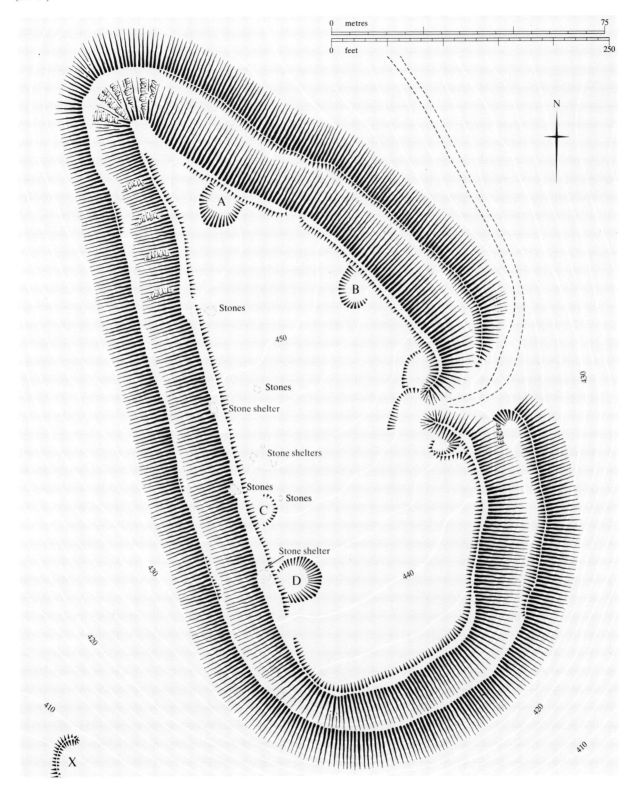

151 Crug Hywel (HF 64): based on a survey by A. W. Pearson, 1983

152 *(opposite, upper)* Crug Hywel (HF 64) from the north

153 *(opposite, lower)* Crug Hywel (HF 64): view of the defences from the saddle on the north

Y may be the remnant of an early field system delineated by boulder-revetted terraces and low stone banks. The S.W.-facing terrace is up to 1.5 m high.

S 1950 a. 7.

Crickhowell/Llanbedr Ystrad Yw
SO 22 S.W. (2255 2065)   25 iii 83

Omitted Sites

These have been suggested as defended sites but their authenticity is very doubtful.

(i) RHIWIAU, S.W. of Llanfrynach. No trace of the supposed hillslope enclosure was found despite exhaustive searching.

Brycheiniog, I (1955), p. 119. SO 02 S.E. (055 240).

(ii) ABERCLYDACH, S.S.W. of Tal-y-bont ar Wysg. In the area of the supposed hillslope enclosure are several natural ridges and escarpments but, excepting field boundaries, no man-made structures are visible.

Brycheiniog, I (1955), p. 119. SO 12 S.W. (102 217).

(iii) LOWER HOUSE, S.S.E. of Hay-on-Wye. There are no convincing surface remains of the "distinct...camp" supposed to occupy this spur.

Trans. Woolhope Naturalists Field Club (1898-9), p. 140. SO 24 S.W. (2375 4115).

Roman Remains

It will never be possible to write a detailed history of the relationships between the Roman Imperial authorities and the native, Silurian tribesmen who occupied the lands later designated Brycheiniog (Brecknockshire). Tacitus, the sole literary source for the history of Wales in the first century A.D., offers too imprecise an account to allow more than intelligent guesswork about the campaigns of the Roman army in the area. Too little archaeological and even less epigraphic data are available to be in any way decisive both within the area and on its periphery. Nevertheless, it is worth briefly considering some of the possibilities that such evidence suggests.[1]

It is generally agreed that the lands of Brecknock were occupied by northern groups of the Silures who from only a few years after the initial Roman invasion of south-east Britain in A.D. 43 were engaged in a bitter and bloody struggle for independence from Rome. Until A.D. 50 they formed the core of Caratacus's army in his struggle with the Roman governor Ostorius Scapula. Caratacus moved to Ordovician territory further north to avoid a decisive engagement with Scapula, an action that may have been forced upon him by a Roman encircling movement up the Wye, Tywi and Usk valleys; in this case Brecknock would have been undoubtedly the scene of considerable activity, but there is not the slightest archaeological trace at present recognisable. Although Caratacus was defeated and later treacherously surrendered to the Romans, the Silures maintained a stubborn resistance involving guerilla tactics which achieved considerable success against the Roman army and culminated in A.D. 52 in the defeat of a legion. The speculation that Brecknock was concerned in the campaigns of Scapula is to some extent dependent on the definition of the eastern boundary of Silurian territory, usually taken to be the Wye. W. H. Manning[2] has recently argued that the Silures extended further east, occupying Herefordshire; and in this case much of the campaigning may have taken place there and in Gwent.

It is unlikely that by the time he died Scapula had arrived at a settled frontier arrangement and it fell to his successor Didius Gallus (A.D. 52-57) to stabilise the situation. From Tacitus's brief and unsympathetic notice we cannot be sure about the extent and nature of Gallus's activities. The excavator of the important fortress at Usk (Gwent) has argued that its foundation belongs to this period.[3] The arrangements of this base, ostensibly for *legio XX*, seem to show an emphasis on storage—presumably to supply an army intent on campaigning. North of Usk is the fort of Abergavenny (*Gobannium*), certainly pre-Flavian, and likely to have been held as a forward post screening the legionary base. Further north, Clifford or Clyro may have been built to control the middle Wye valley.[4] In the other direction, the occupied zone may have extended as far south-west as the Tâf at Cardiff.

The next governor, Q. Veranius (A.D. 57-8), clearly had orders to advance, and was engaged, before his untimely death, in a campaign against the Silures which may have been no more than a preliminary reconnaissance in force.

Veranius's successor, Suetonius Paulinus, is recorded as having fought two campaigns prior to his capture of Anglesey in A.D. 60, defeating tribes and establishing garrisons among them. The first campaign may have continued Veranius's work against the Silures. How extensive Paulinus's system of garrisons was is not known. None of the Brecknock forts or other military works can be assigned to this phase on present evidence.[5]

Between A.D. 61 and A.D. 74 there are no recorded campaigns in Wales. The subjugation of the Silures was achieved finally by the Flavian governor Julius Frontinus (A.D. 74-8). The available evidence strongly suggests that the three forts known in Brecknock were founded during or very shortly after his successful campaigns as part of the tight network of forts and fortlets constructed to control southern Wales.[6] Three or four of the known marching camps probably also belong to these campaigns rather than earlier, if recent

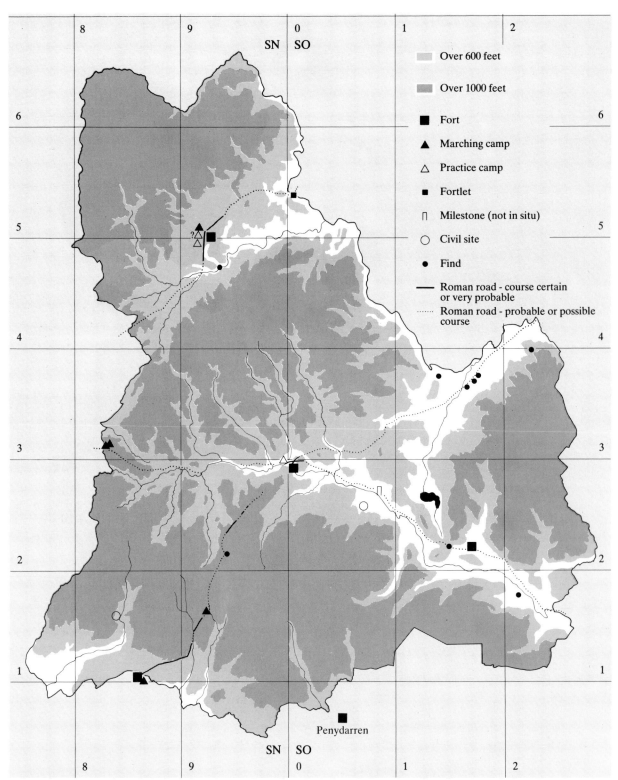

Legend:

Over 600 feet
Over 1000 feet
■ Fort
▲ Marching camp
△ Practice camp
■ Fortlet
∏ Milestone (not in situ)
○ Civil site
● Find
— Roman road - course certain or very probable
⋯ Roman road - probable or possible course

Penydarren

154 Roman remains

views on the chronology of such sites with internal *claviculae* entrances are accepted.[7] The lands of Brecknock from this time fell under the direct control of the commander of *legio II Augusta* based at Caerleon-on-Usk. Y Gaer, Brecon was probably intended at its inception as a base for a quingenary cavalry unit; the *ala Hispanorum Vettonum civium Romanorum* was present in the late first to early second century. The site was clearly pivotal to the system of posts controlling Silurian territory. The garrison of the other forts can only be guessed, but it is likely that Pen-y-gaer and Caerau II housed quingenary infantry units.

The history of Roman Wales in the second century A.D. is poorly known, because archaeology and epigraphy provide the only evidence and it is of variable quality and amenable to different interpretations. As far as the sites in modern Brecknock are concerned, there is evidence of alterations at Caerau (RF 1) where the fort was reduced in size, probably in the first half of Trajan's reign (A.D. 98-117), thus implying a change of garrison. At Pen-y-gaer (RF 3) stone defences were constructed, probably about the same time. The new arrangements of Caerau suggest an alteration in the organisation of the frontier network, but the changes at Pen-y-gaer need be no more than repairs and reconstruction occasioned by natural deterioration. More significantly, a new, smaller unit seems to have replaced the *ala Vettonum* at Y Gaer about this time. Reconsideration of the dating of bricks used in the flues of the bath-house inserted in the *praetentura* of the fort suggests that the building was erected *c.* A.D. 100 rather than at the much later dates proposed by other authorities.[8]

The available evidence indicates that Caerau and Pen-y-gaer were abandoned by the mid-second century but it does not allow of much more precision. The latest likely historical context is *c.* A.D. 140, when Antoninus Pius required troops for the advance in southern Scotland.[9] Coupled with this may have been the decision to strengthen the defences of the surviving garrison at Brecon Gaer where their form hints at a more defensive mode of thinking in military planning. However, Caerau and Pen-y-gaer may have been abandoned earlier; a late Trajanic[10] or early Hadrianic[11] date has been claimed for the withdrawal from Caerau and a later Hadrianic date from Pen-y-gaer.[12] Later finds from both forts can be considered to belong to civil settlements that built up outside them and continued to exist after their original *raison d'être* had gone. However, there is otherwise little firm evidence of non-military settlements or activities from this period. In a secluded valley in the Fforest Fawr the local population seem to have buried their dead in a cave according to their pre-Roman custom of inhumation and accompanied by goods probably obtained from Roman traders.[13] We may speculate that the fundamental patterns of native life, away from the agricultural lands of the Vale of Glamorgan and the immediate vicinity of military establishments, continued, adopting only a few material trappings of the intrusive culture obtained by a limited participation in the market economy.[14]

Difficulties in interpreting the evidence at Brecon Gaer for the latter half of the second century have led to two quite different views of the history of the fort.[15] The site should probably be considered as part of the group of forts maintained in east mid-Wales and the Marches under the Antonines and later because of continuing uneasiness about the trustworthiness of the native population in the often wild and remote countryside. Re-excavation is needed badly before any meaningful attempt can be made to define the nature and extent of late second and third century activity at the site.

Evidence for both military and civil activity in the late third century when the area belonged to the new province of *Britannia Superior* is very scanty. The military road (RR 5) between Brecon and Llandovery was refurbished under the Gallic emperors Postumus (A.D. 258-268) and Victorinus (A.D. 268-270), and may imply a garrison at Brecon Gaer.[16] More significantly, the villa at Llanfrynach may have been established at this time and a peaceful environment is indicated. Coin evidence suggests activity at the end of the third century and in the fourth century at Y Gaer, Brecon but its nature is uncertain. Perhaps it should be linked with the refurbishing of the main arterial route along the Usk valley (RR 3) under Constantius Chlorus (A.D. 296-306) and later under Constantine II (A.D. 317-337 or 337-40).[17] The evident prosperity of the villa at Llanfrynach attests some measure of peace and security for much of the fourth century; the latest coin is of the House of Valentinian. The possibility that the estate remained substantially intact long after the end of formal Roman imperial authority in the area is beyond the scope of this discussion.[18] Coins indicate that Brecon Gaer was occupied or frequented down to the reign of Gratian at least.

[1] The conquest of Wales was recorded by Tacitus in *Annals*, XII, 31-40; XIV, 29-39; *Agricola*, 14-17. *Roman Frontier* summarises knowledge to 1969. J. L. Davies, *Roman Military Deployment in Wales and the Marches from Claudius to the Antonines* in W. S. Hanson and L. J. F. Keppie (eds.), *Roman Frontier Studies 1979, Part i* (Oxford: BAR International, 1980), pp. 255-277 reviews knowledge of the first two centuries A.D. a decade later. G. Webster, *Rome Against Caratacus* (London, 1981) surveys the period A.D. 47-58. The introductory chapters of W. H. Manning, *Report on the Excavations at Usk 1965-1976: The Fortress Excavations 1968-1971* (Cardiff, 1981) are an important contribution to the problems of the pre-Flavian period. The best up-to-date survey of the history of Roman Britain in general is P. Salway, *Roman Britain* (Oxford, 1981).

[2] Manning, *Usk*, pp. 15-23.

[3] Manning, *op. cit.*, p. 34; Webster, *op. cit.*, p. 112; V. A. Maxfield in *Britannia*, XIV (1983), pp. 367-8. The foundation of Usk by Gallus seems more probable than the short-lived governorship of Veranius favoured by Webster (pp. 105, 107) but of course archaeological evidence is no help in distinguishing between these choices.

[4] Manning, *op. cit.*, p. 38.

[5] Webster, *op. cit.*, p. 86 draws attention to some pottery from Pen-y-gaer (RF 3) which is more common on Claudian-Neronian sites but admits its occurrence also in early Flavian contexts. The Claudian coin found at Bwlch nearby (Finds no. x, p. 185) might have been lost about this time; such coins are generally found in military contexts in Wales as late as Nero.

[6] For the role of fortlets in the Flavian system see Davies, *op. cit.*, pp. 262-3.

[7] *Britannia*, XI (1980), p. 57.

[8] George C. Boon, *Laterarium Iscanum: The Antefixes, Brick and Tile-Stamps of the Second Augustan Legion* (Cardiff, 1984), pp. 23-4, 54.

[9] *Roman Frontier*, p. 22.

[10] Davies, *op. cit.*, p. 264 who envisages a more widespread late Trajanic withdrawal of the Welsh garrison.

[11] See RF 1.

[12] See RF 3; Davies, *op. cit.*, pp. 268-70.

[13] See RCS 1.

[14] *Cf.* J. L. Davies, 'The Coinage and Settlement in Roman Wales and the Marches: some observations.' *Arch. Camb.*, CXXII (1983), pp. 78-94 for a discussion of the evidence of coinage for market relations.

[15] See RF 2 for details.

[16] Milestone: *R.I.B.* nos. 2260, 2261.

[17] Milestone: *R.I.B.* nos. 2258, 2259.

[18] W. Davies, *Roman Settlements and Post-Roman Estates in South-East Wales* in P. J. Casey (ed.), *The End of Roman Britain* (Oxford: BAR, 1979), pp. 153-173.

Forts

Three forts are known in the county: Caerau, Llangamarch (RF 1); Y Gaer, Brecon (RF 2); and Pen-y-gaer (RF 3). Only Brecon Gaer has been the scene of extensive excavations, and knowledge of the other two is confined to evidence gleaned from single defence-sections and minor explorations of the interior, and from surface remains and aerial photographs. Pen-y-gaer and Caerau survive as rectangular earthworks partially encumbered with more recent structures and subject to agricultural disturbance. At Brecon Gaer the masonry of part of the defences and three of the gates has been restored and these features may be inspected by the public. The interior, unfortunately, continues to be ploughed. Pen-y-gaer and Caerau are private property and permission to visit them should be sought from the owners.

All the forts were founded, on present evidence, in Flavian times during or shortly after the successful campaigns of Julius Frontinus against the Silures. They belong to a tight network of posts established to control southern Wales. A feature of this system was the construction of fortlets or signal stations between the forts, but the known or probable sites between Llandovery and Caerau and Caerau and Castell Collen fall outside the county, as does the site at the north-west edge of Mynydd Bach Trecastell between Llandovery and Brecon Gaer.[1] It is possible that there were posts of this kind in the uplands between Brecon Gaer and Coelbren, Brecon Gaer and Penydarren, and Brecon Gaer and Caerau. There would have been little need, except possibly at the pass at Bwlch, for such sites between Brecon Gaer and Abergavenny because of the existence of the fort at Pen-y-gaer. The possibility of a site at Trecastell halfway between Brecon Gaer and Llandovery has been raised but the fortlet on Mynydd Bach Trecastell probably sufficed.[2] Examination of the known distribution of forts points to the possibility of a missing site in the middle Wye valley superseding Clyro, thought to have been abandoned before or at the time of Frontinus's campaigns. An iron-smelting site of apparently early Roman date which might have been linked with military activity is known at Gwernyfed School playing fields.[3] More attention should be paid to this vicinity during aerial reconnaissance.

The unit stationed at Brecon Gaer in the late first-early second century A.D. was a cavalry force of five hundred men, *ala Hispanorum Vettonum civium Romanorum*, occupying a site of nearly three hectares. Unfortunately, fort size is not a sure guide to the type of garrison in occupation; thus the first fort at Caerau could conceivably have been occupied by either a *cohors quingenaria equitata* or *cohors milliaria peditata*. The smaller sites, Pen-y-gaer and Caerau II, are of appropriate size for a *cohors quingenaria peditata*, five hundred infantry.

The fort at Y Gaer, Brecon contains several interesting buildings.[4] The stone west gate (*porta praetoria*) with rectangular projecting gate towers of Antonine date is a very early example of an increasing tendency in military architecture towards more defensive planning. The *principia* is notable for its stone forehall, a feature known in the Germanies from late Flavian times but comparatively rare in Britain. There is some dispute as to whether the structure was roofed or not, the former being more likely in the prevailing climate.[5] The building functioned probably as a cavalry drill and assembly hall. The long rooms besides the courtyard of the *principia* have been postulated as armouries[6] and the square foundation inside the courtyard as a shrine.[7]

There is evidence of a *vicus* at all the forts, those at Pen-y-gaer and Caerau probably continuing as settlements after the garrison had been withdrawn. At Brecon Gaer, Wheeler's "Building B" seems to have been an official structure, a *mansio* or *praetorium*.[8] Cemeteries are known or implied at Pen-y-gaer and Brecon Gaer.

[1] See J. K. St. Joseph's remarks on spacing in *J.R.S.*, LXVII (1977), p. 155.

[2] See Suggested Sites 1.

[3] See RU 1.

[4] See RF 2 for full details; A. Johnson, *Roman Forts* (London, 1983) is a recent comparative survey of forts in the W. Empire.

[5] Johnson, *op. cit.*, p. 123 for discussion.

[6] *Britannia*, III (1972), p. 75.

[7] Johnson, *op. cit.*, p. 108.

[8] For a discussion see P. Salway, *The Frontier People of Roman Britain* (Cambridge, 1965), pp. 171-2; on *praetorium*, E. Birley, *Roman Britain and the Roman Army* (Kendal, 1961), pp. 85-6.

(RF 1) The Roman fort at Caerau, Llangamarch (Figs. 155-158)

The fort, 1 km S. of Beulah, stands on the edge of a spur, its long axis lying approximately N.E.-S.W., coinciding with that of the ridge. The highest enclosed part of the spur is in the S.W. half of the fort at about 220 m above O.D., while the N.E. edge of the site is about 7 m lower. There are extensive views of the Camarch valley and the hill country to the N.E. The approach from most sides is not difficult, though marshy in parts, and to the N.E. the ground falls away fairly steeply to the bluffs of Afon Camarch nearly 200 m away.

The main feature of the remains is a slightly trapezoidal earthwork with rounded corners, about 167 m long N.E. to S.W. with the N.E. side 110 m and S.W. side 117 m long measured between the outer crests of the rampart, an enclosed area of about 1.77 ha. The central part of the S.W. rampart has been obliterated by the construction of a Norman motte (now 4.5 m high) and the approach lane and paddocks of the later farm which occupies much of the S.W. half of the interior. Except at the middle of the S.E. side, where it appears as a low bank for about 20 m, the main rampart has been reduced by repeated ploughing to a single scarp about 1.5 m high on average. As recently as 1958 the N.E. corner is recorded as up to 3.66 m high.[1] There is a distinct hollow and possible counterscarp bank at the S. corner and there are vague traces of a ditch along the N.W. side. The interior of the enclosure is subdivided by a scarp up to 1.8 m high whose crest is between 61 and 54 m S.W. of the N.E. rampart. This feature probably represents a later reduction in the area of the fort to about 1.32 ha. The entrance is represented by a depression in the centre of the N.E. rampart scarp which was connected by a causeway, now almost entirely ploughed away, to a corresponding hollow in the centre of the 'reducing' scarp. In front of the N.E. side of the fort is a narrow platform forming the tip of the spur on the edge of which there appears to be an L-shaped stretch of bank

continuing the line of the S.E. side of the enclosure and parallel to the N.E. side, about 40 m apart, but it is not certain that this is an artificial feature.

Material of Roman date including brick, pottery and glassware has been recorded from the area of Caerau since the seventeenth century,[2] but the first detailed study of the site and its environs was made in 1958 when particular attention was drawn to extra-mural structures.[3] In the fields immediately N.W. of the fort the possible remains of a *vicus* were identified. Two small, semicircular terraces at 9229 5035 and one at 9233 5032 were interpreted as building ledges and it was claimed that marks probably representing four rectangular building foundations could be seen at 9224 5021, 9228 5023, 9222 5025 and 9225 5028. A scatter of pottery, brick and tile was found in the fields. In its present-day appearance the sloping surface exhibits several vague undulations, depressions and small terraces which form no distinguishable plan. The farmer remarked (1983) that ploughing brought up much stone, some of it "squared". The 'ledge' at 9229 5035 is a wet hollow. Pottery and tile can still be picked up in the upcast left by mole burrowing.

North of the fort between 9239 5029 and 9252 5038 runs a low embankment about 5.5 m wide, more prominent along its N. edge where it is up to 0.2 m high. A very shallow depression about 2 m wide runs along its N. side. The purpose and date of this feature are obscure. It crosses land which tends to be wet but does not appear to be a metalled causeway as probing found no stone in the structure. Possibly it formed part of an annexe to the fort.[4]

At 9255 5035 S.S.E. of the E. end of the latter bank is a broad, E.-facing shelf on two levels, above the

155 *(opposite)* Roman sites in the vicinity of the Roman fort at Caerau, Llangamarch (RF 1). Background detail based on 1:10 000 O.S. map with additions

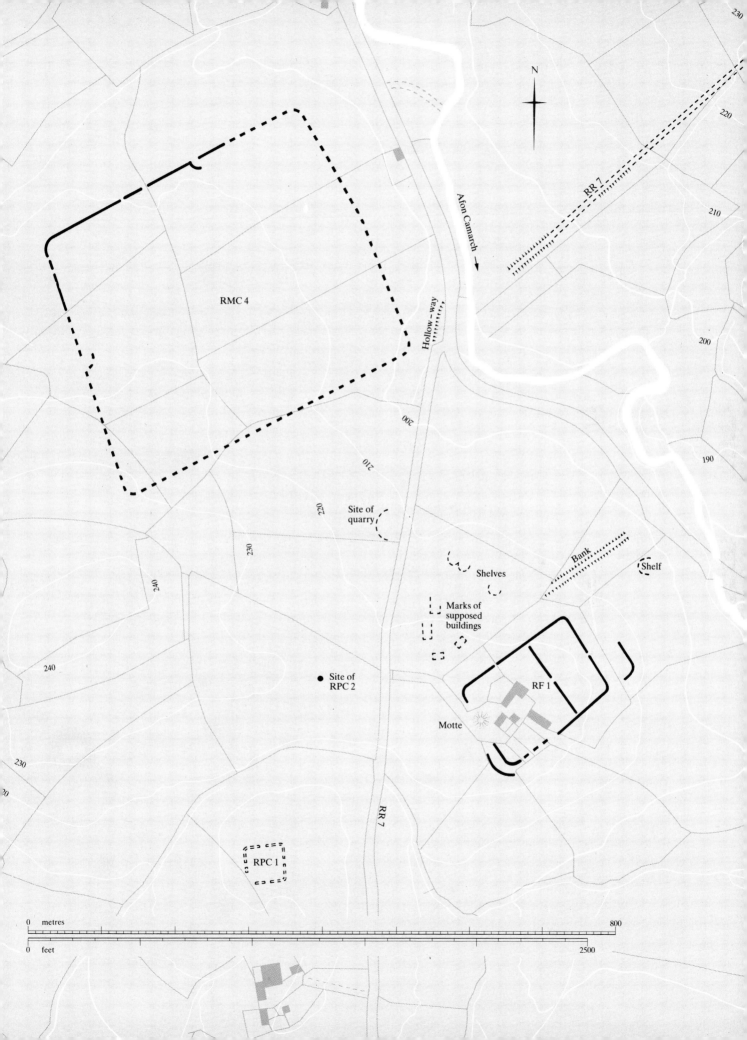

N

230

220

210

200

190

RR 7

Afon Camarch

Hollow‑way

RMC 4

240

230

220

210

200

240

230

20

Site of quarry

Shelves

Bank

Shelf

Marks of supposed buildings

Site of RPC 2

RF 1

Motte

RR 7

RPC 1

0   metres   800

0   feet   2500

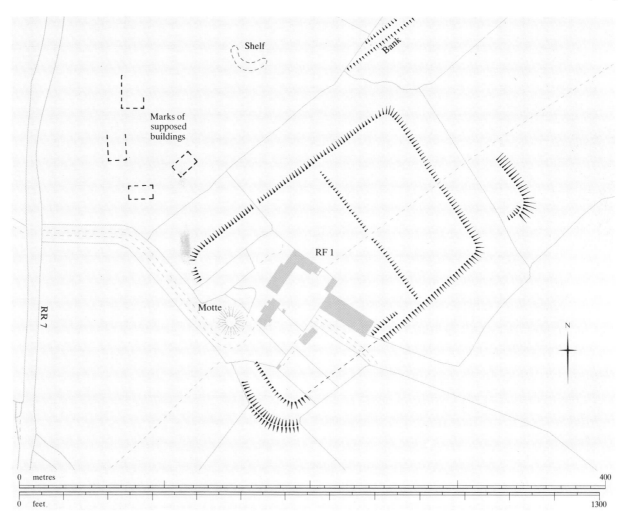

Shelf

Bank

Marks of
supposed
buildings

RF 1

RR 7

Motte

N

0 metres   400

0 feet   1300

156 Roman fort at Caerau, Llangamarch (RF 1). Background detail based on 1:2500 O.S. map with additions

steep bluff of Afon Camarch. The shelf is generally wet and is not definitely of artificial origin although building material appears to have been found on it.

The surface of the fairly level area in front of the N.E. entrance of the fort was found to be covered with building material and the hedgeline crossing it was piled with worked stone, brick and tile, giving rise to the suggestion that the ledge may have been the site of the bath-house.

At 9219 5038 on the W. side of RR 7 is the site of a small quarry which is suggested as a possible source of building material for the fort and *vicus* but could equally well be of much later date.

In addition to the surface finds mentioned above other material collected in 1958 included samian pottery, vessel and window glass, a glass melon bead, iron nails, fragments of hearths, and slag.

A section was cut across the N.W. defences of the fort in 1965.[5] Two main periods were recognised, Flavian and early second century according to the excavators. In the first, the rampart was 7.62 m wide, composed of orange clay revetted in front with turf on a clay-and-cobble footing. Immediately in front of the rampart was a ditch 4.42 m wide and 1.37 m deep. A berm 3.05 m wide separated this ditch from another of similar depth and 4.12 m wide with a low counter-scarp bank on its outer lip. An outermost trap ditch, used in both periods, completed the defences creating

157 Roman fort at Caerau, Llangamarch (RF 1) from the north-east

a 'kill zone' 12.8 m wide. In the second period the two inner ditches were backfilled and replaced by a single ditch cut into the berm between them, of similar depth but about 6.1 m wide. Material was added to the front of the rampart (increasing its width to 8.38 m) and a new turf on clay-and-cobble face was constructed.

In the interior, 4.27 m from the rear of the rampart, were the remains of a timber building, possibly a barrack, belonging to period I which had been demolished and replaced by an *intervallum road*, 3.35 m wide and with side gullies, constructed immediately behind the rampart. The excavations also located in the interior the possible site of the period I *praetorium* underlying a stone granary 11.58 m wide with 1.22 m thick walls, the floor of which was raised on small stone pillars.

The lack of black-burnished wares from the excavation has led to the suggestion that period II had ended by the early years of Hadrian (A.D. 117-138).[6] However, samian collected in 1958 from the supposed *vicus* area probably dates from as late as the Antonine period.[7] More extensive excavation within and without the fort is required before a fully reliable chronology can be established.

In June 1982 a new farm building was constructed within the fort at 9238 5013. Disturbance of the pre-existing surface was limited and nothing of archaeological significance was noted.[8]

B.B.C.S., XVII (1958), pp. 309-15; *J.R.S.*, LVI (1966), pp. 196-7. C.U.A.P. ABU 56-9, AFR 50-1, ANA 5, 13, 14, ASA 72, AUF 64-5, BAK 39, 40, 51, CBN 19, CCT 5, 52-4.

[1] *B.B.C.S.*, XVII (1958), p. 310.
[2] *e.g.* Camden's *Britannia* (ed. Gibson, 1695), p. 591; *Arch. Camb.* (1863), p. 377; *Arch. Camb.* (1879), p. 151; *Arch. Camb.* (1923), p. 156; *Carmarthen Antiq.*, III (1961), p. 128.
[3] *B.B.C.S.*, XVII (1958), p. 309-15; *J.R.S.*, XLVIII (1958), p. 130.
[4] *Roman Frontier*, p. 48.
[5] Precise position not stated but probably about 9230 5019; *J.R.S.*, LVI (1966), pp. 196-7; *Arch. in Wales*, 5 (1965), pp. 15-16.
[6] *Roman Frontier*, p. 48.
[7] *Arch. Camb.*, CXII (1963), p. 16.
[8] *Arch. in Wales*, 22 (1982), p. 22. By Clwyd-Powys Trust observers.

Llangamarch (E), Treflys (C)
SN 95 S.W. (9240 5016)   January 1983

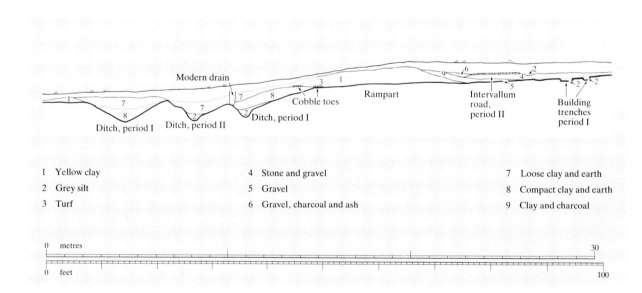

1	Yellow clay	4	Stone and gravel	7	Loose clay and earth
2	Grey silt	5	Gravel	8	Compact clay and earth
3	Turf	6	Gravel, charcoal and ash	9	Clay and charcoal

158 Roman fort at Caerau, Llangamarch (RF 1): section through the north-west defences, 1965 (after *J.R.S.*, LVI), at about SN 9230 5019, looking north-east

(RF 2) The Roman fort at Y Gaer, Brecon (Figs. 159-164)

The fort lies at about 167 m above O.D. at the end of a wide spur overlooking the confluence of Afon Ysgir and the River Usk, 4 km W. of Brecon Cathedral. Immediately beyond the defences the ground to the W. and S. falls away steeply to the rivers. To the N. and N.E. the site is overlooked by gently rising land.

A. The main feature of the remains is a rectangular enclosure with rounded corners formed by an earthen rampart fronted by a stone wall. The enclosure whose long axis lies about 74 deg. W. of N. measures 200 m by 148 m to the outer wall faces, excluding the towers, an enclosed area of about 2.96 ha.

The stone wall is well-preserved along the whole of the E. portion of the N. rampart between the N.E. angle and the site of the N. gate for a distance of about 73 m. It consists of a core of mortared sandstone rubble and waterworn pebbles with a facing of regular courses of rectangular sandstone blocks, up to 12 courses of which are preserved in places above a plinth projecting about 0.15 m. The core at present stands between 2.4 m and 3 m high above the offset. The wall is about 1.2 m thick but behind it are traces of another overgrown stone wall about 2.1 m thick (see below). The back of the grass-covered earth rampart has been eroded by repeated ploughing. In front of the wall is a berm about 2.2 m wide and a ditch between 7.6 m and 9.1 m wide, only about 0.3 m deep near the site of the N. gate but increasing to about 0.9 m at the N.E. angle. The ditch tends to be waterlogged and its present surface is littered with stone rubble. The site of the N. gate (*porta principalis dextra*) and the W. portion of the N. side is occupied by farm buildings, some recently rebuilt.

The curve of the stone wall is visible at the N.E. angle where the interior of the stone corner turret excavated in 1970 is exposed and preserved (see below). The E. side to the E. gate (*porta decumana*) is a bank about 1.8 m to 2.4 m high, thickly overgrown with trees and bushes through which occasional traces of rubble may be discerned but no facing. Ploughed-down traces of ditching are visible in the field outside the fort. Only the N. guard-chamber of the E. gate is now visible, its walls on three sides up to 1.22 m high, but the N. face against the core of the rampart is 2.13 m high. The S. portion of the E. side appears also as a bank thickly masked by vegetation but in places along the exterior the wall core is exposed. The

S.E. corner turret is partly visible but in a ruinous condition. Three courses of masonry of the tower can be seen, as can four courses of the outer wall face at the angle, below which is a tumbled mass of stone.

The E. part of the S. defence line is preserved as a grass-grown bank about 1.2 m high which supports a modern fence and a few trees; there are remains of a previously thicker cover. Rubble is visible in the bank and stretches of wall-core are exposed in its outer face. In front are the remains of a shallow ditch with a hint of a counterscarp bank near the S.E. corner. In the pasture beyond the ditch are patches of nettle and bracken that might indicate disturbed areas.

The S. gate (*porta principalis sinistra*) has been carefully cleaned and preserved by the M.P.B.W. within a fenced area. Both guard-chambers are visible. The E. wall of the E. chamber stands 2 m high and seventeen masonry courses are exposed, but elsewhere the walls are lower. The central piers between the two roadways are preserved as is the stone-built drain through the E. roadway. The threshold of the W. road is also visible. On both sides of the gate short stretches of the stone facing of the rampart are preserved, 4.6 m on the E. and 10.7 m on the W. Two courses of facing about 0.45 m high above a plinth are exposed on the W. and the core stands to a height of 1 m; on the E. the facing is about 0.9 m high and the core 2 m. Between the gate and the S.W. corner the rampart is a grassed bank supporting trees, the base of an old field wall and a wire fence. There is no sign of a ditch in front. From the S.W. angle, which is about 3.7 m high externally, to the W. gate the W. side is of similar character. The W. gate (*porta praetoria*), like the S. gate, has been fenced off and carefully preserved by the M.P.B.W. Both guard-chambers are visible, the S. wall of the S. chamber standing about 1.8 m high, including core, with nine facing courses extant. Also preserved are the bases of the piers separating the roadways and the pivot holes of the gate. The chambers of this gate unlike those of the others project beyond the line of the stone facing of the rampart, short lengths of which are exposed either side of the gate. On the S., the wall stands 1.9 m high including the core, with four courses preserved above the plinth; on the N., seven courses can be seen. North of the gate, the rampart is represented by a grassed rubble scarp up to 2 m high supporting a tree, fence and remains of an earlier boundary.

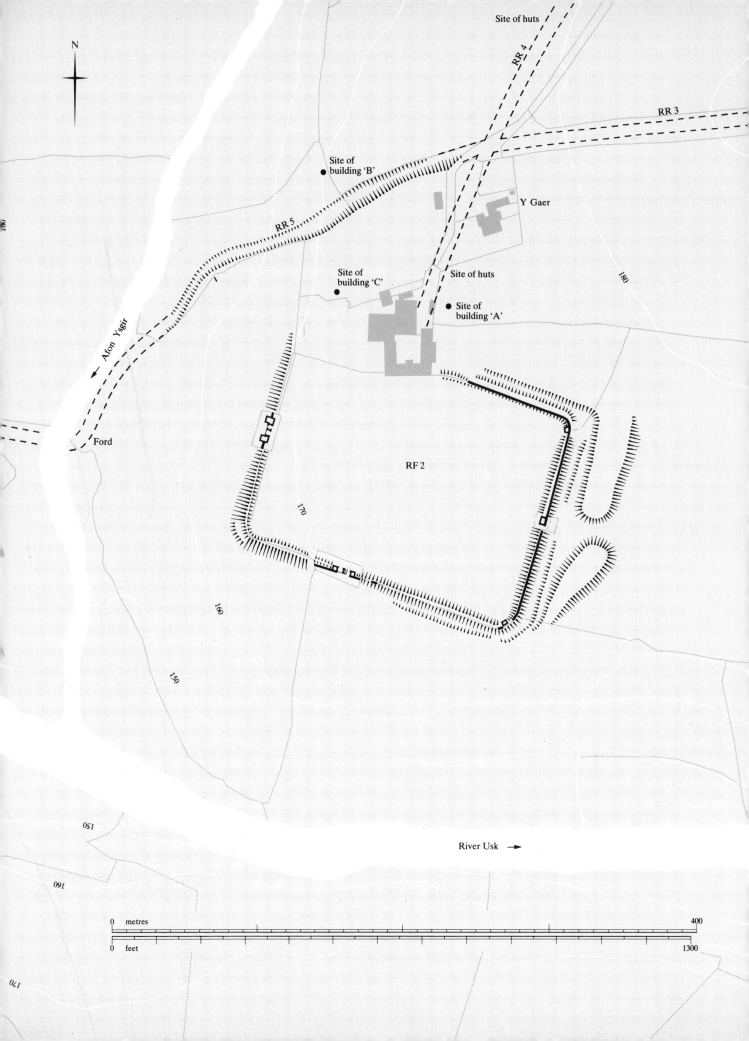

N

Site of huts

RR 4

RR 3

Site of
building 'B'

Y Gaer

RR 5

Site of
building 'C'

Site of huts

Afon Ysgir

Site of
building 'A'

180

Ford

RF 2

170

160

150

150

160

River Usk →

170

0   metres   400

0   feet   1300

The interior is, unfortunately, cultivated repeatedly. In certain crop conditions, for example the severe drought of 1976, the outlines of the street pattern and some buildings can be discerned clearly, especially from the air.[1]

The fort is referred to in documents of the twelfth century and from the seventeenth century onwards there are records of finds of Roman objects.[2] Extensive excavations were carried out by R. E. M. Wheeler in 1924-5 which provided much information about the defences, gates and the principal buildings, though less about other accommodation.

The remains of the original *defences* (period I) consisted of a bank 1.52 m high and 5.49 m wide in front of which on the E., W. and S. were two V-shaped ditches. The inner ditch, 4.57 m to 4.88 m wide by 1.83 m deep was 1.52 m in front of the rampart face and separated by between 4 m and 8 m from the outer ditch, 3.96 m wide and 1.52 m deep. The rampart rested partly on a cobble footing and was composed in its outer half of yellow clay and in its inner of rammed earth with a clay capping. Excavation across the S.E. defences in 1970[3] showed that this part of the rampart was 6.5 m wide and built of clay with a turf front revetment on a cobble foundation. The primary rampart was converted into a more monumental feature by the construction of a stone wall at its front which is still visible about 3 m high on the N. side (period II). The wall, built on a low plinth, consisted of a core of roughly-coursed rubble set in mortar with an external facing of squared sandstone blocks rising above a slightly projecting course on the plinth. Large blocks projected from the rougher inner face of the wall to key it into the rampart which had been raised with earth to a height of 3.05 m. Large chamfered stones found in debris at the foot of the wall may have been part of its capping. The average thickness of the wall was 1.04 m (1.2 m on the S.E.). At 7.6 m E. of the S. gate there was evidence that a section of the wall had collapsed shortly after it had been built, necessitating rebuilding. Later the wall and the front of the guard-room again collapsed but were not repaired for some time and then in a noticeably inferior fashion.

The latest addition to the defences was built on top of the raised rampart and consisted of a revetment wall of re-used building stone built roughly parallel to the

earlier wall between 2.9 m and 4.27 m behind it and holding back a fill of earth, rubble and building materials. This wall does not occupy the whole defensive circuit being absent on the W. Covering the N.E. corner turret, where it was excavated in 1970, the wall was 4 m wide utilising the front of the turret as the footing for its revetment blocks. Large stones had been dumped into the turret to counteract subsidence. At the S. gate the revetment wall, acting as a parapet, ran on a bank of red marl that had been used to block the gate after it had fallen into disrepair. The E. gateway was also blocked with rubble up to 3.05 m wide revetted both sides with dry-coursed masonry and boulders. Wheeler considered this late defence to be post-Roman but no satisfactory evidence for precise dating has been obtained.

Of the four gates, three of which were examined in detail, the W. and E. gates lie on the long axis while the N. and S. stand opposed on a line parallel and W. of the transverse axis of the fort. The original timber W. gate was shown to be smaller than its stone-built successor as the cut-away ends of the period I rampart were found under both later guard-chambers. Details of its structure were uncertain as only four post-holes were extant. The later stone gateway and the stone wall of the period II defences were of the same build. The gate, 18 m by 7.15 m, comprised two roughly rectangular guard-chambers, the N. slightly larger than the S., which projected just over 3 m beyond the wall line, and flanked two roadways separated by a central *spina*. The facade of the entrance had probably some architectural pretension with piers of conglomeritic cornstone on each side of the roadways.[4]

The stone S. gate also had a timber predecessor of which only one post-hole remained. The period II structure, 16.7 m by 5 m, consisted of two nearly square guard-rooms flanking roadways separated by a central *spina*. The guard-chambers did not project beyond the line of the wall. The facade of the entrance was set back slightly from the wall line and again comprised piers on each side of the roadways. A stone-covered drain from the annexe to the *Commandant's house* ran to the front of the gate through the E. roadway. An iron shoe for a door post was found intact in a pivot hole at the outer end of the central pier. When the E. roadway was resurfaced the drain was blocked and when the second surface of the W. roadway was created a stone sill was erected at the front rendering obsolete the original door pivots. The front of the E. guard-chamber in conjunction with the rampart wall had collapsed forward at some period occasioning a coarse rebuild, about 0.3 m thicker than

159 *(opposite)* Roman fort at Y Gaer, Brecon (RF 2) and the sites of Roman remains in its vicinity

previously, of reused stones and poor sandy mortar. In probably post-Roman times the gate was blocked with marl (*supra*).

No remains of a period I E. gate were found. The stone phase was of similar plan to the S. gate measuring 16.5 m by 5.3 m. Only the N. guardroom was examined fully, where the door sill and rebated door jambs were intact. The original pivot stones for the gates were covered by the stone thresholds and slab paving which retained 0.46 m depth of pebble metalling laid when the roadways were renewed. The gateway was blocked by the later rubble rampart.

The N. gate could not be fully excavated but it was established that the guard-rooms did not project beyond the walls.

At each corner of the fort were *turrets* attached to the rear of the wall. All were of similar trapezoid plan and, although not bonded to the wall, Wheeler considered them to be contemporary with it. The N.E. turret was partly cleared by Wheeler and fully excavated by J. Casey in 1970. Internally the maximum width of the building was 3.5 m, minimum width 2.8 m and the length from front to back 3.7 m. The whole structure was built on a foundation of cobbles in yellow clay. The wall-footings were substantial, 0.7 m to 1 m wide, cut into the period I bank. The upper side walls were built into the period II bank, 0.6 m wide and flush with the outer edge of the footings. Attention to the strength of the substructure is a feature of these turrets, reflecting concern over the possibility of slippage.

East of the *via principalis* were the customary buildings although they exhibited some peculiarities of siting and construction. The northernmost structure was a stone *granary* measuring overall 29.9 m by 16.6 m with characteristic side-buttresses and a central partition wall indicating a double-span roof. No trace remained of the supports for the usual raised floor. The space between the granary and the headquarters building was left undeveloped, probably to accommodate wagons and stock, and contained only a stone-lined well, 1.19 m wide at the top and 5.18 m deep, backfilled with domestic rubbish and building debris.[5]

The headquarters building (*principia*) stood in the centre of the fort. The original structure was of timber of which only 14 post-holes survived. Wheeler believed that the main axis of this building coincided with that of the fort and that the central axis of the later stone structure was shifted about 6.1 m N. to allow for the unusual disposition of the commandant's house (*praetorium*). A notable feature of the plan of the

stone *principia* is the forehall along its W. side, overall 46.3 m by 13.3 m, straddling the *via principalis*. The long axis of the hall coincides with that of the street while its transverse axis conforms to the E.-W. axis of the fort. This suggests that the hall either occupies the exact site of a timber forerunner while the rest of the building has been moved N., or is a primary feature or addition associated with a timber main building. The footings of the stone headquarters have been interpeted as being later than the forehall.[6] The position of the *sacellum* does not appear to support the suggestion that it predates the stone *principia*.[7] The stone building measured overall 35.3 m N. to S. by 32.6 m, excluding the forehall, and comprised an open court enclosed on three sides by halls. Behind the most important hall, the E. crosshall, lay three rooms, the central being the shrine of the standards (*sacellum*) with strong, structurally independent foundations indicating at least a two-storey building. In the middle of this room was a small cellar 2.13 m by 1.52 m by 0.61 m deep. Of the small rooms situated in the S.E. angle of the crosshall and the N.E. and S.E. corners of the courtyard, the latter two were later insertions. The corridor or verandah along the N. side may also have been an addition. In the courtyard were a hearth and a backfilled well.

Southernmost of the central range of buildings was the commandant's house. There is evidence of two timber phases in the form of 14 post-holes and two floor levels but little is known of the exact plan. Wheeler thought that the building extended further W. than the stone phase. There is some evidence that the timber period ended with burning. The stone successor was of different design and its plan and positioning are unusual. It was set well back from the *via principalis*, impinging on the *via quintana*, with its long axis parallel to the *via principalis*. It was clearly designed, and under construction, before the stone *principia* as when the latter was built it was necessary to shift its long axis N. to allow for the length of the *praetorium*. The stone building measured overall about

160 *(opposite)* Roman fort at Y Gaer, Brecon (RF 2): plan of excavations (after Wheeler, 1926, with additions)

■	Early 2nd century I	▨	Uncertain Roman periods
▨	Early 2nd century II	▨	Post-Roman re-inforcement
▨	Later Roman		

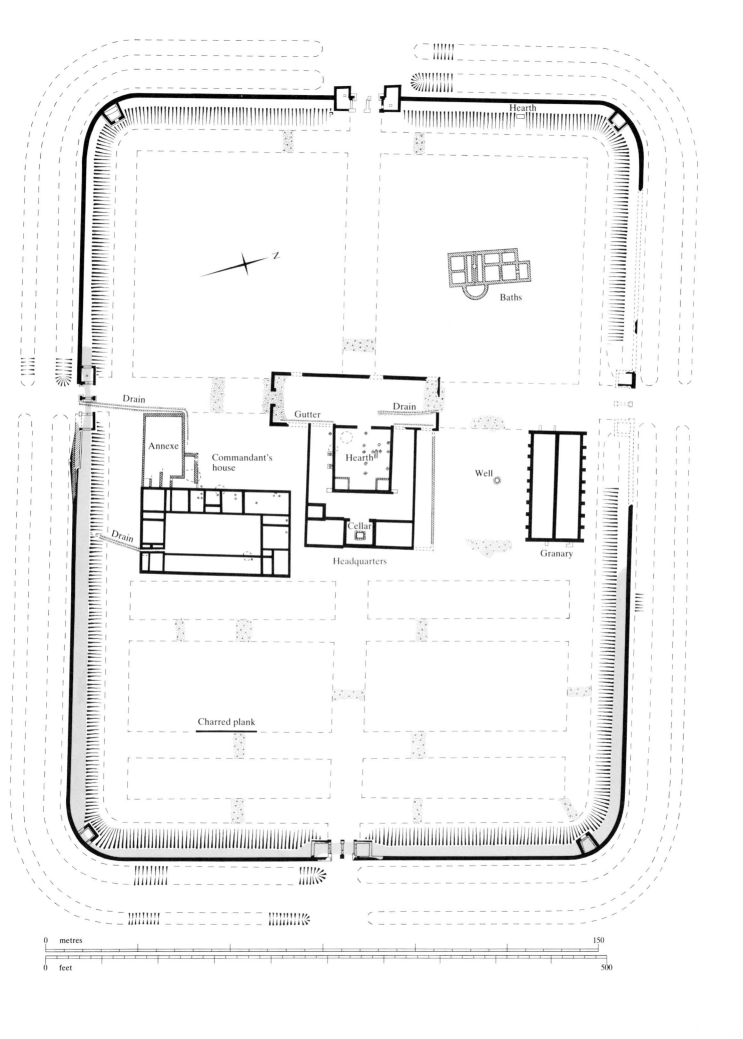

Hearth

Baths

Drain

Gutter

Drain

Annexe

Commandant's
house

Hearth

Well

Drain

Cellar

Granary

Headquarters

Charred plank

0 metres   150

0 feet   500

161 Roman fort at Y Gaer, Brecon (RF 2) from the north-west

41.1 m by 22.9 m and comprised ranges of rooms and halls about a central courtyard which was drained by a culvert through the S.E. corner leading to the rampart. To the W., initially, there was an open yard. Structurally later than the main *praetorium* was an L-shaped annexe to its S.W. side, 15.8 m by 19.8 m. Externally the building was bordered on the N. and W. by a well-built drain which passed along the main street and through the E. roadway of the *porta principalis sinistra*. Wheeler suggested that the annexe may have been demolished during the Roman period as its footings were noticeably less intact than those of the main house and its drain was blocked by the metalling of the refurbished S. gate.

A small bath-house was excavated in the N. half of the *praetentura* measuring 23.2 m by 9.1 m, excluding the apsidal projection. At the N. end of the building was the furnace which heated four hot or warm rooms. The flues from the furnace and between the warm rooms were lined with bricks bearing plain stamps of *Legio II Augusta*.[8] The S. half of the structure contained unheated rooms including the semi-circular cold plunge-bath which emptied through a square outlet into a drain crossing under the floor of the cold room and debouching through an arch in the W. wall. The cold room floor was drained by a large sink near its centre.[9] None of the floors of the original building or their supports survived and it seemed that these had been removed and replaced by a levelled dump of building debris and the structure converted to other use. The long axis of the baths does not conform to the transverse axis of the fort.

163 Roman fort at Y Gaer, Brecon (RF 2): the eastern passageway of the south gate viewed from the interior. Note the drain from the annexe of the Commandant's House

Little information was obtained of the other arrangements in the interior except for the street plan. The *intervallum* road and the subsidiary streets were about 6.1 m wide, metalled with pebbles and broken stone up to 0.3 m thick at the crest, slightly cambered and sometimes kerbed. No signs were encountered of subdivision of the *praetentura* except for the *via praetoria*, 9.14 m wide, but the area was denuded badly. The full street plan of the *retentura* was ascertained, indicating that the barrack-blocks were disposed transversely (*scamna*) to the long axis of the fort on either side of the *via decumana* of similar width to the *via praetoria*. The barracks must have been of timber throughout the occupation of the fort as no traces of stone were found. The charred remains of a plank probably from the front of the verandah of one of the barracks was found in the S.E. half of the *retentura*.

B. Excavations either side of RR 4 from the N. gate of the fort showed it to have been flanked for 275 m by buildings represented by post-holes and clay-and-cobble floors. At 0036 2977 was a rectangular building, probably a workshop, (Wheeler's Building 'A') with rough stone foundations, at least 20.7 m by 7.2 m, overlying an earlier occupation deposit. The structure lay end-on to the road and was subdivided at its E. end. Outside, close to the building's S. wall, was a square, clay-floored oven or kiln near which a small amount of iron slag was found.

162 Roman fort at Y Gaer, Brecon (RF 2): view of the west gate from the rampart immediately to the south

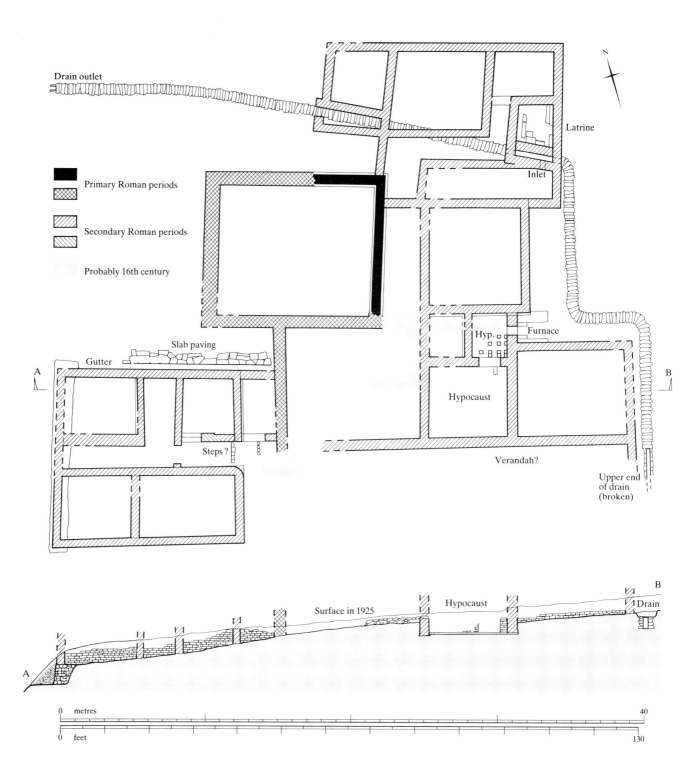

Drain outlet

Primary Roman periods

Secondary Roman periods

Probably 16th century

Latrine

Inlet

Slab paving

Gutter

A

Steps?

Hyp.

Furnace

Hypocaust

Verandah?

Upper end
of drain
(broken)

B

B

Surface in 1925

Hypocaust

Drain

A

0   metres   40

0   feet   130

164 Roman fort at Y Gaer, Brecon (RF 2): plan and section of Wheeler's Building 'B'

C. Limited excavations were made in the area of 0028 2986 of a complex building (fig. 164; Wheeler's Building 'B') set on the edge of the steep W.-facing slope above Afon Ysgir, N. of RR 5. The structure in its latest phase extended at least 34 m by 41 m. The remains were covered partly by those of a probably sixteenth century cottage. The earliest part of the building appeared to be a substantial rectangular room or court 10.5 m by 12.6 m with a wall running S.S.W. from it. Added to the E. of this structure was a block of rooms 28.5 m by 24 m including probably a small bath-suite and a latrine. The latter was flushed by a drain which ran from the S. downslope around the E. side of the building before turning W.N.W. to cross under the N. range, against the E. wall of which the latrine was constructed. Outside the building the drain was about 0.76 m high, constructed with stone side-walls set in a trench and capped with closely-fitted, large, flat slabs covered by less than 0.3 m of loam derived from digging the trench. Under the building the conduit was just over 1 m high, while at the outlet on the hillslope 18.3 m W. of the building it was reduced to 0.3 m. Wheeler considered that the primary function of the drain was to carry water from the external bath-house of the fort (see D). Another block of rooms was added to the S.W. side of the primary building but the relationship with the E. range was not established. The foundations of the W. side of this unit were necessarily deep to compensate for the slope of the hillside. The rectangular block 12.2 m by 15.6 m comprised two rows of rooms either side of a central corridor stepped down E. to W. The function of the whole complex is uncertain but it may have been a *mansio*.

D. At 0029 2978 under the N. side of the old farmhouse, Wheeler excavated fragments of masonry foundations which probably belonged to the original, extra-mural bath-house.

Numerous finds of Roman objects were made during the excavations of 1924-5, including much pottery, glassware, a coin-series running from Republican issues down to Gratian, and tiles and bricks bearing the stamps of *Legio II Augusta*.[10] A variety of metalwork, military and non-military, was found, notably a bronze bath-saucer handle stamped by one of the Ansii, bronze-founders near Capua.[11] The finds are now in the N.M.W. and the Brecknock Museum.[12]

Three inscriptions have been found at or near the fort:

(i) *R.I.B. 405.* A tombstone with two inscribed panels. Now lost. The inscription has been partly reconstructed from a corrupt transcription as:

D[is] Man[i]bus | Val(eri) Pr[i]mi [.]et[.] | fil(i) [e]-q(uitis) [a]lae NER | opt[io]nis | ḥ(eres) f(aciendum) c(urauit)

NER has been taken to be a misreading of VETT (onum), part of the name of the army unit stationed for some time at Y Gaer.

'To the spirits of the departed (and) of Valerius Primus, son of..., trooper of the Cavalry Squadron..., *optio*; his heir had this set up.'

(ii) *R.I.B. 404* (fig. 165).[13] A tombstone once known locally as Maen y Morwynion, The Maidens' Stone, on which a man and his wife are depicted, life-size in relief, above a panel recording details of the husband. Found near the fort in the sixteenth century, the stone was later moved to 0065 2985 by RR 3. It is now in the Brecknock Museum. The stone is severely weathered and only part of the three bottom lines of the inscription can be made out as:

...| [u]ixi [... | ALAN.D I..IV...EI..]|coniunx eius h(ic) s(itus) est

'...(set up by) his wife; he lies buried here.'

(iii) *R.I.B. 403* (fig. 166). A fragment of tombstone found in 1877 about 2.4 km N. of the fort at 0047 3213 (estimated) and now in the Brecknock Museum. The inscription has been restored as:

Diis M[anibus] | Cand[idi....] | ni fili [eq(uitis) alae] | Hisp(anorum) Vett(onum) [c(iuium) R(omanorum) tur(ma)] | Clem(entis) dom[o....] | an(norum) XX stip(endiorum) III H [...

'To the spirits of the departed (and) of Candidus, son of [...]nus, trooper of the Cavalry Regiment of Vettonian Spaniards, Roman citizens, of the troop of Clemens, from......; aged 20, of 3 years' service;....'

This inscription is important as it gives the name of a unit stationed at the fort—*ala Hispanorum Vettonum ciuium Romanorum*—a quingenary cavalry force which may have been Y Gaer's first garrison.[14]

The chronology of the fort has been a matter of some debate. Basing his arguments on contemporary views of pottery dating and on the coin evidence, Wheeler assigned the foundation of the fort to the Flavian period and the rebuilding in stone to the Trajanic era. The latter was considered to be, in part at least, the work of legionaries of *II Augusta* and to have been incomplete *c.* A.D. 120 when there was a marked diminution in the scale of occupation amounting to almost complete abandonment by early

165 Maen y Morwynion (*R.I.B.* 404): partial reconstruction. Scale 1:10

Antonine times. Wheeler believed that after *c.* A.D. 140 there was probably no further intensive occupation by Roman troops, the evidence, such as coins, of occupation down to the later fourth century being explicable in terms of such activity as casual visits or occupation by civilians, the temporary presence of military patrols or the presence of a small caretaker force.

In 1963, Dr. G. Simpson published an important critique of Wheeler's chronology based on a detailed analysis of all the pottery from the excavation, particularly unpublished material. While accepting the evidence for a period I occupation of *c.* A.D. 80-100, Simpson considered that pottery found in positions critical for dating indicated that the period II (stone) defences could not pre-date *c.* A.D. 140. Her revised chronology envisaged a reconstruction in stone of the defences and main buildings by *legio II Augusta* in the Antonine period (i.e. *c.* A.D. 140 or later). Dr. Simpson's views on the later second century to fourth century history of the site have been criticised by Dr. M. G. Jarrett and the meagre evidence from the excavations does not allow the writing of any meaningful account of the site's later history. However, more recent work has shown that earlier ideas about the dating of the small bath-building inserted in the *praetentura* must be abandoned. Stamped bricks of the type used in the flues of the bath-house are now dated *c.* A.D. 100 and it seems probable that the building was erected about this time. Its position and size show it cannot have been meant for the *ala Vettonum* but the kind of garrison that replaced it is unknown.[15]

Dr. Jarrett has advanced an interesting hypothesis concerning the peculiarities of planning in the central range of buildings. Noting the orientation of the axis of the stone commandant's house, its size, and its relationship to the stone *principia* he suggests that the original intention when it was begun was to reduce the size of the fort and alter its orientation to face N. rather than W. The new headquarters was intended for the space to the W. in front of the S. gate, symmetrical to the new N.-S. axis. If this idea is correct, the stone commandant's house must post-date the stone defences which follow the earlier plan, Jarrett suggesting *c.* A.D. 150 and *c.* A.D. 140 respectively. The hypothesis envisages that when work was well-advanced on the *praetorium*, a further change of mind concerning troop dispositions occurred, necessitating the retention of the whole walled area. For some reason it was not considered worthwhile to modify the commandant's house and, instead, when work began on the new *principia* its axis was shifted N., eccentric to that of the fort.

Finds from the excavation in 1970 at the N.E. corner turret support the Antonine dating of the period II defences.

The site at Y Gaer has been claimed as that of *Cicutio* of the Ravenna Cosmography but this identification has been disputed.[16]

R. E. M. Wheeler, 'The Roman Fort at Brecon', *Y Cymmrodor*, 37 (1926); J. Casey, 'Excavations at Brecon Gaer, 1970', *Arch. Camb.*, CXX (1971), pp. 91-100; G. Simpson, 'Caerleon and the Roman forts in Wales in the second century, Part 2', *Arch. Camb.*, CXII (1963), pp. 16-37; M. G. Jarrett, 'The Roman fort at Brecon Gaer: some problems', *B.B.C.S.,* XXII (1966-8), pp. 426-432.

[1] *e.g.* C.U.A.P. BZV 78-82, 84.
[2] Evidence prior to 1924 reviewed in Wheeler, *op. cit.,* pp. 4-6.
[3] Casey, *op. cit.*, p. 93.
[4] Simpson, *op. cit.*, pp. 23-4 suggests that the piers (and the present projecting structure, though not its plan) belong to a rebuild of the front of the gate. Dr. Simpson also proposes a series of rebuildings at the S. and E. gates (pp. 25-7). See *chronology*.
[5] Simpson, *op. cit.*, p. 29.
[6] Jarrett, *op. cit.*, p. 429.
[7] Simpson, *op. cit.*, p. 29.
[8] George C. Boon, *Laterarium Iscanum: The Antefixes, Brick and Tile Stamps of The Second Augustan Legion* (Cardiff, 1984), pp. 23-4, 54.
[9] *Roman Frontier,* p. 171.
[10] Boon, *op. cit.*, p. 54, also p. 51.
[11] Wheeler, *op. cit.*, p. 107; *Britannia*, IX (1978), p. 334.

166 'Candidus stone' (*R.I.B.* 403): scale 1:5

[12] For finds in 1970 Casey *op. cit.*, pp. 96-100 (pottery, glass, metalwork, coin).

[13] See also R. J. Brewer, *Corpus Signorum Imperii Romani. Great Britain.* Vol. i, fasc. 5 (1985), no. 26.

[14] *Roman Frontier*, p. 17.

[15] Boon, *op. cit.*, pp. 23-4, 51, 54.

[16] I. A. Richmond and O. G. S. Crawford, 'The British Section of the Ravenna Cosmography', *Archaeologia*, XCIII (1949), pp. 6, 17, 28, followed by A. L. F. Rivet and C. Smith, *The Place-Names*

of Roman Britain (London, 1979), p. 307 who propose *CICUCIUM* as the original form. The identification is, however, questioned by M. G. Jarrett and J. C. Mann, 'The Tribes of Wales', *Welsh History Review*, 4 (1968-69), p. 169.

St. John the Evangelist Brecon (E), Fenni-fach (C)
SO 02 N.W. (0033 2966)   14 iv 83

(RF 3) The Roman fort at Pen-y-gaer (Figs. 167, 168)

The fort stands at about 110 m above O.D. on a small knoll, possibly in part artificially shaped,[1] 2.2 km S.W. of St. Michael's church, Cwm-du. The site lies in the bottom of the narrow valley of the Ewyn Brook where it broadens to join the flat W. alluvial plain of the Rhiangoll valley. There are unrestricted views towards the Black Mountains to the E. but to the W. the little valley narrows rapidly towards the pass at Bwlch and the site is overlooked by steep hillslopes to the N. and a short distance to the S.

The status of the earthworks in the light of discoveries made at the beginning of last century had been a matter of discussion[2] until the military nature of the site was demonstrated conclusively by excavation in 1966.[3]

The present visible surface remains consist of a discontinuous outward-facing scarp that indicates that the fort was rectangular, its long axis about 128 m E.N.E. to W.S.W. by 90 m, an area of 1.15 ha. The E. part of the site is crossed by a winding lane which may represent the general position of the *via principalis*. The interior is occupied by the buildings, fields and paddocks of Pen-y-gaer farm and Greenhill farm. The defences are most definite to the E. of the lane. The S.E. part is a grassy earth and stone scarp between 1.3 m and 2 m high, capped by the wall of a post-medieval garden. This scarp continues round the E. side, generally 1.7 m to 2 m high, though at 1692 2193 reduced to as little as 0.4 m. In hollows created by grubbing trees out of the old orchard beyond the S.E. corner, Roman brick and roof-tile are visible. Around the N.E. side, where excavation about 1687 2199 confirmed the line of the defences, the rampart has been so spread by ploughing that a genuine crest and toe cannot be identified. The defences on the N. enhanced the naturally steep slope of the knoll. W. of the lane, below the wall leading to Greenhill farmhouse, there is an indistinct scarp

continuing the N. side. The N. part of the W. side is a scarp which diminishes from 2 m high below the W. end of Greenhill farm until it peters out about 1679 2193. The details of the S.W. corner and W. part of the S. side have been obscured by ploughing and construction of an orchard although a faint scarp 0.3 m to 0.4 m high, roughly in line with that E. of the lane, can be traced in the orchard.

Additional data concerning the defences and internal buildings of the fort are supplied by aerial photographs[4] which show a mark representing the W. ditch nearly 7 m wide between 1678 2192 and 1681 2185. Others taken in the drought conditions of 1975[5]

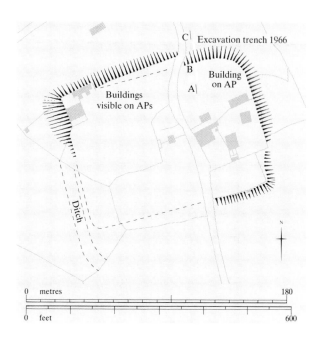

167 Roman fort at Pen-y-gaer (RF 3)

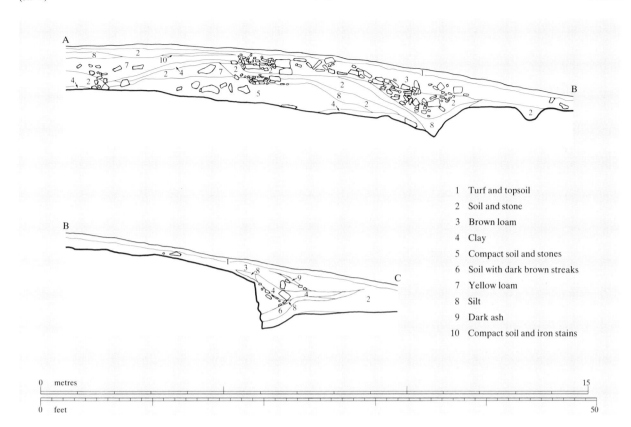

1   Turf and topsoil
2   Soil and stone
3   Brown loam
4   Clay
5   Compact soil and stones
6   Soil with dark brown streaks
7   Yellow loam
8   Silt
9   Dark ash
10   Compact soil and iron stains

0   metres   15

0   feet   50

168 Roman fort at Pen-y-gaer (RF 3): section through the north defences, 1966 (after *Arch. Camb.,* CXVII)

confirm the rounded shape of the N.E. and S.E. corners and the line of the N. part of the E. side. The same series seems to indicate several buildings with stone foundations in the interior. Near the centre, W. of the lane and partly obscured by the ruins of much later farm buildings, are, possibly, the traces of a square building which St. Joseph identified tentatively as the *principia.* Lying close to and parallel to the N. defences between about 1680 2197 and 1683 2198 is a long narrow building, and a short distance to the S. is possibly another similar building on a roughly parallel axis. Also on a similar alignment is a much larger rectangular building between 1680 2194 and 1684 2195, probably buttressed, the characteristic of a granary. In the N.E. corner at 1689 2197 is a smaller structure consisting apparently of one rectangle inside another. Elsewhere there are other marks of uncertain significance.

Several interesting observations were made in the survey of 1803.[6] In about 1801, just outside the centre of the E. defences, 1.52 m below the ground surface,

"a kind of vault" was discovered made of stones and brick set in very hard cement. The chamber measured 1.83 m by 0.91 m by 0.91 m high and was considered to have been an ossuary as human bones were found in it. Freestone, which Payne considered to be Bath stone, was used to cover the entrance which was from the top. Throughout much of the interior and the area to the E. of the fort finds of the remains of wall foundations, bricks, "well worked Blocks of Freestone", cement and pottery are recorded as well as the occasional coins and urns. At one point an arched drain had been uncovered. Payne notes three coins from the site: Marcus Aurelius as Caesar (A.D. 145-61), Constantine I (*c.* A.D. 307 or 8) and Constantius II as Caesar (A.D. 332-3). If truly from the fort area the latter two indicate that there may have been frequentation of the site long after the apparent abandonment of the fort (see below). An entry in Colt Hoare's diary suggests that a cemetery may have lain to the N. where large numbers of samian vessels had been found. Depicted N. of Maes-llechau farmbuildings (W.N.W. of the site) is a semi-circular mound or terrace, which is described as the site of a building from which large stones "having the appearance of Hearth Stones and Chimney Pieces", pottery and "two paterae of mixed metal" had been recovered. In the hillside at 1658 2208, corresponding to the depicted point, there is now a semi-circular, scarped terrace about 80 m E. to W. by 40 m which C. S. Briggs has pointed out as a suitable position for the fort bath-house. Thick wall foundations are shown leading W. for a considerable distance from the semi-circular feature of which traces no longer survive. About 1801 a very large urn containing small bones, probably a cremation, was found some distance W. of the fort. Printed versions of the plan show the spot surrounded by a building for which there is no authority in the MSS.

In 1966 a trench was cut across the E. part of the N. defences and a small square cutting examined the interior just W. of the main trench. The primary defences comprised a stone and soil bank about 7.6 m wide, piled on the original ground surface and probably revetted in front with upright timbers and by a stone kerb at the rear; no ditch was found, for it was probably destroyed by the later works. No dating evidence was recovered. The period II defences consisted of a stone wall about 1 m wide built on top of the first rampart, which was heightened behind it. The excavator considered that the period I ditch remained in use. In period III, the wall was demolished, and a terrace of dumped stone and soil was formed at the front of the rampart. On this was built a new, wider wall and further additions were made to the rampart at its rear. In front of the terrace (or berm) was cut a roughly V-shaped ditch nearly 3 m wide and over 1 m deep. The latest fill of this ditch comprising soil, stone, brick and tile, contained potsherds of c. A.D. 80-130.

169 Centurial stone (*R.I.B.* 401): scale 1:5

In the interior, the fragmentary remains of stone and timber structures belonging possibly to period III were excavated. 12.2 m N. of the defences a steep-sided depression in the rock, possibly a dried-up spring, was discovered containing deposits of rubbish including pottery. Other than pottery, the only noteworthy find from the fort was a poorly stratified coin of Nero (c. A.D. 67). Crossley considered that the pottery evidence pointed to occupation between c. A.D. 70 and A.D. 130-40. The initial period might tentatively be assigned to the campaigns of Frontinus and the stone building might be Trajanic. A Hadrianic occupation was indicated by the presence of pieces usually dated post-A.D. 120 but the lack of exclusively Antonine wares suggests abandonment by c. A.D. 140.

Two inscriptions (figs. 169, 170) which come most probably from the fort are built into separate buildings in Tretower nearby. Both are small *centurial stones* and read: *R.I.B. 401: c(enturia) Peregri* | *ni fec(it)*; *R.I.B. 402: c(enturia) Valentis*. They record that particular pieces of building work were executed by the unit named.

170 Centurial stone (*R.I.B.* 402): scale 1:5

[1] *J.R.S.*, LXVII (1977), pp. 150-1.

[2] T. Jones, *Hist. of Brecknock,* II (1805-9), p. 499; H. T. Payne, *Archaeologia Scotica*, III (1831), pp. 91-98; F. Haverfield, *Trans. Cymmr.*, (1908-9), pp. 74-5; H. J. Randall, *Arch. Camb.,* C (1949), pp. 262-6 and *Arch. Camb.*, CI (1950), pp. 21-2.

[3] D. W. Crossley, *Arch. Camb.*, CXVII (1968), pp. 92-102.

[4] C.U.A.P. ABI 69, 71.

[5] C.U.A.P. BUA 101, 105.

[6] MSS sources: Payne MS, Brecknock Museum; 'Mortimer MS', N.M.W. (see *Arch. Camb.*, CI (1950), pp. 21-2); Colt Hoare's diary: M. W. Thompson (ed.), *The Journeys of Sir Richard Colt Hoare through Wales and England 1793-1810* (Gloucester, 1983), p. 238.

Llanfihangel Cwm Du

SO 12 S.E. (1686 2195)   26 x 76

Other Military Works

Generally, the large lightly-embanked enclosures classified as *marching camps* are considered to be the overnight defences of the Roman army on summer campaign (*castra aestiva*), but some were almost certainly practice works constructed during manoeuvres. On Y Pigwn, a smaller camp on a new alignment was constructed on the site of an earlier one. The pre-existing banks may have been too extensive for the later force, and it has been suggested[1] that waterlogging of the north perimeter of the earlier enclosure accounts for the new arrangments. Nevertheless, it is noticeable how the S.W. entrance is positioned at the mid-point of its side, despite the fact that this is an unsuitable spot, and suggests that this is an example of construction following textbook rules, perhaps in a time of peace. (See RMC 2.)

All four known sites possess internal *claviculae* at their entrances. This feature has been considered to indicate a Flavian date,[2] in which case all the sites (with the possible exception of RMC 2 noted above) should belong to Frontinus's campaigns.[3] Other sites belonging to earlier wars may await discovery, but some may have suffered destruction if sited in valleys subject to later agricultural development.

The accepted view seems to be that one legion required a camp of about 8 hectares, in which case Y Pigwn I (RMC 1) and Beulah (RMC 4) could have held the equivalent of nearly two legions while a force just above legionary strength could have occupied the other two.

Practice camps are small, squarish earthworks with carefully rounded corners that were constructed by Roman soldiers as part of their training. One definite and two possible examples are known close to the fort at Caerau (RPC 1, 2) and Brecon Gaer (RPC 3).

Signal stations are not known in Brecknock.

[1] In J. E. Lloyd (ed.), *A History of Carmarthenshire, Vol. I* (Cardiff, 1935), pp. 94-5.
[2] *Britannia*, XI (1980), p. 57.
[3] In this connection, it is interesting to note a gold coin of Vespasian from Ystradfellte (Finds: No. ii, p. 184).

(RMC 1 and 2) The two marching camps on Y Pigwn (Figs. 171-173)

These camps, 5.5 km W.N.W. of Trecastell, stand between 390 m and 413 m above O.D. enclosing a dome-shaped, undulating area of open moorland at the N.W. end of the long ridge of Mynydd Bach Trecastell where it reaches its highest point. The camps have a commanding outlook in all directions. They are easily approached along the axis of the ridge from the S.E. but there are steep slopes to the N. and W. and marshy ground to the S.

The remains consist of two superimposed, almost rectangular earthwork enclosures with rounded corners. The outer and larger camp (1) is everywhere slighter than the inner (2) and is undoubtedly older as the inner enclosure crosses it in the S. part of its S.W. side and probably did so in the E. part of its S.E. side. The long axis of the outer camp lies on a True Bearing of about 42½°, measuring 420 m. The shorter N.E. and S.W. sides have True Bearings of about 310½° and 311½° respectively, the transverse axis measuring about 360 m. The enclosed area was about 15 ha. The long axis of the well-preserved inner camp lies on a True Bearing of about 58½°, the N.W. and S.E. sides measuring respectively 327 m and 361 m internally. The shorter N.E. and S.W. sides have True Bearings of about 326° and 332° respectively and measure 292 m and 274 m. The enclosed area was about 9.8 ha.

Each camp probably had four internal *claviculae*, one to each side. In both enclosures the surviving *clavicula* in the long side is eccentric to the transverse axis of the camp. Those in the shorter sides of both camps are also eccentric to the long axis but much less markedly so; that in the S.W. side of the later enclosure is at the mid-point.

The Outer Camp (1)

On the S.W. side the defences consist of an earthen bank 4 m wide and up to 0.8 m high in front of which are traces of a shallow ditch up to 0.4 m deep. A faint *clavicula* exists at SN 8265 3106. The inturn is on the S.E. and is about 16 m long measured along its curve, 7.3 m deep measured from the entrance gap inwards, and the gap itself is 10.7 m wide. The N.W. side consists of a bank 3.7 m wide and 0.3 m high with faint indications of a fronting ditch. A good *clavicula* exists at 8262 3130. The inturn is on the S.W. and is 16 m long and 9.1 m deep; the entrance gap is 9.1 m wide. The N. angle can be traced as a very low bank at the head of ground falling steeply to the N.W., and the N.E. side to the *clavicula* at 8291 3140 is also slight.

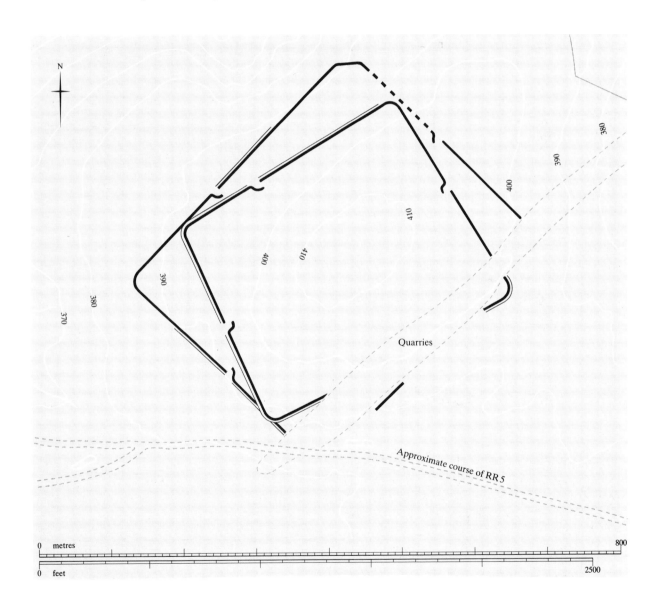

171 Two Roman marching camps on Y Pigwn (RMC 1 and 2)

The inturn of the *clavicula* is on the N.W. and is 11 m long and 9.1 m deep; the entrance gap is 8.2 m wide. South of this the defences are 5.2 m wide, of which the bank is 3 m wide and 0.4 m high with a shallow outer ditch. Later mining which has left a broad band of hollows N.E. to S.W. has destroyed the E. angle and most of the S.E. side except a 53 m length of bank preserved S.W. of the centre. The S. angle is no longer visible in marshy ground. Here the turnpike road crosses the site and possibly RR 5 did so also.

The Inner Camp (2)

On the S.W. the defences are 7.3 m wide and comprise a bank of orange-brown clay 4.6 m wide and 0.6 m

high with a slight outer ditch and counterscarp bank. The *clavicula* at 8264 3113 is in a very unsuitable position where a steep natural scarp breaks through the defences. The inturn is on the S.E. and measures 16 m long and 8.5 m deep; the entrance gap is 9.1 m wide. The S. angle crosses the line of RMC 1 and the W. angle also seems to impinge on the rear of the defences of the earlier camp. The N.W. side consists of a bank 4.6 m wide, 0.3 m high internally and 0.6 m externally, with a barely perceptible outer ditch. The *clavicula* at 8266 3131 has an inturn on the S.W. 20 m long and 10.7 m deep; the entrance gap is 8.9 m wide. On the N.E. side the defences are well preserved, 6.4 m wide, of which the bank is 4.6 m wide and up to 0.9 m high with a narrow but well-defined outer ditch. The

172 Two Roman marching camps on Y Pigwn (RMC 1 and 2) from the west

clavicula at 8294 3132 has an inturn on the N.W. 14 m long and 10.7 m deep, the entrance gap being 8.5 m wide. Towards the S. end of the N.E. side a 30 m length has been destroyed by mining but the E. angle with traces of the fronting ditch are preserved. Most of the S.E. side and the S. angle are preserved where the defences are 6.1 m wide of which the bank is 3.7 m wide and 0.3 m high internally and 0.8 m externally above the bottom of the ditch. There is a possible trace of a counterscarp bank here.

B.B.C.S., XXIII (1968-70), pp. 100-103; *Roman Frontier*, pp. 123-6.

173 Roman marching camp on Y Pigwn (RMC 2): the north-west *clavicula* seen from rising ground inside the camp

Llywel (E), Traean-glas (C). The W. angles of the camps lie in Carmarthenshire

SN 83 S.W. (8280 3123)　　　　　　　　29 i 69

(RMC 3) The marching camp at Plas-y-gors (Figs. 174, 175)

This camp is situated on a moderate S.E.-facing slope about 400 m above O.D. on the W. side of the valley of Afon Llia. It commands a N. to S. pass through the uplands of Fforest Fawr with unobstructed views right to the head of the valley. This pass was partly utilised for the line of the later Coelbren to Brecon road (RR 1: *Sarn Helen*), the approximate course of which crosses the E. part of the site. Discovered by aerial reconnaissance[1] when it stood in stream-dissected moorland, the site has been afforested and considerably damaged, despite the line of the defences having been left unencumbered by trees in a system of firebreaks. The defence line is in the form of a parallelogram. The shorter sides are 240 m long on a True Bearing of about 346½° and the longer 376 m long on a True Bearing of about 275½°. The preserved corners are rounded. The enclosed area would have been about 8.47 ha (21.6 acres). Aerial photographs indicate an internal *clavicula* entrance to the N. of the centre of the eastern side though this has been obliterated by tree-planting. Lengths of the defences are still visible on all four sides but the N.W. corner is no longer traceable on the ground. The W. side is a low turf-covered bank up to 4 m wide and 0.6 m high, in parts severely damaged by a track and water erosion. The W. half of the S. side is of a similar nature. The best-preserved section occurs towards the S.E. corner where the bank is about 2 m wide and 0.6 m high with a fronting ditch 0.4 m deep. The low bank up to 0.5 m high forming the E. side has been partly destroyed by stream action. There is a hint of the fronting ditch in the S. half of this side. The N.E. corner is obscured by a trackway. A 76 m length of bank up to 5 m wide and 0.6 m high with a shallow accompanying ditch represents the line of the N. side.

A section across the S. line of the defences has been excavated by G. D. B. Jones[2] at about 92513 16236. Set on the pre-existing turf and soil of the site was a rampart 1.42 m wide, constructed of turf blocks. The inner face was well-preserved, constructed vertically on a single plinth course of turf 6.35 cms thick which projected 5 cms outwards from the rampart face. The outer face had weathered and its precise form was lost. The ditch was separated from the rampart by a berm 0.4 m wide. It had been cut through the old land surface into the yellow clay subsoil and was a symmetrically sloping feature 1.78 m wide at the top and at least 0.86 m deep. Clearly, some care had been taken in the construction of this defence and Jones has suggested that the camp conforms to a type described by Vegetius for use in hostile territory.

Another section cut by D. Webley and C. Crampton[3] suggests that the method of defence construction was not uniform. The rampart consisted

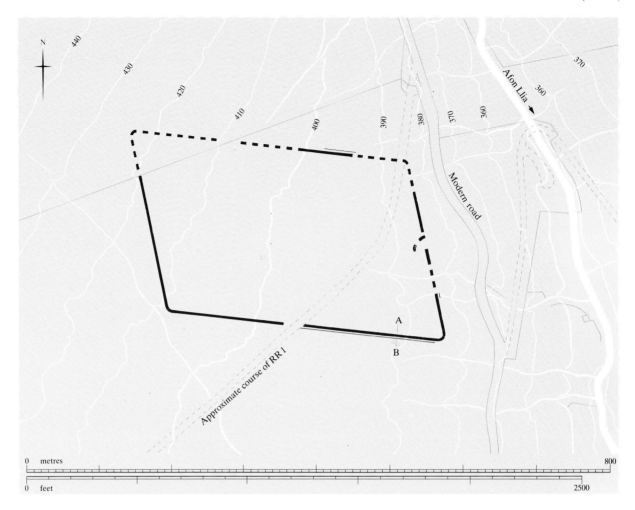

0   metres   800

0   feet   2500

174 Roman marching camp at Plas-y-gors, Ystradfellte (RMC 3)

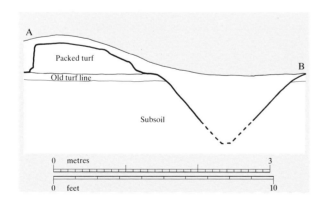

of an earth bank erected on a flagstone foundation laid on the pre-existing ground surface. Pollen sampling indicated that there may have been some tree clearance in the locality during the construction of the camp, followed by the gradual recovery of the vegetation.

[1] J. K. St. Joseph, *J.R.S.*, XLVIII (1958), p. 96. C.U.A.P. SY 26-29, 31-34, ACX 59-60, ARF 94-6.

[2] *B.B.C.S.*, XXI (1964-6), pp. 174-8.

[3] *B.B.C.S.*, XX (1962-4), pp. 440-446. The location of this section is not given, but was a little to the E. of the track, along the S. side of the earthwork (*ex. inf.* Mr. G. C. Boon).

175 Roman marching camp at Plas-y-gors, Ystradfellte (RMC 3): section across the south defences, 1965 (after *B.B.C.S.*, XXI)

Ystradfellte
SN 91 N.W. (9237 1638)   16 xi 82

(RMC 4) The marching camp near Beulah (Fig. 155)

This camp 300 m S.S.W. of the Camarch bridge at Beulah stands between 200 m and 230 m above O.D. on ground sloping moderately upwards N.N.E. to S.S.W. There are commanding views to the N., N.W. and N.E. but the site is overlooked by a small knoll to the S.S.W. Marshy ground lies to the N. and much of the interior has been subject to water-logging. The N.E. side lies just W. of the edge of steep bluffs forming the W. side of the River Camarch valley at this point.

The site lies in several fields of improved or partly improved pasture. The only well-preserved parts of the defences are the N.W. side, W. angle and part of the S.W. side. The N.E. is visible on aerial photographs but is very difficult to discern with any certainty on the ground. The details of the rest are conjectural. The N.W. side lies on a True Bearing of about 61° and measures about 373 m long. Only a 92 m length of the S.W. side survives on a True Bearing of about 340°. The N.E. side is on two alignments, the change point being probably the site of an entrance. The N. part of this side, 172 m long, has a True Bearing of 328½° while the S. part, estimated length 174 m, has a True Bearing of 336½°. The estimated enclosed area was about 13.9 ha.

There are no surviving traces of the S.E. side, S. angle or most of the S.W. side of the defences but their general position can be ascertained from the alignment and surviving lengths of the other sides. The N. part of the S.W. side is preserved as broken lengths of low, grassed bank. There is no trace of the internal *clavicula* detected on this side.[1] The W. angle survives showing the camp to have had the standard rounded corners but is plough-damaged. Much of the bank of the N.W. side to the internal *clavicula* at 9190 5087 is preserved, 2 m to 3 m wide and up to 0.4 m high. The *clavicula* has an inturn on the S. and measures 16 m long and 10 m deep; the entrance gap is 10 m wide. N.E. of the entrance the defence is reduced to a grassed scarp which peters out as a readily definable feature after about 40 m. Although visible on air photos the N. angle, N.E. side and the start of the E. angle are very difficult to locate on the ground, but a very low bank or ridge just perceptible intermittently may be a remnant.

C.U.A.P. AQD 57, AYF 97-8, BAK 41, 44-6, BEX 38-9.
[1] *J.R.S.*, LIX (1969), pp. 123-4.

Llangamarch (E), Treflys (C)
SN 95 S.W. (919 507)   4 i 83

(RPC 1) Probable practice camp near Llwyncadwgan (Fig. 155)

The site lies at about 216 m above O.D. on land falling gently to the S.W. Aerial photographs indicate a rectangular earthwork with rounded corners and at least one entrance in the centre of the E. side.[1] The overall dimensions are approximately 52 m N. to S. by 55 m. The only traces visible on the ground are very slight ridges.

J.R.S., XLVIII (1958), p. 96; *ibid.*, LIX (1969), pp. 123-4 (C on plan).
[1] 106 G/UK 1471, Nos. 1110-1112.

Llangamarch (E), Treflys (C)
SN 94 N.W. (9200 4995)   January 1983

RPC 2 (Fig. 155)

Professor St. Joseph reports[1] a rectangular enclosure with rounded corners and at least one entrance in the centre of the W. side, at about 230 m above O.D on very gently sloping ground nearly 200 m W. of RF 1.

The site is visible on aerial photographs as a parch-mark in grass but there are no surface indications. The enclosure measures about 48.8 m by 38.1 m. The ditch of a later enclosure overlies much of this probable camp.

An enclosure of similar dimensions is visible on an aerial photograph[2] of a narrow saddle between two knolls 200 m to the W. (9189 5017). The photograph indicates at least a rounded S.W. corner. There are no traces apparent on the ground.

[1]*J.R.S.*, LXVII (1977), p. 151.
[2]C.U.A.P. BYR 9 (1.7.76).

Llangamarch (E), Treflys (C)
SN 95 S.W. (9209 5017)   January 1983

(RPC 3) Probable practice camp near Y Gaer, Brecon

The site is on flat ground about 300 m W. of Y Gaer, Brecon (RF 2). The site is revealed as a grassmark on aerial photographs but there are no visible surface remains. The enclosure is univallate, approximately square with sides about 27 m to 30 m long and with rounded corners.

Arch. in Wales, 21 (1981), p. 37; *Britannia,* XIV (1983), p. 280.

Aberysgir
SO 02 N.W. (000 298)   2 xii 81

Roads

It has been necessary to reconsider the whole network of Roman roads in Brecknock, partly because earlier authorities have suggested a multiplicity of routes far in excess of the likely number of engineered ways,[1] and partly because these same writers have made modern Brecon the focus of the system, although there is no evidence of Roman occupation there and the large fort at Y Gaer (RF 2), 4 km to the west, is the obvious destination.[2] The Commission has restricted itself to considering the most likely routes. Others, less likely, have been examined cursorily but several highly improbable suggestions have been ignored. There is still a pressing need for detailed fieldwork to establish the medieval and early modern pattern.

In considering likely routes the following types of evidence (in order of decreasing importance) have been considered satisfactory enough to establish the course of a Roman road: a) excavated structural remains; b) unexcavated *agger* or paving; c) milestones, not necessarily *in situ* but found close to a likely line; d) terracing, usually in conjunction with other evidence and with e) fairly long alignments and changes of direction on sighting points. The juxtaposition of inscribed stones of the Early Christian period with a likely route may be taken in some instances as additional confirmation of a course. The task of identifying the precise route of a road has been made difficult by the probable slightness of the original works in places.

Our knowledge of the complete system of Roman roads in Brecknock is thus imperfect. It is not possible to indicate with any certainty the course of the presumed road from Y Gaer (RF 2) to the forts in the north, and the evidence for a connection in the opposite direction between Y Gaer and Penydarren is far from satisfactory. Five routes, however, can be confirmed on evidence of varying quality, though in two cases only can extensive lengths of the actual line of the road be demonstrated (Coelbren-Y Gaer; Caerau, Beaulah-Castell Collen). Although the first kilometre of a road N.E. from Y Gaer has been verified by excavation, its further course is almost entirely hypothetical. The existence of milestones and short lengths of probably ancient road confirm the general route of the Abergavenny-Y Gaer, Brecon-Llandovery road.

If in addition to the five certain routes we assume the existence of the other two, it is clear that the vicinity of Y Gaer is the focal point of the system in the county. The Abergavenny-Llandovery road is a major arterial valley route for most of its length. Y Gaer was also at the W. end of another arterial valley route from Kenchester (Her.). The other routes crossed generally barren uplands between major valleys.

There can be little doubt that besides the constructed highways other routes were in use during the Roman period, but it is impossible to demonstrate this conclusively. We may envisage that some pre-Roman ridgeways associated with a pastoral economy continued in use,[3] and, in the valleys, on the slopes above the ground liable to flooding, tracks still connected permanent settlements laterally and also ran between upper and lower valley pastures. The imposition of the Roman pattern would have greatly facilitated communication between settlements.

The basic road system was probably constructed soon after the establishment of permanent military garrisons in the later first century; however, if the hypothesis of an earlier large fort at Coelbren is accepted,[4] 'Sarn Helen' hereabouts may not have been constructed until the later fort was erected, towards the mid-second century. Milestones provide evidence of later refurbishing of the main S.E. to N.W. arterial route under Postumus (A.D. 258-68), Constantius Chlorus (A.D. 296-306) and Constantine II (either A.D. 317-37 or 337-40).[5]

The entries dealing with the roads fall into two parts: a general account of the route, which will be sufficient for most purposes; and a detailed description of the actual remains, based primarily on grid references, which will enable anyone who wishes to study the road in greater detail to locate its traces with precision on the ground or on a large-scale map.

[1] For example S. O'Dwyer, *The Roman Roads of Brecknock and Glamorgan* (Newtown, 1937) who considered the many sunken lanes in the county to be of considerable age—the more wear, the older—and often of Roman origin.

[2] *op. cit.*, p. 9. O'Dwyer explains his alignment on the fords at Brecon by considering the roads to have been built after the abandonment of Y Gaer; Margary, *Roman Roads.*

[3] Marching camps such as those on Y Pigwn may have been sited in relation to such routes.

[4] *Inv. Glam.*, I, ii, p. 84.

[5] *R.I.B.*, nos. 2260, 2258, 2259.

(RR 1) Coelbren to Brecon Gaer (Sarn Helen) (Figs. 176, 177)

The general course of this road has been known from the eighteenth century and there have been several descriptions of it,[1] the most recent by G. D. B. Jones,[2] which deals in detail with the stretch between the Llia valley and Blaengwrthyd. In 1940 Sir Cyril Fox demonstrated the structure of the road at Maen Madog.[3] There is reasonably good evidence that this route was an artificial construction for almost its entire length although the N. termination is lost. The surveyors seem to have attempted the most direct route possible, deviating only when topography such as the marshes of Pant Mawr dictated. The main characteristic of the course is the alternate crossing of high moorland ridges and the narrow upper reaches of rivers and streams dissecting Fforest Fawr.

General Description

A causeway interrupted by modern lanes runs from the site of the E. gate of the Roman fort at Coelbren (Glam.) to a ford of the small Afon Pyrddin which forms the county boundary. Where the course of the road is visible again, about 45 m E. of the stream, it has assumed a more northerly alignment and the *agger* forms an almost continuous feature for about 1.6 km. Under the modern road by the covered reservoir 400 m E.N.E. of Cefn Gwenynawg there is a change of direction to the S. and a series of minor adjustments in alignment carry the road E. and N. across the ridge to a major change of course at Gwaun-y-maerdy. To the S. lie extensive forestry plantations and to the N. bleak, marshy moorlands. In this stretch the ancient road is less well defined, obscured by the modern metalling of the track following its line. It appears to have been generally a raised construction but for 260 m W. of B.M. 300.81 m there is a S.-facing terrace.

At Gwaun-y-maerdy the road turns abruptly N. to follow the W. side of the upper valley of Afon Nedd. The present track to Cefn Ucheldref must follow closely the original. Between Cefn Ucheldref and the ford at Blaen-nedd-isaf there are now no certain traces but the alignment of the stone piles from the *agger* in the field above Coed y Garreg leaves little doubt as to the fording point and the general direction of the road. The road climbs N. from the ford out of the narrow valley onto the open moorland. At Maen Madog, Fox showed that the present track is nearly 11 m N.W. of the original road which suggests that the modern line from N. of Coed y Garreg to the Afon Llia valley only approximates to the ancient one. North-north-east of Maen Madog is a change of alignment, and the modern track, and presumably the Roman road, cross the site of the earlier marching camp at Plas-y-gors (RMC 3) changing to a more N. alignment in its E. half and running to join the narrow modern road running almost due N. between Ystradfellte and Heolsenni, which represents the course as far as a point 800 m S. of Maen Llia where the ancient line is taken up by a moorland track across Bryn Melyn. There is no trace of a suggested alternative route further W. passing W. of Maen Llia and descending into and running along the lower slopes of the E. side of the Senni valley to Gelliau-isaf. The line of the road N.N.E. across Bryn Melyn to Nant Cwm-du is represented by the modern rough-metalled track, formerly part of a toll road, which is in some places a terrace, in others a shallow cutting. A ford at Pont Blaen-cwm-du is the only feasible crossing point of the stream, to the N. of which the road continues in the form of a generally derelict, terraced track[4] running along the upper E. edge of the Senni valley towards Plas-y-fan. The more easterly road to Forest Lodge has been suggested as the route but is a later turnpike road. South-south-west of Fedwen-unig is a change of alignment to the E. In the fields between here and the A4215, E. of Gwern Lle'r-tai, are sporadic traces of the ancient causeway. Further N.E. traces are absent or ambiguous from the A4215 to where the *agger* with associated ditches and quarries

176 Sarn Helen (RR 1), showing the course between about SN 870 112 and Coelbren Roman fort (SN 858 106)

reappears on the same alignment in a large field W. of Nant y Llest. It is from here, looking N.E. or S.W., that the general alignment and topographic objectives of the road can best be observed. A slight deviation is made to cross the stream but the actual ford has disappeared, as have positive traces immediately to the N.E. Two fine sections of causeway aligned to the presumed crossing of the Nant y Llest extend across open moorland for 400 m S.W. to N.E. from the drain at SN 9597 2557. Between the end of the causeway and Cwm Camlais-fach and to the N.E. of this stream, the details are obscure, but it seems reasonably clear that the moorland track N. of Pantcilgatlws marked *Sarn Helen* on O.S. maps represents approximately the course and there is a good piece of *agger* continuing its line to the entrance lane of Blaengwrthyd farm. A change of alignment to a more easterly direction takes place in this section. Short lengths of *agger* survive in the lane to Blaengwrthyd. North-east of the farm the road curves N. as a slight causeway and terrace petering out 110 m E. of the Fish Pond near Pen-y-parc. Beyond this its course is uncertain. Jones considered that the road crossed the Usk where the Pen-pont/Llansbyddid parish boundary meets the river, envisaging a route E. of Twyn y Gaer (HF 10). Such a course would entail a sharp change of alignment near the Fish Pond, climbing and crossing a ridge and another marked alteration of direction S. of Pant-y-gaer. This area was examined but no traces of ancient road were found. Similarly no signs were encountered in the relevant area N. of the river. The suggested descent in a straight line through Pen-y-wern Wood is impracticable due to the steep slope and there are no signs of engineering to overcome this. Morgan[1] notes a local tradition that the route ran through Pen-pont Park. The road appears to point towards the ford at Pen-pont where it could have crossed and possibly joined the Brecon Gaer-Llandovery road (RR 5) at Pentre-bach. The O.S.[5] suggests another plausible but unsubstantiated route represented by the stone-cored track passing Wernfawr with a change of alignment to the N. of the farm via one or other of two old fieldways leading N.E. to a joint path to Pen-pont farm. A steep-sided stream here forces the present lane to make a short deviation to the N. coming to a junction with the A40 (T) by the Old Forge. The modern highway is supposed to mark the course for 450 m E. before deviating S., the earlier line following, possibly, a slight terrace above the flood plain of the Usk running E.N.E. for about 1.45 km to a good ford of the river near its junction with the Pen-pont/Llansbyddid parish boundary.

Details of Route

The road from the E. gate of Coelbren fort crossed the Afon Pyrddin at about SN 8611 1075 where a paved ford has been observed.[6] For about 45 m E. of the stream there are no remains. The first probable trace is a mound about 10 m long by 14 m wide and up to 1 m high, lying W. of a streamlet at 8616 1076 on the alignment of known lengths of *agger* further E. Between the stream and the boundary of an old lane at 8623 1080 there is a well-defined length of *agger* about 13 m wide and up to 1 m high. The *agger*, now 12 m wide, continues N.E. of the lane, partly obscured by superimposed field boundaries from 8630 1084 to 8649 1095. Beyond the latter point it is unencumbered to 8664 1103 being about 10 m wide, 0.2 m high on the N. and 0.5 m on the S. with an indistinct ditch to the N. about 0.3 m deep. Some metalling and possible limestone kerbing are visible and it is about here that Morgan observed well-preserved pavement and "curbs" in 1907. From 8665 1103 to 8690 1117 the *agger* is between 8 m and 10 m wide, its N. side largely under a field boundary but the S. side is plainly visible about 0.6 m high. After a short break the *agger* continues to 8729 1139 as a grassed causeway 9 m to 10 m wide, 0.3 m high on the N. and 0.4 m high on the S. Several minor breaches caused by erosion and stone robbing occur in the W. part of this length where traces of metalling are exposed and on aerial photographs[7] side ditches are visible. S. of Cefn Gwenynawg, Morgan considered the ancient road visible but mended with modern material. There are slight traces of the N.W. side of the *agger* from 8730 1140 to 8737 1144 but from the latter point to 8751 1150 across marshy ground the indications are vague. In the small triangular field between 8751 1150 and the modern tarmac road at 8756 1153 a possible short length of *agger*, 0.2 m high, and a bunch of rushes marking the line of the N. ditch of the road have been observed. The modern road as far as 8790 1166 follows the ancient line but obscures the details. The O.S. record for 17 m N.E. from 8757 1153 the possible remains of the *agger*, 0.6 m high, in a drainage ditch on the S. side of the modern road and possible traces of ancient metalling in the modern ditch on the N. side. A track with modern metalling follows the course from 8790 1166 to the crossing of Nant Hir at 8864 1179. It probably lies over an *agger* to about 8835 1176 but from here to about 8860 1179 it runs along a S.-facing terrace 2 m to 3 m wide descending towards the stream. The details of the crossing of Nant Hir are uncertain but the modern metalled track

recommencing its ascent of the ridge here follows the course, possibly on the low remnants of the *agger* about 10 m wide between 8873 1180 and 8956 1206. There are no visible ancient features from the latter point to the highest part of the ridge crossed by the road at 9009 1223, 334 m above O.D., the present metalled moorland way presumably following the course, and the same is true as the track descends into the Afon Nedd valley towards Gwaun-y-maerdy, near where there is a major change of alignment to the N. at about 9053 1233. Also, the present track between Gwaun-y-maerdy and Cefn Ucheldref must follow approximately the line of the ancient road of which no certain traces are visible although Morgan noted portions of pavement in gullies eroded across the track. The road encounters a series of streams in this sector which would have required a certain amount of small-scale engineering to facilitate their crossing. The track passes through a cutting at about 9066 1264 which is possibly original and towards the N. end of this sector it runs on a grass-grown natural terrace with a stone surface. The course between Cefn Ucheldref and the probable ancient ford at Blaen-nedd-isaf is uncertain. Morgan claimed that the road was visible across two successive fields N. of Cefn Ucheldref and that the hedge between 9097 1389 and 9102 1425 probably followed the line. Stone piles were observed along this course similar to those associated with the road at Coed y Garreg. The lack of present-day surface remains and indications on relevant aerial photographs[8] make it difficult to decide the course though it should be noted that a more westerly line than Morgan's, after that immediately N. of Cefn Ucheldref, would avoid an awkward crossing of the small W. to E. ravine joining the Nedd valley S. of Pont Cwm Pwll-y-rhyd. The crossing of the Nedd was certainly very near or at the Blaen-nedd-isaf ford at 9110 1449. For about 220 m N.N.E. from the ford in the field S. of Coed y Garreg there are no certain traces but in the enclosure between 9120 1469 and 9131 1491, ascending the valley side, are remains of the *agger* about 8 m wide on which are piles of stones derived from the road pavement which was lifted in the later nineteenth century. To the N. of the field the *agger* with a hint of a ditch on the W. comes onto the open moorland merging into the present metalled track which represents the approximate line N.N.E.

177 *(opposite)* Sarn Helen (RR 1): view of the road, looking south-west from SN 8672 1107

Maen Madog is an inscribed stone commemorating the burial of *Dervacus* in the fifth or early sixth century A.D.[9] During its re-erection in 1940 at 9182 1576 Sir Cyril Fox examined the area immediately to the S. and E., finding that the N.W. margin of the Roman road on a bearing of 38° magnetic for a length of at least 20 m ran 10.67 m (35 ft) S.E. of and roughly parallel to the S.E. margin of the modern track. The memorial had been erected originally on the N.W. edge of the R. road 5.18 m (17 ft) S. of its present position. The road paving of river pebbles and boulders lay under about 0.25 m of peaty soil. The surface was 4.88 m (16 ft) wide set on a make-up of clean pink clay 0.064 m to 0.089 m (2½ to 3½ ins) thick which lay on a thin, black soil horizon over the weathered sandstone bedrock.[10] No ditches were noted. Between the Roman and the modern road just over 10 m S.W. of Maen Madog was another possible roadway of uncertain date made of looser, angular stones. Fox suggests the following sequence of activity in connection with the stone and its vicinity: I Roman road built in the first century A.D. and in use until the sixth century or later. II Complete disuse of the route. The road becomes overgrown and lost; the *Dervacus* stone falls? III The route is reopened; coal traffic creates hollow-ways in slopes. *Dervacus* stone 'discovered' prostrate. Period ends *c.* 1813. IV Sarn Helen reconstructed as metalled road approximately on R. line. *Dervacus* stone set up in new position *c.* 1820-1850. Morgan records that another stone, the Penymynydd, was found to the left (W.) of the road near Maen Madog. The course is probably represented approximately by the metalled track between Maen Madog and 9255 1661 which crosses the site of the Plas-y-gors marching camp (RMC 3) and by the modern road to 9250 1840 but no ancient remains are now apparent although Morgan mentions that pitching was visible by the side of the modern road in 1896. The old toll road across Bryn Melyn to Pont Blaen-cwm-du at 9423 2149 probably follows the Roman line although there are no unequivocal traces of ancient work. Jones describes several constructional features including fords along this stretch but none are demonstrably Roman and several could be relatively recent. The embankment at about 9376 2107 is almost certainly a ruined boundary wall, not part of the road structure. The alignment of undoubtedly ancient remains N.E. of Plas-y-fan seems to support Jones's identification of the road course with that of a derelict lane between Pont Blaen-cwm-du and Fedwen-unig. From the stream crossing to 9397 2171 a S.W.-facing terrace leads across marshy moorland. A section cut

by Jones seems to show that the road was founded on a shelf created by excavating into the rock of the steep hillside to the N. and by building up clay over sandstone blocks on the S., downslope side. A metalling of broken sandstone about 4.65 m wide and 0.15 m thick was laid on the levelled surface created, and capped with gravel. However, the structure is not necessarily Roman and could be much later. The lane continues N. as a west-facing terrace of varying width, encroached upon and bounded by more recent field boundaries. At approximately 9382 2227 the track was sectioned again by Jones revealing broken sandstone metalling about 4.3 m wide and 0.25 m thick capped with gravel on a shelf cut into the rock of the hillside. Continuing further N. the track remains essentially a terrace-way intermittently becoming a hollow-way at stream crossings. Between 9398 2322 and 9403 2327 the lane becomes a slightly raised causeway unenclosed on the S.E. A section cut by Jones revealed a cambered structure flanked by shallow gullies measuring about 5.7 m wide overall. The *agger* measured about 4.45 m wide by 0.46 m high and was composed of a thin basal layer of gravel covered by a main core of clay which was capped successively by thin layers of broken sandstone and gravel metalling.

From 9405 2330 to 9408 2334, in a field between Fedwen-unig and Plas-y-fan,[11] the line of the causeway is only faintly visible on the ground and further N.E. it is represented between 9409 2334 and 9419 2346 by an ill-defined ridge flanked by probable quarry hollows, though Jones states that the stones of the road surface could be felt by probing, less than 10 cm below the surface in places. A much more distinctive ridge, 0.25 m to 0.3 m high, continuing the alignment, runs between 9419 2346 and 9445 2377 with the disturbed surface metalling and flanking quarry hollows visible. The Commission was unable to examine the land between the crossing of Cwm Brynych and the A4215 but details are supplied by Jones and the O.S. Between 9446 2379 and 9459 2394 the course is ill-defined although a number of quarry hollows can be seen. When the area between 9459 2394 and 9466 2402 was ploughed for forestry the line of the road was shown by disturbed foundation stones and a strip of lighter, gritty soil contrasting with the black, peaty soil of the field. Substantial quarry hollows were also observed. Between 9466 2402 and a stream crossing at about 9476 2415 the surface of the road was located by probing 0.1 m to 0.13 m (4 in to 5 in) below ground level. At the stream crossing "the remains of a roughly-worked sandstone ramp" were unearthed. Between there and 9489 2430 are the intermittent remains of a prominent causeway up to 8.5 m wide and 0.5 m high bordered by quarry pits. At 9495 2436 Jones found "a pair of stone supports, in the shape of a rough circle 4 ft (1.22 m) in diameter" under reeds and grass which he supposed to be the remains of a bridge across marshy ground. About 18 m N.E. of this a "ramp of rough sandstone" is incorporated in a later turf wall across the road. From 9498 2440 to 9514 2458 is a low, indistinct stony ridge to the S.E. of which are quarry hollows.[12] At the entrance of the field N. of the crossroads is a short length of metalled track over the causeway but N.E. of this there are no certain surface remains until 9557 2507 although in Morgan's time the road was apparently traceable. Aerial photographs[13] suggest that the road may have made a short deviation to the E. in this sector to avoid wet ground. Between 9557 2507 and 9575 2531 is a stretch of fairly prominent *agger* up to 10 m wide in places with a distinct line of quarry scoops along the N.W. side and a suggestion of side ditches. Jones sectioned the structure at about 9562 2513 revealing a cambered causeway with shallow side ditches about 5.56 m wide overall. The *agger* was about 4.32 m wide and up to 0.33 m high consisting of a foundation of large sandstone blocks covered by smaller sandstone and gravel and capped with gravel. There is a slight change of alignment at the N.E. end of this stretch of *agger* prior to the crossing of Nant y Llest. The exact details of the crossing are uncertain and there are no longer any clear traces, such as the line of stones noted by Morgan, in the field to the E. of the brook and the aerial photograph evidence is equivocal. Positive remains of the road are encountered again crossing the moorland between 9597 2557 and 9604 2564 and between 9605 2568 and 9624 2586. The *agger* is a well-defined grassed mound averaging about 8 m wide with rushes growing along the line of the side ditches and several quarry depressions flanking it, especially to the S. Jones cut a section at about 9607 2569 revealing a cambered causeway with shallow side ditches about 5.49 m wide overall. The *agger* was about 4.32 m wide and up to 0.58 m high composed of a core of sandstone with the larger pieces towards the base capped with gravel. It is apparent that the dimensions of the road between Fedwen-unig and Cwm Camlais-fach were almost constant, suggesting a single construction design and execution.

From 9624 2586 to Cwm Camlais-fach only the occasional hollow, possibly metalling quarries, indicates the course of the road on the ground.[14] No ancient remains are visible at the likely crossing point of Cwm Camlais-fach. The modern track between 9640 2609 and 9652 2619 probably follows approximately the ancient course and several small hollows of uncertain age are found to the S.E. of it. Across gorse- and bracken-infested moorland from a small stream at about 9653 2621 to an undoubted length of causeway beginning at 9686 2648 there is no unequivocal trace of the ancient road, the modern track probably following approximately the line. However, Jones claimed that the earlier causeway, 4.57 m (15 ft) wide, could be discerned firstly to the S.E. of the modern line, demarcated near the stream by large stones which are still visible, and then crossing under and running along the N.W. side of the present track further uphill. Small-scale quarrying of unknown date is visible either side of the modern track. The causeway between 9686 2648 and 9696 2654[15] lies partly to the N. of the present route and has a shallow ditch along its N. side. Overall the road is about 7.8 m wide, the causeway being 0.25 m high with a level top 3.3 m wide. Fragments of causeway, some with traces of metalling, are extant on either side of the green lane leading to Blaengwrthyd Farm. E.N.E. of the farmyard[16] between 9729 2669 and 9742 2679 are traces of *agger* about 0.2 m high, partly encroached upon by field boundaries. At 9744 2681, E. of a small stream, the causeway is about 6 m wide. Metalling is visible where the stream cuts the route.[17] The course curves N. to 9750 2688 as a N.W.-facing terrace up to 5 m wide with a downslope scarp about 1 m high. Between 9750 2688 and 9754 2700 the terrace continues with its E. side apparently masked by a lynchet accumulated behind a hedge built along its line. A stony-surfaced ledge below the hedge, 1.6 m to 1.7 m wide, represents its W. side. A final length of terrace about 5 m wide is encountered between 9754 2704 and 9753 2712. Beyond this the presumed extension to Brecon Gaer (RF 2) is uncertain. Aerial photographs[18] show a line of very low relief between 9756 2700 and 9776 2729 but nothing is visible on the ground at present and no N. continuation can be traced.[19] There are no indications N. of the Usk that there was a direct connection to the S. gate of Brecon Gaer.

Margary, *Roman Roads*, p. 338 (Route 622). The N.E. continuation of *Inv. Glam.* I, No. 755.

[1] *e.g.* W. Ll. Morgan, *Arch. Camb.* (1907), pp. 129-135.
[2] Jones, *Arch. Camb.*, CVI (1957), pp. 56-63.
[3] Fox, *Arch. Camb.*, XCV (1940), pp. 210-216.
[4] Designated *Sarn Helen* on the 6-in O.S. map, SN 92 SW, Provisional Edition, 1964.

[5] Unpublished notes O.S. RR 662 (1973).

[6] O.S. Records, RR 662.

[7] For side ditches, see C.U.A.P. AJB 86. For Coelbren to Cefn Gwenynawg in general see RAF 58/1452/F 21, Nos. 0037-0039. Also C.U.A.P. AQF 52.

[8] RAF CPE/UK 2079, Nos. 2115-6, 4113-4.

[9] V. E. Nash-Williams, *The Early Christian Monuments of Wales* (Cardiff, 1950), p. 82. L. A. Alcock, *Arthur's Britain* (London, 1971), pp. 247-8.

[10] Fox does not give a full cross-section, the structure being inferred from cuts at either edge of the road.

[11] A.Ps. covering the area between Plas-y-fan and the A4215 include O.S. 72.330.992, August 22nd, 1972.

[12] A.Ps. RAF CPE/UK 2079, Nos. 2288-9.

[13] A.Ps. RAF CPE/UK 2079, Nos. 2286-9 cover the line to Cwm Camlais-fach.

[14] A.Ps. RAF CPE/UK 2079, Nos. 4284-5 and 2286-8 seem to indicate faintly the continuation in the same alignment.

[15] A.P. O.S. 72.329.804, August 22nd, 1972.

[16] A.Ps. RAF CPE/UK 2079, Nos. 4283-5 and f.n. 15.

[17] According to a local farmer, metalling was encountered about 10 m N.E. of the stream in a cutting made in August 1979.

[18] A.Ps. RAF CPE/UK 2079, Nos. 4283-5.

[19] S. O'Dwyer, *The Roman Roads of Brecknock and Glamorgan* (Newtown, 1937), pp. 21-22 gives another possible line W. of Twyn y Gaer but this is no better evidenced than other suggestions and difficult to locate precisely; but he established the line immediately N.E. of Blaengwrthyd partly by probing apparently along the course described above. The "small settlement" mentioned may be the ruins at about 9755 2701 which are post-Roman.

(RR 2) Penydarren towards Brecon Gaer

There is no indisputable evidence for an engineered road between these forts although a connection is likely. The traditional line is up the Taf Fechan valley, across the Beacon's watershed at Bwlch ar y Fan and on to Llan-faes. The lack of positive traces and the alignment on the medieval town of Brecon rather than the vicinity of the Roman fort has led to the alternative suggestion of a course further W. incorporating an engineered track across Pen Milan.[1] As neither route has been demonstrated satisfactorily the main characteristics of each, with suggested variants, are given below.

(i) The Eastern Route

Margary, describing the road as lost between Gelli-gaer Common and the Taf Fechan (Pontsticill) Reservoir, takes no account of the fort at Penydarren. If a road did exist between Penydarren and the Taf Fechan it has been destroyed almost certainly by housing and industrial development. There is disagreement as to the line of the possible road until SO 0548 1422 near Tŷ'n-y-coed at the N.W. end of the main Taf Fechan Reservoir. The O.S.[2] has suggested a course firstly E. of the river with the crossing to the W. side obliterated now by the reservoir, while O'Dwyer[3] maintains that having crossed the river at Pont Sarn on the county boundary the road runs entirely to the W. through Vaynor and Pontsticill to Tŷ'n-y-coed. There is general agreement that the line is followed by the modern, narrow, metalled road running on a terrace above the river N.N.W. for about 2.2 km between 0548 1422 and the fork 250 m S.S.E. of Pont Cwmyfedwen at SO 0431 1611. There is renewed disagreement as to the course N. from the latter point. Margary and O'Dwyer favour a line W. of the river, represented by the present track to the S. end of the Lower Neuadd Reservoir. As with previous suggestions there is no evidence of Roman construction for this small road which is generally a track on a terrace above the river, hollowed in places. Immediately S. of the reservoir between about 0295 1776 and 0296 1788 the track is a sunken trail, typically 2.3 m wide and 0.5 m deep. Between here and 0287 1942 on the N. side of the Upper Neuadd Reservoir none of the present paths or tracks show any evidence of Roman construction. O'Dwyer considered that the road was now lost but originally ran to the W. of the cairn at 0282 1922 at present on an island in the Upper Neuadd Reservoir. North of the lake a track ascends the W. side of the steep, narrow valley of Nant Yr-hen-heol to join at about 0316 2051 the old coach road over Bwlch ar y Fan. The track is an alternating series of terraces and narrow hollow-ways, some embanked, with a maximum width of about 3 m. This suggestion is dismissed by the O.S. on topographic grounds and because of the lack of typical Roman structure. The track is considered to have served a later, deserted settlement N. of the Upper Neuadd Reservoir at 026 194. The O.S. favours a route represented by the modern metalled road on a terrace between Pont Cwmyfedwen and Blaen Taf Fechan continued by the track ascending the W. side of the Tor Glas, marked "Roman Road" on maps,[4] between Blaen Taf Fechan and Bwlch ar y Fan. This track is considered to be typically Roman. At its S. end it is a 3 m wide, gravel-metalled roadway on a W.-facing terrace. Approaching Nant y Gloesydd, the track becomes a narrow path falling sharply towards the river and broken by stream erosion. After a steep rise out of the stream valley for about 60 m the track resumes a more gently ascending gradient as a 3 m to 4 m wide gravelled terrace, slightly hollowed in places and ditched on the E. At approximately 0344 1860, for about 20 m, the road is in a shallow cutting 2 m to 3 m wide and 0.3 m deep. Continuing N. for about 1.5 km the track is a well-defined, W.-facing terrace up to 4 m wide but generally between 3 m and 3.5 m, with gravel metalling. A stone revetment about 1 m high is exposed for 25 m along the W. side of the track at about 0331 1998. The terrace fades as the road approaches the mountain top, broadening to 5 m at about 0330 2022 and becoming a level track 3 m wide, without terracing, from 0328 2031. There is no doubt that this is a well-engineered and relatively well-preserved roadway, as is its N. continuation, but other authorities dispute its Roman date, considering it more likely to have been an eighteenth century coach road between Merthyr and Brecon. A. H. A. Hogg[5] applies this interpretation to its N. continuation also but other authorities accept that the coach road follows an earlier, Roman, line N. from Bwlch ar y Fan. The O.S. considers it a "typical, direct, high, undulating route." At about 0316 2051 the track descends the valley head in a cutting 3 m wide and 4 m deep. By 0308 2065 the road is 5 m wide with gravel metalling as it drops into Cwm Cynwyn. Further N. the route travels over bare rock and at 0294 2084 it widens further to 10 m. Shortly after, the tracks narrows rapidly and at 0292 2094 runs in a cutting 2 m wide and between 0.5 m and 1 m deep. The road continues in a cutting to about 0300 2140 and then runs alternately on a terrace or in a cutting, 2 m to 3 m wide. As it descends further the track becomes a more consistent terrace and by about 0334 2244 broadens to 4 m to 5 m in places. An irregular trail and path diverging from the road at 0309 2160, running up to 70 m to the W. and rejoining at 0337 2275, shows no sign of ancient structure. The road descends to the entrance Cwmcynwyn farm at 0364 2353 as a slightly sunken, winding, roughly metalled track 2 m to 3 m wide. After this the road becomes a hollow-way, very broad at first and bounded by field banks but at 0372 2364 it narrows to 2 m, and 60 m N.W. of here has a cobbled surface. The line is continued past Bailea and across Nant Sere at Pont Caniedydd by the modern lane in a hollow-way, up to 2.5 m deep and 3 m wide. The modern road deviates sharply E. just N. of the bridge but there is no trace of ancient structure where the direct route

would have crossed. The authorities consider that from here the Roman line is followed by the modern lanes via Mynydd-ffernach and Bailyhelig to Llan-faes. O'Dwyer states that the road crossed the Usk at the Bernard Ford. The alignment on Brecon seems a major objection to this course.

O'Dwyer[6] supposes that a route branched off somewhere near Pont Cwmyfedwen (0416) crossing the mountains further to the E. and descending to crossings of the Usk via either Llanfrynach or Pencelli, but there is no evidence to support the identification of a Roman road between these points.

(ii) The Western Route[7]

No satisfactory evidence for this proposed route has been found on either side of the Taf Fawr valley between Penydarren and Cwm Crew. On the W. side of the valley between the modern Beacons Reservoir and Pant Brwynog (SN 9817) are the remains of a road system which is reasonably well aligned on a track across Y Gyrn and Pen Milan (see below) and conceivably Roman in origin. It is most easily traced from N. to S.[8] In a small plantation on the W. side of the A4059 just above the bridge crossing the Taf a road appears as a terrace between SN 9881 1803 and 9878 1798, the alignment suggesting a river crossing near the present bridge. At a large natural slab about 20 m S. of the plantation there is a change of course to closer to due S. and for 100 m there is a very fresh-looking metalled section following the terrace. Adjacent to this is a deeply-worn hollow trail which must pre-date the present metalling but not necessarily the cutting of the terrace. The terrace narrows to 3 m with light metalling visible in places as it approaches a ford across Nant yr Eira at 9874 1779 and continues S. below HF 6 (Rhyd Uchaf), at first reasonably well-made but sometimes degenerating into irregular shelving and a hollow trail, multiple in places, becoming indistinct in the boggy moorland of Pant Brwynog. Hogg has suggested tentatively that the terrace-way may be basically Roman, part of an uncompleted road between the forts. The development of the deep hollow-way N. of Nant yr Eira is ascribed to the breakdown of the Roman surfacing. The visible metalling may represent an attempt in more recent times to re-establish the road which, before any appreciable wear had taken place, was replaced by a new road now the A4059.

Modern reservoir and road construction will have obliterated any traces between the latter section of road and the possible route ascending Blaen Taf Fawr.

Running between 9903 2005 at the N.E. boundary of a forestry plantation and the beginning of the well-defined track on Pen Milan at about 9954 2307 is a variously-preserved trail which might represent the line of a Roman road although no certainly Roman structure has been identified. The route ascends along the W. side of Blaen Taf Fawr and is a poorly-defined path or track in its S. part running sinuously along the top of crags for some of the way. At 9913 2085 it becomes a grassy, hollowed trail about 1 m wide, flanked in places on the E. by a low stony bank. Sixty metres further N. the track broadens into a grassed, partly-revetted, E.-facing terrace up to 3 m wide but shortly after becomes a hollowed trail again. At 9915 2102 the track widens into a terrace 2 m to 3 m across and continues for several hundred metres N. as an irregular shelf which becomes vague as the head of the valley is approached. Commission investigators[9] observed kerbstones in this stretch and at about 9917 2180 to the E. of the track a large slab of dimensions appropriate to a fallen milestone. Crossing the watershed the track is poorly defined and it continues N. for several hundred metres as a somewhat irregular W.-facing terrace, in places twin-pathed.

The descent of the steep E. and N.E. slopes of Pen Milan is made on a steady gradient by a well-defined terrace 1.5 m to 3 m wide beginning about 9954 2307. As the track approaches the sharp bend it makes at 9990 2367 it becomes hollowed. At the turn it forms a broad terrace but continues its descent on a new alignment S.E. for 130 m as a winding hollow-way up to 2.0 m deep in places. Another sharp bend occurs at 9998 2357 and the trail becomes a 1.5 m deep hollow-way/cutting about 1.5 m wide, decreasing in depth as it winds N. down the hillside. At SO 0002 2407 the track is better defined as a hollow-way flanked on the E. by a grassed terrace but from here

to 0007 2464, where it ends, it deteriorates gradually into a vague, dissected trail. The Pen Milan section of the route has an engineered appearance and is plausibly of Roman origin. However, no satisfactory continuation has been proposed or identified. O'Dwyer notes that the alignment is continued to Llanfaes by lanes passing Clwydwaunhir Farm, Hollybush Hall, Cilwhybert and Ffrwdgrech but the same objection applies to this line as to the proposed N. end of the E. route, namely the alignment on Brecon. A direct route to Brecon Gaer implies a crossing of Afon Tarell N.E. of Libanus, possibly to link with the lost section of RR 1 on Mynydd Illtyd.

O'Dwyer also suggests a more westerly route across Y Gyrn via a track followed by the Glyn/Modrydd parish boundary E. of Storey Arms. From where the parish boundary leaves to follow the course of the Byddegai brook this path continues N.N.E. to join the route described above. No evidence of Roman structure is given or is visible now.

Margary, *Roman Roads*, p. 337 (Route 621). N. continuation of *Inv. Glam.*, I, No. 754.

[1] A. H. A. Hogg, *Arch. Camb.*, CXXII (1973), p. 17.

[2] O.S. Records, RR 621.

[3] S. O'Dwyer, *The Roman Roads of Brecknock and Glamorgan* (Newtown, 1937), p. 16-17.

[4] For example: 6-in O.S. map, SO 01 NW, Provisional Edition (1964).

[5] A. H. A. Hogg, MS. notes in R.C.A.M. files (1969).

[6] *op. cit.*, p. 28.

[7] *Arch. in Wales*, 9 (1969), p. 17.

[8] A. H. A. Hogg, MS. notes in R.C.A.M. files (1978).

[9] In 1970. The slab is 1.73 m long and 0.3 m by at least 0.25 m in section. No lettering was observed but the underside was not seen as the block was too heavy to move with available equipment.

[10] *op. cit.*, p. 20.

Penydarren to the Usk valley

Several routes have been proposed but none have been substantiated. The characteristics of the main suggestions are outlined below.

Margary considers that a road branched from the supposed Penydarren to Brecon Gaer route (RR 2) near Dol y Gaer, the actual junction having been obliterated by the Taf Fechan Reservoir. He proposes

that the line is represented by the lane running N.E. up Cwm Callan between Neuadd, SO 059145, and Blaencallan, 066150, and continued by the track across the ridge of Bryniau Gleision to Pen Bwlch Glasgwm, 090162. In the vicinity of Neuadd, the lane is a modern metalled road on a terrace above Nant Callan but by about 200 m N.E. it has degenerated to a roughly metalled track. 100 m N.E. of Blaencallan the track is on a well-formed, S.E.-facing terrace 2.5 m to 3 m wide. At 0682 1519 there is a change of alignment to a more easterly course. The moorland track forms a terrace in places but otherwise has no definite structure. There are no remains in this portion of the proposed route to suggest a Roman origin.

At Pen Bwlch Glasgwm there is another change of alignment to N.N.E. and for a short distance the route is in a rock-cut, hollowed terrace 2 m wide and 1.2 m deep. The course to a change of alignment to N.E. at 0917 1667 is a winding, E.-facing terrace high on the ridge overlooking the upper reaches of the Afon Crawnon. Margary considers that the line is continued by the track passing W. of Bryn-melyn and by the modern road W. of Tor y Foel which passes Pantywenallt and descends to Tal-y-bont. This latter stretch is marked "Roman Road" on earlier editions of O.S. maps but the authority for this has not been ascertained.[1] The track to the junction at 109187 is generally on a terrace and roughly metalled but shows no signs of Roman structure. The road to the B4558 at Tal-y-bont ar Wysg has a modern surface and runs on a W.-facing terrace on the slopes of Tor y Foel and then on an E.-facing terrace from near Pantywenallt whence it descends steeply across the hillslope. E. of Tump Wood (HF 43). Margary claims that an old terrace was clear on the E. side of the lane near Pantywenallt but this has not been identified. From Tal-y-bont, Margary supposes that the road is represented by the modern B4558 via Cross Oak and Pencelli joining RR 3 at 077 274, S. of Groesffordd. No satisfactory evidence of a Roman origin for the route is presented.

Alternative origins and endings for this general route have been proposed by O'Dwyer[2] and A. H. A. Hogg.[3] In the S., O'Dwyer describes vaguely a route from E. of Dowlais N. along the ridge of Cefn yr Ystrad and joining Margary's route at Pen Bwlch Glasgwm. O'Dwyer's course coincides with Margary's to the B4558 at Tal-y-bont but here he considered that the road ran through Maes-mawr farm and crossed the Usk at Llansantffraid to join his suggested route between Abergavenny and Brecon. No supporting evidence is given for these views.

Hogg notes that modern roads, not necessarily on an old line, run from 054078, Penydarren, to 066098 and 066100 connecting with an old track running N.E. from 066114. Although the alignment is suggestive no remains of any ancient road are visible and it seems probable that the present track along the W. side of the Twynau Gwynion quarries is of no great antiquity.

The moorland track N. from the county boundary at 0645 1109 is a grassy path about 2 m wide occasionally slightly cut or terraced but otherwise unremarkable. It ascends gradually to Cerig y Llwyni with a major alignment change to the N.E. at 0685 1248. At Cerig y Llwyni as it approaches and runs parallel to Cwm Criban the track is very vague, 2 m to 3 m wide in places with no visible structure. At 0732 1320, 40 m N.W. of the track, stands the "Ystrad Stone",[4] a standing stone with an Ogham inscription of fifth or sixth century date. The erection of this stone in the vicinity of the track and the local placename "Ystrad" may imply some considerable antiquity for it. The track ascends, running parallel and E. of Cwm Criban at the foot of the crags of Cwar yr Ystrad. Quarry installations have disturbed the area at the highest point of the mountain and N. of these the track makes for Pen Bwlch Glasgwm deviating W. from a more direct line to avoid the marsh of Gwaun Nant Ddu. Quarry traffic has eroded the track in this sector. Although the presence of the memorial stone and the placename 'Ystrad' suggest the existence of an ancient road, no structure has been located. Hogg follows Margary's route until 1098 1876 from where he prefers the lane to Cwm Crawnon which is a plausible route if a connection with the Abergavenny to Brecon Gaer road near Pen-y-gaer was intended. The crossing of the Usk would have been at Llangynidr bridge with a series of modern lanes representing the general course towards Pen-y-gaer. The W. half of the route runs parallel to the S. slopes of Tor y Foel. A modern metalled lane leads to Bwlch-y-waun, 116188, but W. of the farm the line is continued by a rough track on a terrace 2 m to 3 m wide which is enclosed by field boundaries and hollowed and overgrown in places. A change of alignment occurs at 129193 and the track is a hollow-way up to 2 m deep as it ascends to Pen-y-bailey, 134193.

O'Dwyer also noted the possibility of the Bwlch-y-waun to Pen-y-bailey lane and suggested two routes continuing it to the Usk. One, not closely specified, ran by Llwyn-yr-eos, 139194, to the ford at Cwm Crawnon and thence to Bwlch via Llangynidr bridge. Another, he supposed, ran N. from near Llwyn-yr-eos connecting with a track through the wood behind the house named Glawcoed, 1409 2000. When the garden of this house was extended in c. 1937 part of a "heavily paved" road was found. The crossing of the river was suggested as the old ford by Llanddeti vicarage. N. of the river it is proposed that, possibly, the road went either to Bwlch or, represented by the lanes passing Buckland House and Tal-y-bryn-isaf, joined the ridgeway over Allt yr Esgair. The significance of the paving at Glawcoed is uncertain and, although a route S. of Tor y Foel seems more satisfactory than one via Tal-y-bont, no reliable evidence is available for any of the course.

Margary, *Roman Roads*, p. 336 (Route 620).

[1] O.S. Records, RR 620.

[2] S. O'Dwyer, *The Roman Roads of Brecknock and Glamorgan* (Newtown, 1937), p. 15-16.

[3] A. H. A. Hogg, MS. notes in R.C.A.M. files (1969).

[4] V. E. Nash-Williams, *The Early Christian Monuments of Wales* (Cardiff, 1950), p. 79.

(RR 3) Abergavenny to Brecon Gaer

The existence of a road between *Gobannium* and Brecon Gaer is undoubted but very little positive evidence of its exact course is extant. The milestone found at Millbrook Farm was not *in situ*, but must surely have come from this road.

Description of the Probable Course

It is generally agreed that the A40T between Abergavenny and Crickhowell, the modern representative of a long-standing route between the towns, follows approximately the line of the Roman road on the N. side of the Usk Valley. The original route probably involved several minor alignment adjustments and a major one immediately W. of the crossing of Afon Grwyne (SO 2316).

At 207 194, N.W. of Crickhowell, a narrow lane leaves the main road and ascends the valley side to Cwm-gu. At 199 210 the roadway makes a sharp turn to W.N.W. and descends on a terrace towards Tretower. Margary favours this lane to represent the Roman line and although no ancient structure is apparent, it does continue the general alignment from Glangrwyne and the turn at Cwm-gu points towards the pass at Bwlch which must have been taken by the road. The recent excavations of the Neolithic chambered tomb at Gwernvale (211 192)[1] failed to locate any sign of a Roman road along the old line of the A40, and it possibly ran further uphill, for example directly between Pont Cwmbeth (214 190) and Llanfair (208 195).

In 1803 Thomas Payne recorded[2] a length of causeway, destroyed by a local farmer, which ran from the vicinity of Lower Gaer Farm (171 218) to a point very close to the S.W. corner of Pen-y-gaer Roman fort (RF 3) and continued W. for some distance. The juxtaposition of this evidently old causeway and the Roman fort suggests *prima facie* that it was the Roman line that was broken up by the farmer, but unfortunately there are no surface indications at present of the precise course. There is no visible structural evidence of a Roman road on any of the possible alignments between Tretower and Pen-y-gaer but the narrow, sunken lane between 1746 2179 and 1716 2183 immediately N. of Lower Gaer Farm possibly continues the alignment of the causeway recorded by Payne.

Three hundred metres W. of Pen-y-gaer, Margary[3] proposes that the course is taken up by a modern lane on a slight terrace at the foot of a steep slope between 1647 2189 and Tymawr, 1563 2188. The line of the lane is continued to the A40T at 1509 2187 by a S.-facing terraceway about 3 m wide. West of the modern road to the centre of Bwlch village, a short length of modern track, slightly sunken and embanked, 2.5 m to 3 m wide, and further N.W. a footpath, represent a possible course across the pass. From Bwlch to 1419 2253 it is assumed that the A40T follows the ancient course. There is no evidence of Roman structure along any of this plausible route. O'Dwyer[4] proposes a branch off the route at Bwlch represented by the B4560 to Cathedin-fawr and thence by lanes past Cae Cottrel, Caenant and Whitelow farm joining the lane between Genffordd and Talgarth at 167 309. No evidence is quoted and the suggestion may be dismissed as highly improbable as may another that a road ran between Blaenllynfi, Trebinshwn, Treberfydd and Pennorth at the E. foot of Allt yr Esgair.

The course N.W. from Glanpant (140 225) favoured by Margary and earlier versions of O.S. maps runs along the ridge of Allt yr Esgair. The proposed route from Glanpant to 1307 2327 is at present a narrow, embanked, sunken green lane gradually ascending the S.E. slopes of the hill. The continuation of the line N.N.W. is uncertain but may be indicated by the course of the Llansantffraid/Cathedin parish boundary along which field boundaries and grassy paths lead to the hill-fort (HF 47) crowning the ridge.

Such a route implies an alignment change to N.N.W. at about 1295 2337. A hollow-way, in places up to 3 m deep and as narrow as 0.5 m, runs steeply downhill from the N. entrance of the hill-fort to 1231 2537 where it turns through a right angle and carries on almost due W. for almost 350 m before realigning N.W. at 1198 2543. From here a much less entrenched, grassgrown path, 3 m to 4 m wide at first but narrowing northwards to as little as 1 m, runs to join the modern metalled road E. of Pennorth at 1140 2601. This lane, on a new alignment generally W. then N.W. by Manest Court, is supposed to represent the line as

The best evidence for the existence of the road is a milestone (fig. 178) found built into the steps of a granary at Millbrook farm, 650 m N.W. of Llanhamlach (0849 2713) and now in the Brecknock Museum. Although not *in situ* it is very likely that it came from the side of the Abergavenny to Brecon Gaer road, no great distance away, and indicates that the present A40 represents approximately the line. The stone has been published with full discussion by R. P. Wright in *R.I.B.* and *Roman Frontier (RFW)*,[6] from which the following extract, with original entry numbers is taken with permission.

R.I.B. 2258

R.I.B. 2259

178 Roman milestone from Millbrook Farm: scale 1:5

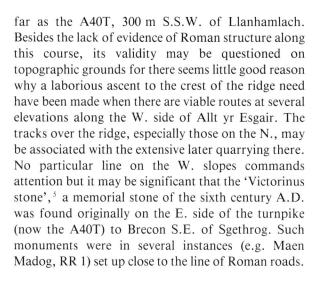

far as the A40T, 300 m S.S.W. of Llanhamlach. Besides the lack of evidence of Roman structure along this course, its validity may be questioned on topographic grounds for there seems little good reason why a laborious ascent to the crest of the ridge need have been made when there are viable routes at several elevations along the W. side of Allt yr Esgair. The tracks over the ridge, especially those on the N., may be associated with the extensive later quarrying there. No particular line on the W. slopes commands attention but it may be significant that the 'Victorinus stone',[5] a memorial stone of the sixth century A.D. was found originally on the E. side of the turnpike (now the A40T) to Brecon S.E. of Sgethrog. Such monuments were in several instances (e.g. Maen Madog, RR 1) set up close to the line of Roman roads.

Main inscription: *R.I.B.* 2258; *RFW* 15.

Imp(erator) C(aesar) | [F]l(auius) Val(erius) C|onsta|ntius|[...

'The Emperor Caesar Flavius Valerius Constantius [....'

Constantius Chlorus; after the recovery of Britain, A.D. 296.

Back of *R.I.B.* 2258: *R.I.B.* 2259; *RFW* 19.

[Imp(erator) C(aesar)] | Fla|uius | Cla(udius) Co|nsta|[n]tin|[us

'The Emperor Caesar Flavius Claudius Constantinus [....'

Constantine II, A.D. 317-37, or 337-40.

From Millbrook it is generally assumed that the recently improved modern main road to Brecon follows the general course of the Roman road. The alignment of the route suggests a crossing of the River Honddu between Brecon castle and the confluence with the Usk. West of Brecon, the lane running from the tithe barn at 034 289 via Pennant to Y Gaer is presumed to represent the course to the N. side of the Roman fort. A major change of alignment occurs N. of Coed Fenni-fach at 015 299. John Strange seems to be referring to the W. part of this lane in a letter to the Society of Antiquaries,[7] 1769: "... *within half a mile of the farm house* (= Y Gaer), *the present road from Brecknock joins an old Roman causeway; which, though much broken and over-run with bushes, is still very discernible. It was originally a raised way near forty feet wide, and seems to have been chiefly made with large round pebbles of various sizes, collected probably from the bed of a neighbouring river. This causeway runs in a direction nearly at right angles with the Eskir* (= Ysgir), *a small brook which joins the river Usk just below The Gaer.*"

The lane is described most intelligibly from W. to E. (004 298-034 289). N. of the fort, at 0045 2989, there is an apparent *agger* about 10.5 m wide. On the N. side is a partly-backfilled ditch 2 m to 3 m wide. A few metres to the W. on the S. of the *agger* the other flanking ditch is about 3 m wide and the crest of the causeway is between 0.7 m and 1 m above its base, increasing to 2.3 m 30 m further E. The modern rough-metalled track has quarried into the *agger* crest which shows no sign of consistent metalling. The causeway is made up of red clay and sandstone boulders. A Roman tile was observed at 0.2 m below the present surface. At 0058 2989 the upper layers of boulders at the crest of the causeway are more consistent, suggesting deliberate metalling. Forty metres to the E. the *agger* flattens out and the side ditches are very faint. At 0068 2991 the modern track has hollowed into the crest revealing boulder metalling. East from here for nearly 600 m the remains of the *agger* and side ditches are slight but at 0126 2993 they

become marked. The *agger* is 5 m wide and its crest about 1 m above the largely infilled N. ditch. The S. ditch is between 3 m and 4 m wide. One hundred metres further E. the *agger* is flattish-topped, 7 m wide and about 0.5 m high above the base of the N. ditch. Both ditches are about 2.5 m wide. By 0155 2990 the traces are fainter and the S. ditch is largely obliterated. In the woodland W. of Llyn Gludy the forest track may follow the line of the N. ditch with the slight *agger* emphasised by the down-cutting of the track. The probable S. ditch is emphasised by a former pathway about 2.6 m wide by 0.3 m to 0.5 m deep. At Coed a linear bank from 0182 2963 to 0177 2967 resembles superficially a length of *agger*. Near Coed, O'Dwyer[8] mentions a branch from the road running N.N.W. to join the putative road to Hay via Llan-ddew but there is no evidence to support a Roman identification for this track. E.S.E. from Coed there are no traces of Roman structure. Between Coed and Pennant the lane is now a stream course up to 2 m deep and from Pennant to the tithe barn the road is narrow and sunken to varying degrees, particularly so at 0323 2909 where it runs below a S.-facing escarpment. A modern metalled lane carries the line towards Brecon.

The W. continuation of this road towards Llandovery is described below (RR 5).

Margary, *Roman Roads*, pp. 333-34 (Route 62 a).

[1] W. J. Britnell and H. N. Savory, *Gwernvale and Penywyrlod: Two Neolithic Long Cairns in the Black Mountains of Brecknock* (Cardiff, 1984), p. 94.

[2] Payne MS., Brecknock Museum.

[3] Followed e.g. by O.S. 6-in map, SO 12 SE, Provisional Edition, 1964.

[4] S. O'Dwyer, *The Roman Roads of Brecknock and Glamorgan* (Newtown, 1937), pp. 13, 29.

[5] V. E. Nash-Williams, *The Early Christian Monuments of Wales* (Cardiff, 1950), p. 79. Reset at 1105 2485 but now in Brecknock Museum.

[6] *R.I.B.*, p. 706; *Roman Frontier*, pp. 187-8.

[7] *Archaeologia*, I (1804 ed.), p. 317.

[8] *op. cit.*, p. 14.

(RR 4) Brecon Gaer to Kenchester (*Magnis*; Herefordshire)

The existence of an engineered road between these sites is probable but there is little direct evidence for its course in Brecknock, except in the vicinity of Y Gaer. Margary's alignment on modern Brecon may be

dismissed in favour of a route from Y Gaer running to the N. of Pen-y-crug. Consequently the sunken green lane from Bishop's Meadow to the modern road 1 km E. of Llan-ddew Church must be regarded as a later, probably medieval, route, subsequently used as the coach route to Hay. Margary favours a crossing of the Wye at Hay to pass Clyro Roman fort. Excavations[1] at Clyro suggest that the fort was abandoned before the road system in the area was established and it is unnecessary therefore to consider that the course of the road would have taken account of the site. Hogg[2] has proposed tentatively that the route E. of Hay ran S. of the Wye. Most authorities consider that modern roads represent the greater part of the course forming several long, straight alignments, although these are attributable most probably to turnpike construction.

General Description

Excavation by Sir Mortimer Wheeler[3] proved the line of the road from the N. gate of the Roman fort although he considered it to be the S. end of a route to Castell Collen. The road ran in a broad curve N.N.E. and E.N.E., W. of the modern track to Y Gaer farm until 005301 and then S. of the lane between Pont-ar-ysgir and Cradoc to just S. of Pool farm (see *Details*). A grassed ridge approximately on this line is visible in the large field S. of the entrance to Pool. Originally the medieval (?) road between Pont-ar-ysgir and Cradoc was virtually straight but the construction of the railway line and Cradoc station diverted the road S., W.S.W. of Cradoc leaving abandoned a hollow-way between 0117 3041 and 0149 3050. The road identified by Wheeler aligns on the road to Cradoc from the E. end of this hollow-way rather than the line of the hollow-way itself, opening to question the suggestion that this represented part of the Roman line.

The thoroughly modernised road between Cradoc and Tairderwen (034 310) continues the alignment of the road excavated by Wheeler, with an adjustment to a more easterly couse S. of Danycrug. The route E. of Tairderwen is conjectural. Margary claims that traces of *agger* could be seen at Lower Penwaun (079 316) but these were not visible to R.C.A.M. investigators. If the features noted by Margary were genuine, and had been destroyed before the Commission's visit, a course through Llan-ddew might be implied. Such a route would be represented approximately by the B4520 for 600 m S.E. from Tairderwen, the narrow lane via Pont Cwm Anod at Llan-ddew and the lane from Llan-ddew to Lower Penwaun. Several minor adjustments in alignment are made during this course to accommodate to the local ridge and valley topography but at no point is there

any evidence of Roman structure. At Lower Penwaun there is a break in the continuity of the line for 400 m before it is taken up again by an old, slightly sunken, green lane to Pen-isa'r-waun (Penishawain). Margary suggests a major alignment change in this vicinity with the line of the ancient road represented by the hedgerow between 0881 3222 and 0889 3282, E. of the modern road. The O.S. have suggested[4] that a low linear bank 14 m W. of and parallel to the S. part of this hedgerow may be an *agger* though the positive identification of short isolated pieces such as this is questionable. The bank runs from 0883 3229 to 0886 3237 and is between 6 m and 8 m wide.

The modern A470T is supposed to represent the line to Felin-fach where there is a major change of alignment from N.N.E. to E.N.E. From Felin-fach to Three Cocks first the A470T and then the A438 in several long straight alignments follow a plausible route for the ancient road but their appearance is probably attributable to the turnpike era. North of Three Cocks the modern A438 runs W. of the turnpike line, a deviation which took place when the railway line was constructed. The old course is now a minor lane E. of the old railway, between the Vicarage (177 382) and Glasbury. Beyond Glasbury the B4350 from near Llwynau-bach to N.E. of Pen-y-maes (216 417) and then Gipsy Castle Lane, a minor road into Hay-on-Wye, are supposed to follow the Roman line.

Details of Route

The only proven part of this road in the county is the first 900 m leading from the N. gate of the Roman fort at Y Gaer. The course was visible as scorch marks in 1925 and subsequently demonstrated by excavation. Three sections were cut between 0041 2990 and 0045 2997 revealing a road 9.14 m wide (30 ft) with 0.61 m (2 ft) depth of metalling, the surface of which was marked by traffic ruts. Further N.E. at 0095 3028 another section showed a less substantial structure just over 6.1 m (20 ft) wide with about 0.3 m depth of pebbles and fractured stone as metalling. The surface had a camber of about 0.1 m and lay between a coarse kerbing of larger stones. For 275 m N. of the fort gate the road was flanked by buildings (see RF 2).

Margary, *Roman Roads*, p. 342 (Route 63 b).

[1] *Roman Frontier*, pp. 77-80. More extensive excavations are required before the chronology is established securely.

[2] *Arch. Camb.*, CXXII (1973), Map, p. 9.

[3] R. E. M. Wheeler, 'The Roman Fort at Brecon,' *Y Cymmrodor*, 37 (1926), p. 56.

[4] O.S. Records, RR 63b, 30 v 73.

(RR 5) Brecon Gaer to Llandovery

The existence of a road between these sites is unquestioned but there is no unequivocal evidence for its precise course within the county. The route in Carmarthenshire is better attested and supported by the discovery of a milestone of the third quarter of the third century during the making of a turnpike in 1769.[1] Modern authorities tend to place the course from Brecon Gaer to Trecastell N. of the Usk but this ignores John Strange's[2] insistence on the Roman date of a causeway that he observed at Rhyd-y-briw which, if true, would imply a course S. of the Usk from, possibly RR 1 to Sennybridge. A. H. A. Hogg[3] has suggested the possibility of a missing fort at Trecastell. The road over Mynydd Bach Trecastell, W. of Trecastell, is confidently marked "Roman Road" on O.S. maps but the lane and metalled trackway owe their present form to turnpike construction begun in 1769 and probably represent only the approximate course of the ancient road (see *Details*). One major change of alignment occurs in the likely general course on the ridge 2 km W. of Trecastell, just over 14 km W. of Brecon Gaer and just under 11 km S.E. of Llandovery.

General Description

North-west of the Roman fort the line of RR 3 from Abergavenny is continued by a curving hollow-way between SO 0038 2988 and 0012 2969 which descends the steep E. side of the Afon Ysgir valley to a ford opposite Aberysgir church. The route in its present form is, in places, a small, water-eroded ravine and exhibits no typical Roman structure but its continuity with RR 3 may imply a course for the Llandovery road N. of the Usk. The road is supposed to have crossed through Aberysgir churchyard.[4]

The course to Sennybridge is uncertain but may be represented in part by the modern valley-side road, generally a fairly narrow lane often on a S.-facing terrace, passing through Trallwng to Llwyncyntefin, Sennybridge. There are several possible alternatives along this stretch of the route, none of which, however, can command any greater acceptance. Any details at Sennybridge have been destroyed by building since Strange's day but a N. route might have been continued on a line represented by a terraced track W. from Beili-bedw which joins the A40T 400 m E. of Pont Clydach. The course of the latter track aligns equally well with a crossing of the Usk at Rhyd-y-briw from a S. course.

The A40 from Pont Clydach to Trecastell with a change of alignment at about SN 890294 may run approximately on the Roman line. Roman coins were reputedly found near the Norman castle at Trecastell. The course of the Roman road from Trecastell is supposed to be represented by an enclosed lane with modern metalling climbing steeply the hillslope W. of the village to emerge onto the long ridge of Mynydd Trecastell. Along the crest of the moorland ridge from the gate at 8455 3000 to the county boundary at 8264 3098 the track marked as "Roman Road" on O.S. maps[5] is a coarse-metalled trackway owing its present form to eighteenth century turnpike building. A long earthen boundary bank about 2 m wide and 1 m high flanks, with occasional interruptions, the N. side of the track. Neither show any signs of Roman structure. Earlier maps[6] designate as "Roman Road" a track running S.E. to N.W. from the main one, immediately N.E. of the cairn at 8315 3098. The feature is a rounded bank about 3.7 m wide and 0.3 m high, running very straight, with a narrow ditch along its S.W. side, but not certainly on the other. A very similar bank and ditch run at right angles to this line to the S.E. of the *Stone Circles* (8335 3109) suggesting strongly that the structure is part of a defunct boundary system.

Although there was no visible sign of an *agger* along the present main track, excavations between 838 305 and 835 308 were undertaken by Mrs. E. Alcock in March 1956[7] in the hope of revealing some Roman constructional features (see *Details*). No structures that are likely to be related to a Roman road have been identified S. of the main track. Near the county boundary the modern track appears to cross the site of the S. corner of the earlier of the two marching camps at Y Pigwn (RMC 1 and 2) but while it is very probable that the Roman road was built after these camps were occupied, the uncertainty as to the exact course of the road does not allow the relationship of the camp with the turnpike to be used in support of this. About 100 m W. of the county boundary (in Carms.) are possible remains of an *agger* and a course can be followed S. of the modern track, with a change of alignment at 822 309, passing to the N. of the Roman fortlet at 8206 3103,[8] whence it descends the steep hillslope to Hafod Fawr.

Details of Route

Mrs. Alcock excavated three sections on Mynydd Bach Trecastell. *Trench I* was cut at right angles from the N. side of the present track at 8388 3051 across a slight, apparent *agger* between two banks. A thin road surface (IA) made up of sandstone chippings embedded in the natural subsoil was preserved under the *"agger"* and S. bank. The road was at least 8.7 m wide bounded on the N. by a shallow ditch 1.76 m wide, the upcast from which formed a low bank on its outer edge. Use of the road seems to have been limited as the surface showed no signs of wear and turf had been allowed to encroach upon its S. half. The S. edge of the road had been dug away by a shallow trench cut through the turf. The S. bank, composed of red sandy soil, lay over this trench and the turf covering the road and was formed probably during the construction of the main track to the S. (the turnpike). The N. bank and ditch do not extend very far N.W. before vanishing in marshland and old peat excavations. The S. bank, however, can be traced running in a virtually straight line for 475 m N.W.

Trench II was cut at about SN 8352 3080 across the visible course of the S. bank of trench I where it crosses a slight ridge avoided by the modern track. A road (IB) of similar construction to that in trench I lay under and to the N. of the bank but had no ditch to the N. To the S., in a zone indicated on the surface by terraces, was a better-made road (II A, B) about 8.5 m wide. This was constructed on two levels with a difference of about 0.3 m, separated by a central spine of large stones. At both levels a layer of rounded pebbles had been laid carefully onto a prepared surface of bedrock and capped with sandstone chippings. The surface showed some signs of wear. The S., lower, edge of the road was bounded by a shallow ditch 3.8 m wide, the line of which is represented on the surface by a slight hollow. The S. toe of the bank overlying road I B coincided with the N. edge. Originally this bank seems to have been crudely revetted in stone on both faces. Underlying it and cutting through road I B was a trench of similar though narrower shape to that encountered in trench I, which seemed to be unweathered and devoid of silting, indicating that it was open for a short while only. It is possible that this trench served as a marker indicating the intended line of road II to the builders and if so road I would pre-date the better-made highway.

A further section dug about 15 m E. of trench II confirmed the contemporaneity of the differing levels of road II and showed also that the difference in height

decreased substantially eastwards.

A few metres W. of trench II the visible bank changes alignment (18° S.) and can be traced to the rough track at 8346 3083 beyond which it is lost, though clearly the projected line would run to the N. of the present road. The disappearance of the road may be accounted for by peat cutting.

The excavations provided no direct dating evidence. It is possible to interpret the remains as representing three periods of construction: Road I—Road II—turnpike, but the chronological placement of the first two is uncertain and need not be Roman. The construction technique of road II is unusual for a Roman road. It would allow two-way traffic and might be related to the extensive quarrying at Y Pigwn. Road I has general similarities with the poorly understood surface identified near Maen Madog.[9]

The Reverend Canon Jones-Davies[10] suggested a route between Brecon Gaer and Carmarthen represented in the county by a series of lanes and tracks connecting places with Early Christian monuments. The devious course proposed between Sennybridge and Cwm Wysg is totally unconvincing and displays no Roman characteristics. However, the suggested route from Cwm Wysg to Tal-sarn coincides with earlier views of a connection between Carmarthen and Brecon Gaer passing through Trecastell. An impressively direct course between Trecastell and Tal-sarn with a series of minor alignment adjustments is made up for the most part by lanes and minor upland roads with modern metalling, but between Cwm Wysg and SN 840 279 is an embanked hollow-way, no longer used for through traffic. The course crosses the N.W. corner of the Arhosfa'r Garreg-lwyd marching camp (Carms.) (SN 802 263). No signs of ancient structure have been noted in the 11 km between Trecastell and Tal-sarn.

Margary, *Roman Roads*, pp. 334-5 (Route 62 b).

[1] *R.I.B.*, p. 707, nos. 2260-1; *Roman Frontier*, pp. 185-6, nos. 7 and 11.

[2] *Archaeologia*, I (1804 ed.), pp. 317, 321. Read 1769.

[3] *Arch. Camb.*, CXXII (1973), p. 13.

[4] S. O'Dwyer, *The Roman Roads of Brecknock and Glamorgan* (Newtown, 1937), p. 13.

[5] *e.g.* O.S. 6-in map, Provisional Edition, 1964, SN 83 SW.

[6] O.S. 25-in map, County Series, 2nd Edition, 1905, XXV.8.

[7] Unpubl. account in R.C.A.M. files. Detailed description here by kind permission of the author.

[8] *Roman Frontier*, p. 123.

[9] See RR 1, pp. 158-163.

[10] *Arch. Camb.*, CXXIV (1975), pp. 3-10.

(RR 6) Route(s) north from Brecon Gaer

It has long been assumed that there was a route between Y Gaer, Brecon and Castell Collen forts crossing the Wye at the strategic site of Builth. The weakness of the evidence for such a course has led one authority[1] to deny its existence and favour a connection between the two sites through the military position near Beulah (see RR 7). The latter would involve little additional mileage. The discovery of the fortlet guarding a crossing of the Wye at Penmincae (Rads., SO 0055 5396)[2] appears to strengthen this idea without entirely ruling out the possibility of a branch from the Beulah-Castell Collen road (RR 7) E. of the Wye to a crossing at Builth.

The S. end of the route proposed by O'Dwyer[3] and Margary is entirely unsatisfactory being aligned on modern Brecon. The old lane supposed to represent the line between Brecon and Tairderwen (034 310) is the remains of a turnpike. The part of RR 4 between Tairderwen and Brecon Gaer has been seen as only a branch road connecting the fort to the through route to Penydarren. The route suggested by O'Dwyer over Cefn Sarnau is ruled out by its alignment on Brecon. Margary appears to favour the course of the modern B4520 up the Honddu valley through Lower and Upper Chapel as representing the ancient line; but the route is thoroughly 'unRoman' in its meandering alignments, and there is no suggestive structural evidence at any point. A more promising course lies to the E., represented by the lanes and track over the rolling moorland from near Castle Madoc (026 367), passing Twyn-y-post (028 409) and rejoining the modern road at 020 432 by the 11th milestone from Brecon. The track was known as the "Flemish way" in 1241.[4] Short lengths of mutilated *agger* are claimed to be visible N. of Twyn-y-post[5] but these have not been confirmed. Generally, the trail over the moorland is slightly sunken and up to 2 m wide. At the highest spot by Twyn-y-post it is only 1 m wide in a 1.5 m deep cutting. An excavation made in 1956[6] demonstrated that at one point at least, at 022 426, the track had a definite structure. Under about 0.15 m to 0.23 m of earth was a very irregular, slightly-cambered surface of sandstone rubble set on red clay. The surface was approximately 3 m wide and revetted on either side by larger, more regularly-shaped kerb stones between 0.3 and 0.37 m wide. A layer of small stones and pebbles immediately above the coarse surface may have been the remains of displaced upper metalling. The structure

of this road has similarities to that of the Roman road running S. from Tomen-y-mur (Mer.)[7] but such an essentially simple design could have been effected at other dates. The route seems to have served as a main highway between Brecon and Builth before the Honddu valley route came into prominence and milestones were erected along its course.

There is no evidence to support either Margary's or O'Dwyer's route N. of the 11th milestone from Brecon (0243) to Builth. Any traces of the remains supposed by O'Dwyer to exist to the E. of the modern road at Cwm Owen have disappeared during roadworks and the earlier line of the road at Llangynog is a hollow-way functioning as a drainage ditch E. of the present road.

The existence of a route direct between Brecon Gaer and Castell Collen must be regarded as unproven and, in the light of the discovery of the Penmincae fortlet, improbable.

Nevertheless, it is hardly likely that there was no connection between Brecon Gaer and the forts to the N. and it may be suggested that a route ran further to the W. to connect Brecon Gaer with the Llandovery to Caerau, Beulah road (RR 7) just S. of its ford across Afon Irfon at Glan Camddwr. At present there is no compelling evidence for such a route but one or two suggestions for a likely course may be made.

In N.G. area SO 0030 N. of RR 4 from the N. gate of the Roman fort at Y Gaer there are no signs of a route branching off N. However further E., beginning at 0418 3051 very close to the proposed line of RR 4, a derelict, terraced track followed by field boundaries and, in part, by the Fenni-fach parish boundary runs N.W. towards Battle. The terrace faces W. and is up to 10 m wide where well-preserved. At their junction at 0117 3096 the present lane between Battle and Cradoc is clearly later and it seems that the track must be of medieval origin at latest. The course has been interrupted by the construction of Upper Lodge, Battle, but resumes immediately above the house, ascending the ridge as a broad hollow-way which can be traced to 0098 3150. Traces of the route are lost for a short distance to the N. until a partly ploughed-out, terraced track descending the ridge side between 0098 3163 and 0095 3182 presumably continues it. A terraced lane and track with modern surfacing runs in a series of straight alignments almost due N. across the W. crest of Battle Hill. The track is at 379 m above

O.D. at the highest point of its course before descending across the E. side of the narrow Ysgir Fawr valley to 0072 3560, about 400 m N. of Nant-y-gwreiddyn, where it changes to a N.W. alignment. O'Dwyer prefers a more easterly course represented by a track branching from the aforementioned route at 0095 3321, running via Bedd y Forwyn and passing 100 m E. of Gaer Fach hill-fort (HF 36). The course is taken up by a lane with modern surfacing from 0028 3706 to Merthyr Cynog. This route keeps to the crests of the uplands until N. of Gaer Fach, unlike the other suggested course which runs along the lower valley side N. of Nant-y-gwreiddyn. The latter is represented by a narrow lane on a terrace which crosses the Ysgir Fawr at SN 9954 3666 and joins on the W. side of Jubilee Bridge a broader tarmacadamed lane to Merthyr Cynog.

North-west of Merthyr Cynog a course can be projected ascending the S.E. end of Cefn Merthyr Cynog ridge that is represented for about 200 m N.W. of the village by a coarsely metalled trackway between 2 m and 4 m wide, in places hollowed and embanked, and then successively by unstructured hollowed trails and a grassy pathway to the edge of the artillery range at 9760 3840. It has not been practicable to examine

potential courses across the range and there is no reliable aerial photograph evidence for a route with Roman-type features in the likely area. The general alignment might be represented by the moorland trail running between 967400, 950439 and 941450. There is no evidence for a line beyond the N.W. edge of the artillery range to a presumed junction with the Llandovery-Beulah road near Glan-yr-afon, 921469.

It must be admitted that although in light of the doubts that must be entertained about the existence of a road between Brecon Gaer and Castell Collen a route between Brecon Gaer and Beulah must be sought, there is at present no satisfactory evidence for either its existence or likely course.

Margary, *Roman Roads*, pp. 336-7 (Route 621).

[1] A. H. A. Hogg in *Arch. Camb.*, CXXII (1973), pp. 13, 17.

[2] By Dr. J. K. St. Joseph. *J.R.S.*, LXIII (1973), pp. 240-1.

[3] S. O'Dwyer, *The Roman Roads of Brecknock and Glamorgan* (Newtown, 1937), pp. 17-18.

[4] *Calendar of Charter Rolls*, I, pp. 260-1.

[5] O.S. Records, RR 621. 1 xi 81.

[6] By members of King's College, Taunton Rover Crew, 10 April 1956 under the supervision of Mr. J. J. Pytches who kindly supplied details to R.C.A.M.

[7] R.C.A.M. Records, SO 04 S.W. (Earthworks).

(RR 7) Carmarthen-Llandovery-Beulah-Castell Collen

The existence of this road is not in doubt and several lengths of visible remains can be described in detail. For most of its course in Carmarthenshire[1] the route follows river valleys. N.E. of Llandovery it crosses the bleak, dissected uplands of Crychan Forest on an alignment indicated by the positioning of possibly Roman military works at SN 807 393[2] near Cynghordy and at 8494 4152 near Abererbwll.[3] There is no evidence to support suggestions of a road N.E. via Tirabad[4] and the supposed fort at Caerau, Llanddulas[5] must now be discounted (see p. 187). Lengths of *agger* identified N.E. of Beulah and the discovery of the fortlet at Penmincae (Rads.)[6] help to establish most of the line between Beulah and Castell Collen across rolling hill country although some doubts remain, for example the exact course between Penmincae and Llandrindod Common. These discoveries rule out earlier suggestions, in particular that favoured by Margary which envisaged a crossing of the Wye at Newbridge-on-Wye and the course of the modern B4358 representing the route between

Beulah and Newbridge. Similarly Dr. St. Joseph's suggestion of a direct route between the Wye crossing at Penmincae and Caerau, Beulah via the col near Dolderwen, SN 952 513, must be discounted except at the E. end.

General Description

Between the county boundary at SN 853 421 and 881 435 the course of the road is represented probably by an E.N.E. bearing track through Crychan Forest. At its W. end the track runs along the ridge of Cefn Llwydlo for 800 m to its highest point of 358 m above O.D. at about 860 425. From here it gradually descends on a S.-facing terrace below the hillcrest, slightly sunk in parts with a surface of either bare rock or coarse rubble metalling. There are slight traces of quarrying on the N. side of the track at 8680 4295. Between the lanes to Bryn-bedw and Sarn-cwrtau (a possibly significant name) the track continues its descent, partly sunken, particularly at the higher W.

end where it is eroded severely by streams. This erosion has revealed that the coarse surface metalling is only about 10 cm thick and rests on either natural clay or rock. There is no reason to think that this surfacing is ancient. East of Sarn-cwrtau there is a minor change of alignment and the track is a coarsely metalled strip, sunken in places and flanked by relatively recent earthen banks running along the undulating top of the ridge. In 881 435 there is a major change of alignment to the N.E. in the probable course. The present minor road to Aberdulas-uchaf (916 466) with a minor adjustment of line 400 m N.E. of Cae-du follows the most likely ancient course along the top of the long ridge N.W. of the River Dulas. However, for the first 400 m of this stretch the modern road appears to deviate from the general line which is more directly continued between 8816 4355 and 8840 4383 by a derelict, spread bank with a modern-looking ditch on the N.W. but also a trace of a ditch along the S.E., and by a large field bank further N.E. These two features may lie over the remains of an earlier road.

Aerial photographs[7] suggest that the crossing of the River Irfon was not at the present ford but about 100 m further W. A linear mark appears on the photographs between about 9195 4708 and 9199 4723 which is a direct continuation of the lane to the N. leading to Glan Camddwr and probably represents the remains of the early road. The diversion to the present ford probably occurred after the construction of the railway. The precise crossing of the River Dulas is uncertain but the alignment of the road N. of the River Irfon suggests that it was in the vicinity of the present Pont ar Ddulas.

North of the ford at Glan Camddwr a farm lane and the modern minor road to Beulah runs for 3.3. km in a single alignment fractionally E. of due N. At the S. end the modern farm lane deviates W. from the old line which is followed by a grassed hollow-way for about 150 m. Similarly at the N. end of this stretch the modern road deviates to the E. and the original line is represented by a 40 m length of reed-choked hollow-way. The course described above is impressively straight and despite the fact that it nowhere exhibits any characteristic Roman structure there can be little doubt that it approximates to that of the ancient road. In close juxtaposition to the line are several Roman military structures: to the E., the fort at Caerau, 9235 5017 (RF 1); to the W., probable practice camps at 9200 4995 and 9209 5017 (RPC 1 and 2) and the marching camp at 919 507 (RMC 4). The road presumably dates to after the establishment of a permanent garrison at Caerau.

Post-Roman river movement has obliterated probably all traces of the crossing of Afon Camarch but the alignment of stretches of *agger* to the E. of the river indicate approximately its position. The road changed direction at the crossing and was now aligned N.E. There are several short stretches of *agger* preserved along a course of 3.25 km with two minor adjustments in alignment between the crossing of Afon Camarch and Glanddulas (see *Details*). Green lanes and tracks connect these lengths to form a coherent and plausible route.

In the field immediately E. of the likely crossing of the River Dulas is a short length of causeway that is probably another piece of *agger*. N.E. of this for nearly a kilometre the most likely course is that followed for 150 m by a well-defined terrace representing the former course of the modern B4358 and then by the present road to Pen-rhiw-dalar 150 m W. of which there is a marked change of alignment. Between Pen-rhiw-dalar and Esgairgoch the remains are ambiguous but there are hints of a causeway (see *Details*). The course between Esgairgoch and the crossing of the Wye at Penmincae is uncertain. Dr. St. Joseph has described a track (SO 0017 5396 to 0034 5395) on the S. side of the Wye which he considers to represent part of the Roman line. A curving terrace, now a hollow-way, has been cut down the steep slope covered by Goetre Wood. From the foot of the scarp a causeway about 61 m long runs across marshy ground towards the river but stops about 3.7 m short of it.

The causeway is about 4.6 m wide and between 1.83 m and 1.07 m high, decreasing from W. to E. Dr. St. Joseph considered the work "very Roman in character" and the termination at the river end " as if at a bridge abutment." The O.S. have suggested a course between Esgairgoch and St. Joseph's crossing which although plausible has no definite structural evidence to support it. The proposed course runs via Sarn Helen (a significant name) where a realignment to a course only a few degrees N. of E. is made. Aerial photographs[10] suggest that the line ran between about 9700 5429 and 9743 5434 N. of Nant Carrai and there is a slight rise in the ground between these points which could be either the remains of an *agger* or a natural, turf-covered rock ridge. The suggested course changes to a more southerly alignment about 9793 5442 and runs to 9887 5407, just over 200 m of the E. end being represented by a green lane. The next stretch runs almost due E. to Goetre, represented for about 150 m by a raised track, for another 150 m by a hollow-way and then by a hypothetical line across the S. end of

Comin Coch and several fields. A sharp change of alignment to the S.E. is proposed at Goetre, the course represented by a modern minor road for 250 m until it makes an equally abrupt alteration in direction to the E. as a track continued by that through Goetre Wood.[11]

Details of Route

The first definite length of *agger* to be encountered E. of the River Camarch occurs between 9234 5073 and 9240 5077. The feature is plough-spread and measures about 14 m wide by 0.5 m high. N.E. of this to 9251 5086 the remains are badly damaged although the S.E.-facing side N.E. from 9247 5083 survives as a scarp 0.4 m high. There are no further definite traces of the probable course until 9297 5126 although a vague terrace is discernible at 9259 5093. From 9297 5126 to 9302 5130 is a length of causeway across the hill crest about 0.5 m high and of similar width to that to the S.E., Jones and Thomson[12] sectioned the *agger* in this vicinity and found the road to be between about 5.5 m and 5.8 m wide composed of 0.23 m of rammed stone over 0.1 m to 0.18 m of foundation stone set in natural red clay. A fragment of *samian* pottery was found over the foundation layer. An embanked, hollowed trail 3 m to 4 m wide continues the alignment, the lane diminishing to a narrow cutting about 1 m wide at 9326 5145. A path with no structure follows the line until 9354 5167. A further causeway 5 m to 6 m wide and averaging 0.4 m high lies between 9356 5170 and 9367 5177. The alignment is continued to a ford of the Deuffrwd by an irregular hollowed trail. The probable course changes to a more N.

direction at this point and is represented by a series of tracks and lanes leading to Glanddulas. To the E. of the River Dulas between 9474 5301 and 9478 5304 is a length of possible *agger* about 8 m wide and up to 0.2 m high. The orientation of this stretch suggests that the modern lane and the ancient course W. of the river divert at about 9462 5287 but there are no traces in the intervening area although this may be due partly to river erosion.

From 9597 5379 to 9640 5400 a low rise is visible between 6 m and 8 m wide but only 0.2 m high which may represent a spread causeway.

Margary, *Roman Roads*, pp. 339-40 (Route 623).

[1] For the route in Carms. see: *Trans. Carmarthenshire Antiquarian Society*, 12 (1917-8); *Arch. Camb.* (1873), pp. 129-31; T. Codrington, *Roman Roads in Britain* (1919), p. 296; *Carmarthen Antiquary*, 7 (1971), pp. 15-17; *ibid.*, 8 (1972), pp. 3-16.

[2] *Roman Frontier*, p. 130.

[3] O.S. Record card, SN 84 SW 6.

[4] *Trans. Cardiganshire Antiquarian Society*, 8, p. 21.

[5] *Roman Frontier*, p. 200.

[6] *J.R.S.*, LXIII (1973), pp. 240-1.

[7] A.Ps.: RAF 106/UK 1471, No. 3110; 58/RAF/3618, Nos. 0167-0172; O.S. 75.250, Nos. 244-6.

[8] Several of these can be seen on A.Ps. e.g.: RAF 540/498, Nos. 3043-4; 58/RAF/3618, Nos. 0167-0172; F41 58/RAF/3916 1142 Z, Nos. 0123-4; O.S. 75.250, Nos. 244-6.

[9] O.S. Records, RR 623.

[10] F41 58/RAF/3916, Nos. 0128-0130.

[11] Lt.-Col. Ll. Morgan mentions traces of a road on rising ground at 'Pen Caer Helm' (994538) and suggests a crossing of the Wye at 'Nant y Goitre'. *Arch. Camb.* (1911), pp. 135-6.

[12] G. D. B. Jones and R. D. Thomson, *B.B.C.S.*, 17, pp. 314-5.

Other Routes

In addition to the routes discussed in detail above, the following have been considered:

(i) A road *W.N.W. from Coelbren* towards either Carmarthen or a hypothetical military post between Llandovery and Carmarthen.[1] A causeway with side ditches was observed at the N. entrance of Coelbren Roman fort in a drainage trench cut by machine in May 1983.[2] There is no other evidence for an engineered road beyond the immediate vicinity of the defences. The intervening terrain is a formidable obstacle to a direct connection between the proposed destinations. A short length of road was constructed at the N. gate, probably to lessen erosion of the

entranceway caused by frequent military traffic, and to serve the immediate locality only. The line on an aerial photograph[3] which suggests a road from the W. gate to about SN 8530 1055 is not relevant as it runs too far S. If it does represent one end of a longer route the alignment is to the S. of the county except where it might cross for about 400 m a S. tip of the county N. of Seven Sisters although there are no visible traces there.

[1] A possible fort at Llandeilo (SN 633222: Britannia, XI (1980), p. 348) is rejected in *Arch. in Wales*, 23 (1983), p. 34.

[2] *Ex inf.* Mr. W. Chouls. Records in N.M.R. (W).

[3] RAF CPE/UK 2079, No. 1134.

(ii) A road between *Coelbren and Llandovery* Roman forts. The marching camp at Arhosfa'r Garreg-lwyd (Carms.)[1] is on the direct line between these places, 16.5 km N.N.W. of Coelbren and 9.25 km S.S.E. of Llandovery. Roman period occupation is attested in the caves of Craig-y-nos in the Tawe valley.[2] The mountainous terrain of the direct route would have made road building very difficult and it is highly improbable that any connection was attempted. No traces of any likely structure have been found.[3] The settlement at Craig-y-nos need not imply the existence of an engineered route nearby and there is no evidence, and none is given, to support O'Dwyer's suggestion[4] of a road along the E. side of the Tawe valley which is supposed to head N. across Bwlch Cerrig Duon to join the Brecon Gaer-Llandovery road W. of Trecastell.

[1] *Roman Frontier*, p. 124 for references.
[2] See p. 182.
[3] See p. 176 for the N. gate at Coelbren.
[4] S. O'Dwyer, *The Roman Roads of Brecknock and Glamorgan* (Newtown, 1937), p. 23.

(iii) A road between *Coelbren and Penydarren*[1] (Glam.) Roman forts. Such a connection is not prohibited by the intervening terrain but searches in several possible locations failed to find any structure.

[1] *Inv. Glam.*, I, No. 732.

(iv) Several routes S. to N. across the moorlands between Afon Mellte and Afon Tâf Fawr are suggested by O'Dwyer.[1] There is no evidence of the great antiquity of any of the following: a) the track between Craig y Ddinas and Penderyn; b) the small road from Rhigos to Penderyn; c) the line of the modern road from Penderyn to Ystradfellte; d) the line of the A4059 from Penderyn to the junction with the A470T (but see RR 2, p. 164); e) the line of the modern road between Penderyn and the Llwyn-on Reservoir (previously to the Merthyr-Brecon road).

[1] O'Dwyer, *op. cit.*, p. 19.

(v) The Rev. Henry Payne in a letter to Sir Richard Colt Hoare dated September 14th, 1804[1] proposes the existence of a road between Caerffili (Glam.) and the settlement at Llanfrynach (RV 1). The suggested course runs from Caerffili to Bedwellty (SO 1600) between which Payne describes a causeway with broken pitching and kerbstones which he considered certainly ancient. His route ran from Bedwellty along

the ridge between the Rhymni valley and the Sirhywi valley to an unspecified crossing of Nant-y-bwch which formed the old boundary between Monmouth and Brecknock. Here a metalled causeway across marshland was observed, which an informant described to Payne[2] as originally wider, well-made and showing considerable wear. Subsequent development has probably obliterated any traces of this feature. The proposed course to the N. is only generally described as across Trefil Ddu Hill and via "Blaen-Cwm-Carawnant" to Pen Rhiw-calch. The green road that Payne states ascended Trefil Ddu has probably been partly destroyed by quarrying, and the modern metalled road which presumably represents its line across Ffos-y-wern shows no ancient structure. At 110 150 it is probable that the modern road and the route intended by Payne part company, the latter being represented now by a N.E.-facing terraceway descending steeply N.W. across the S. slopes of Cwm Pyrgad to a ford across Afon Crawnon between Pyrgad and Glawgwm-isaf (099 160). The route is continued nearly due N. to Pen Rhiw-calch by a track and path ascending the steep W. slopes of the upper part of Dyffryn Crawnon. Payne supposes that the line continued to Llanfrynach via Tal-y-bont along the course suggested by Margary (see p. 166). Payne makes the interesting speculation that his suggested road was used for the transport of cast-iron pigs from workings in the vicinity of Bryn-oer to workshops at Llanfrynach.

There is no visible structural evidence for the proposed route in Brecknock and its existence is unlikely in the light of the remains on Gelli-gaer Common.

[1] N.L.W., MS 15257 D, fol. 13.
[2] Later letter to Sir R. Colt Hoare, December 11th, 1804: N.L.W., MS 15257 D, fol. 14.

(vi) *Tretower to Bronllys*. A. H. A. Hogg[1] has postulated the existence of a lost Roman fort at Bronllys, possibly on the site of the later castle bailey. No direct evidence of such a site has yet been found. If a fort did exist there, it is likely that a road connected it with Pen-y-gaer (RF 3). The road that preceded the A479T as the route between Tretower and Talgarth along the E. side of the Rhiangoll valley may have followed an earlier, Roman course but shows no sign of Roman structure in its present state. Most of the route between Tretower and Tŷ Isaf is a lane with modern metalling running on a W.-facing terrace. At the S. end between SO 183 217 and 180 231 the road has degenerated to a field track but still shows signs of the original engineering where it is sometimes rock-cut as it ascends on a W.-facing terrace. Between 182 235 and 184 239 the route is represented by a derelict hollow-way. From 180 291 to the modern road which takes the line to Pengenffordd the lane has deteriorated into a bridle path. An alternative, more westerly route from 189 267 via Twynffrwd to 181 291 also shows no evidence of Roman structure and is generally a track on a terrace but in some places a hollow-way. The lane between Genffordd and Pen-y-bont, Talgarth continues the line N.N.W. The road is sunk to varying degrees between hedgebanks and has a modern tarmac surface throughout. The A479 represents the line between Talgarth and Bronllys.

[1] A. H. A. Hogg, *Arch. Camb.*, CXXII (1973), map p. 9.

(vii) North of Bronllys to a crossing of the Wye near Llys-wen.[1] The line of the previously considered route (vi) is continued N. to the upper edge of the Wye valley at 137 370 by a narrow lane with modern metalling. The road is generally either sunken or on a weak terrace depending on whether it is negotiating a slope or running on relatively level ground. No evidence of Roman structure is visible.

[1] A. H. A. Hogg, notes in R.C.A.M. files. Regarded as very doubtful.

(viii) O'Dwyer proposed several routes connecting the Usk valley with the N.E. of Brecknock and the Wye valley, mainly along existing roads and lanes, for none of which there is any evidence of Roman origin. His suggestions included: (a) Brecon-N. of Slwch Tump-Ty'n-y-caeau-Llechfaen-Glandŵr-Tredustan-Talgarth-Felindre-Tre-goed-Fforddlas-Hay. (b) Brecon-Llan-ddew-Warle-Cwm Gwilym-Llandyfalle Hill-Penrheol-Crickadarn. N. of Brecon, near Pen-lan (SO 0529), a raised causeway is mentioned but no demonstration of Roman date offered. (c) RR 3-Groesffordd-Llechfaen-Yr Allt-Llanfilo-Hay road. (d) Llanfrynach-crosses RR 3-Groesffordd-Troedyr-harn-straight N. to join route to Crickadarn. Branch from this by Alexanderstone, N.E. to join Hay road. (e) Partly Wye valley. Builth-Pant-y-llyn Hill-Waun Hirwaun-Erwood-Llyswen-Three Cocks-Hay.

(ix) A conjectual road due W. from Caerau, Beulah. No traces were found of any such road which would have traversed very difficult, wild country.

(x) A conjectual road due E. from Caerau, Beulah. No traces were found of any such road. There is no reason to believe in the existence of a Roman road between Llangamarch Wells and Builth suggested by O'Dwyer.[1]

[1] *op. cit.*, p. 25.

(xi) Castell Collen to Trawsgoed (Cards.). O'Dwyer[1] describes an upland route between Newbridge and Strata Florida but there is no reason to consider it to be of Roman origin. The difficult topography of the mountains of N. Brecknock and W. Radnorshire probably dictated a N.W. rather than due W. course for any route towards the coast from Castell Collen.

[1] *op. cit.*, p. 29.

Civil Sites

Until at least Hadrianic times the Brecknock area fell under direct military rule. Settlements of camp followers and, later perhaps, retired soldiers (*vici*) sprang up outside the military posts but nothing is known of the pattern of native settlement beyond their immediate vicinity, although a continued occupation of some of the weaker defended enclosures may be supposed on analogy with south-west Wales. The status of the late first century iron-smelting site at Gwernyfed School playing fields (RU 1) is not certainly civilian.

It is unknown whether or not the northern boundary of the *civitas Silurum* was extended to include some of the south-east part of the county after the abandonment of Pen-y-gaer (RF 3). The north and central parts of Brecknock may have remained under military control throughout the Roman occupation.

The close proximity of the villa at Maesderwen to the fort at Y Gaer, Brecon is notable.[1] The site is poorly known from a late eighteenth century excavation and no intelligible surface remains can be seen. The villa may have begun in the later third century and was certainly prosperous in the fourth century, the owner being able to afford good quality mosaic floors in the bath suite; it also lies near (but not in) the estate of Llan-gors (Lann Cors) recorded in an early eighth century document. It has been claimed that such early post-Roman estates are the "direct successors" of those of Roman south-east Wales and that some even retained their fourth century shape;[2] but if the theory is to apply in the present case, it is necessary to envisage that the villa lay at the edge of its estates.[3]

The practice of utilising caves for burial and habitation noted in Glamorgan and elsewhere[4] is found in the far south-west of the county. Excavations are continuing in the caves at Dan yr Ogof.

[1] I. Richmond in I.Ll. Foster and G. Daniel (eds.), *Prehistoric and Early Wales* (London, 1965), p. 172.
[2] W. Davies in P. J. Casey (ed.), *The End of Roman Britain* (Oxford: BAR, 1979), p. 153.
[3] *ibid.*, p. 160.
[4] *Inv. Glam.*, I, i, p. 15; ii, p. 110.

(RV 1) Roman villa at Maesderwen (Figs. 179, 180)

A villa bath-house and another building were discovered in 1783 0.5 km W. of Llanfrynach.[1] The site in general lies at about 152 m above O.D. between two tributaries of the River Usk, Afon Cynrig to the N.W. and Nant Menasgin to the S.E., in parkland generally sloping gently upwards to the S.W., but the bath-house stood at the foot of a scarp. Flat valley land stretches to the Usk, 1.5 km distant. No walling is visible today, and low and vague surface irregularities in the area of the eighteenth century discoveries are of uncertain significance.

The wealth of this establishment, witnessed by its mosaic pavements, is remarkable given its location, and attests to conditions as peaceful as anywhere in western Britain in the reign of Constantine I.

The bath-house which seems to have been very accurately surveyed, measured 21.64 m E. to W. by 14.48 m N. to S., the external walls being about 0.61 m thick. The building consisted of a range of rooms which may be described and interpreted as follows (nos. as in fig. 180); *Room 1*, 9.45 m by 1.83 m, was apparently a corridor entered on the N.W., in which

179 Roman villa at Maesderwen, Llanfrynach (RV 1): physical setting

many blue slate tiles were found.[2] *Room 2*, about 2.7 m square, contained a coloured mosaic pavement with a square central panel of network pattern bordered by a guilloche design itself contained within unpatterned zones of white and coloured *tesserae*.[3] *Room 3*, 5.94 m by 3.66 m had a recess in the N.E. side about 3.15 m long by 0.91 m deep. The whole room was floored with concrete and probably functioned as a changing-room (*apodyterium*) with clothes lockers possibly standing in the recess. A door in the centre of the S. wall gave access to *Room 4*, the *frigidarium* or cold room, 4.06 m by 3.66 m, containing in its N. half a mosaic floor depicting, within plain surrounds, intertwined sea monsters, a fish and a sea shell.[4] The S. half of the room contained a brick- mortar-lined bath, 1.83 m wide about 1.2 m deep. An apparently identical bath (*5*) to the S., separated by what looks like a dwarf wall or kerb, may best be regarded as belonging to the final arrangements, an earlier and larger bath having been reduced in size, and its site filled in and floored over by the mosaic as far as this kerb; the mosaic was clearly once considerably larger than the portion recorded on Charles Hay's plan. From a door in its E. wall, *Room 6* was entered, 2.08 m by 5.79 m. A flue 3.58 m long by 0.53 m wide leads into the N. side of the room probably from a furnace (*praefurnium*) on the N. side

of the building (not shown on original plan). In the room, closely-spaced brick pillars (*pilae*) of a hypocaust system supported a tessellated floor. The pillars, 0.99 m high, stood on the natural ground surface and were built of brick tiles 0.18 m square and 0.025 m thick which were capped by inverted roof tiles (*tegulae*) to support the floor. The mosaic was of a chequer and step pattern in blue and white *tesserae* with a plain border on the W.[5]

Hay's plan shows the partition wall between *Room 6* and *Room 7* as abutting the external walls, suggesting that it is a later insertion. It is possible that in the original plan there was a single large square room (*6* and *7*) that had acted as a *tepidarium* (warm room), later subdivided so that *Room 6*, which has its own furnace to the N. could function as a hot dry room (*laconicum*). This explanation implies that the mosaics in both rooms were laid after the alterations (as in *Rooms 4-5*). *Room 7*, 5.79 m by 3.28 m, contained in its W. half a mosaic with two panels bordered by multiple narrow plain bands. The subject of the smaller (N.) panel was possibly a scallop shell while the larger contained a design of linked *peltae*.[6] The E. part of the room had a plain concrete floor. *Room 8* was the *caldarium*, a hot room containing in its N. part a hot bath. Both the concrete floor of the room S. of the bath and the base of the bath were supported on brick pillars, those under the bath 0.61 m high. The room measured 5.28 m by 2.44 m generally, and at its narrow S. end, there probably stood a heavy stone *labrum*, or basin, of cool water. The bath was lined with *opus signinum* 0.06 m thick, formed into a quarter round moulding around the basal edges. Overall the bath was 1.22 m deep and entered on its S. side by two steps 0.61 m and 0.38 m deep. At its bottom S.E. corner was a small arched opening through which it was drained. In the walls E. and W. of the bath was a single vertical flue, 0.1 m by 0.11 m, built of superimposed box tiles. The sub-floor exterior of the S. wall of the bath seems to have been lined with flue tiles; the function of these features is uncertain. A door in the S. half of the E. wall leads to a smaller chamber (*9*) nearer the furnace, 2.26 m by 1.37 m. This will likewise have been the site of a hot bath. The very wide foundation on the E. side would have supported the bronze or leaden boiler, which was carried on at least one substantial iron beam (see below). *Room 10* was the furnace-room (*praefurnium*).

Besides the bath building there is a record of a further structure, already much ruined, where the ground rises about 24 m to the S. Two human skulls were found inside it and were thought to be of "late date", but the possibility of a mausoleum belonging to the villa should be borne in mind. Foundations of other buildings in the close vicinity were said to be easily visible in the late eighteenth century. In an adjoining field some years before 1783, a large quantity of "iron cinders" was dug up, suggesting that iron-working was undertaken at the site; indeed a beam of wrought iron, 1.22 m long by 0.15 m square, was found in the E. *praefurnium* flue. This will have been a lintel-beam to support the boiler, the only one known from Wales.[7]

Two spoons, now in Brecknock Museum, were found at the site. Both are of tinned or silvered bronze and typically late form, one broken, the other with a decorative twisted handle. Twelve coins are known from the site[8] ranging from a *denarius* of Severus Alexander (A.D. 222-235) to a *nummus*, probably of Valentinian I (A.D. 364-375), eight falling in the first half of the fourth century. Five are in the Brecknock Museum. The area of the site also produced several large antlers.

Archaeologia, VII (1785), pp. 205-210; V. E. Nash-Williams, *B.B.C.S.*, XIII (1948-50), pp. 105-108 offers a re-interpretation of the plan and description in *Arch.*

[1] The name under which the villa appears in the literature.

[2] If, indeed, "slate" as described, then it may have come from Pembrokeshire (Prescelly Hills) and have been brought to the site up the River Usk. For Pembrokeshire slate used as ballast, discharged at a quay at Caerleon, see George C. Boon, 'Excavations on the site of a Roman Quay at Caerleon, and its significance', *Monographs and Collections*, I, pp. 11-12 (Cambrian Archaeological Association, Cardiff, 1978).

[3] A. Rainey, *Mosaics in Roman Britain* (Newton Abbot, 1973), p. 111. Rainey compared these mosaics with others at the Lydney temple (Gloucs.). The same company of mosaicists may have been responsible for both sets.

[4] *Cf.* W. H. Bathurst, *Roman Antiquities at Lydney Park, Gloucestershire* (London, 1879), pl. viii. For sea-creatures in a similar

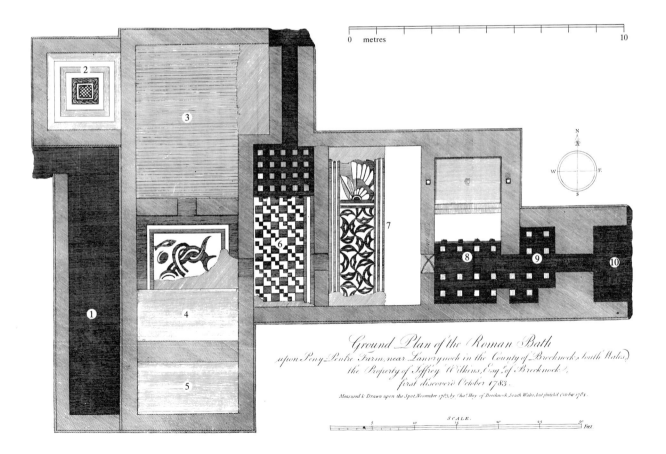

Ground Plan of the Roman Bath
upon Peny-Pentre Farm, near Llanvrynach in the County of Brecknock, South Wales;
the Property of Jeffrey Wilkins, Esq of Brecknock,
first discovered October 1783.

Measured & Drawn upon the Spot November 1783, by Cha.¹ Hay of Brecknock, South Wales, but finished October 1781.

180 Roman villa at Maesderwen, Llanfrynach (RV 1): plan of bath-house, 1783 (after *Archaeologia*, VII)

style, though not entwined, see B. Cunliffe, *Roman Bath* (Res. Rept. Soc. Antiq. Lond. No. xxiv, 1969), pl. lxxxi, and Rainey, *op. cit.*, pl. 15b, Great Witcombe, Glos., and across the Severn at Caerwent (O. Morgan, *Monmouthshire and Caerleon Antiq. Assn. Papers,* 1882, facing p. 22); at Cirencester entwined, Prof. Buckman and C. H. Newmarch, *Illustrations of . . . Roman Art in Cirencester, the Site of the Ancient Corinium* (1850), pl. vi facing p. 36. Dr. David Smith has claimed that the Llanfrynach mosaic is an outlier of his 'Durnovarian School' (D. T. Smith, 'Roman mosaics in Britain, a synthesis', *III Colloquio internazionale sul mosaico antico, Ravenna 1980* (Edizioni del Girasole, 1984), pp. 369-70), the key being 'the representations of deities and other figures and creatures associated with water.' The 'school' was originally centred in Dorchester (*Durnovaria*) but must clearly have spread very quickly far beyond the confines of south Dorset; indeed, it is chiefly reflected by mosaics in Wiltshire, Somersetshire and the Cotswolds (Smith, p. 359, tav. ii) with outliers, of which the Caerwent and Lydney, perhaps also the Kingscote (Gloucester) examples trend in the direction of the upper Vale of Usk and Llanfrynach (see the list, *ibid.*, p. 376). Smith would date the activity of the school to *c.* A.D. 340/50-370+ but the coins from Llanfrynach are mostly of the reign of Constantine I and an earlier date may perhaps be claimed in view of the rapid suppression of coin-types in the fourth century. We may note also that the aquatic mosaic in Lydney temple itself (Bathurst, *op. cit.*, pl. viii), which shows entwined creatures, may very well be earlier than the Wheeler date of A.D. 367+, for it is

not well-centred with regard to the triple shrine, and so may be related to an earlier building on the same site: it had unfortunately disappeared by the time of Wheeler's excavations, and when first found in 1805 the decayed traces of an upper floor may not have been noticed (this suggestion is made by Mr. G. C. Boon).

[5] Rainey, *op. cit.*

[6] Rainey, *op. cit.* There is a close parallel for the *peltae* design at Lydney: Bathurst, *op. cit.*, pl. XVII and see also *ibid.*, pls. V, XIV; it is, also, reminiscent of the mosaic in Room 14 at Chedworth (R. Goodburn, *The Roman Villa Chedworth* (London: National Trust, 1979), pl. 7.2, p. 25) but the design scheme is different. For scallops *cf.* the Littlecote Park Orpheus mosaic (*Britannia*, XII (1981), pl. I), which Smith (*loc. cit.*, note 2) would also claim for the 'Durnovarian School'. The drawing suggests that the surveyor had no understanding of the remains, which may indeed have been badly damaged; interpretation is therefore open to question.

[7] For a discussion of such boiler supports, see J. S. Wacher, 'Roman Iron Beams', *Britannia*, II (1971), pp. 200-202.

[8] T. Jones, *Hist. of Brecknock*, II (1809), p. 599 and pl. XV (includes two mentioned in *Arch.* account).

Llanfrynach
SO 02 N.E. (0692 2585)   13 iv 83

(RCS 1) Ogof-yr-esgyrn

A detailed description of this cave in Carboniferous limestone cliffs forming the W. side of the upper Tawe valley is given in *Inv. Brecknock*, I, i (forthcoming) with a discussion of its pre-Roman occupation.

Remains of Roman period activity have been discovered in excavations made in 1923[1] and from 1938 onwards.[2] The finds have been interpreted as belonging to two separate phases.[3] The earlier phase is represented by disarticulated human bones found throughout the cave but with a particular concentration towards the N. wall. The bones representing about 40 individuals belong almost certainly to the Roman period and probably come from disturbed inhumation burials of mainly Antonine date to which the majority of the finds, probably grave goods, can be assigned. A few pieces hint at the possibility of earlier Roman activity. The likely date distribution of the artefacts suggests a gap in the usage of the cave between *c.* A.D. 180 and *c.* A.D. 330, when renewed activity, apparently entirely domestic, is represented by a series of hearths near the entrance. More recent excavations may indicate that the occupation at this period was more significant than previously thought.[4]

Finds include: coins: Vespasian (2), Trajan, Hadrian (3), Constantine I (5), fourth century (unspecified), Constantius II;[5] bronze: several fine brooches, ring, bracelet, strap-end, seal-box, steelyard arm, *ligula* or ear-scoop, spatula, awl and other fragments; silver: finger-ring (fourth century), ring for pendant; iron: finger-ring, ring, pins, nail and other fragments; piece of lead; bone: pins, needle, bodkin, handle, ring; antler comb (fourth century); fragments of glass vessels; piece of linen; pottery (second and fourth century); stone tessera; bones of domestic animals especially sheep. The finds are mostly in the N.M.W., with some replicas exhibited at the Dan yr Ogof caves.

[1] *Arch. Camb.*, LXXIX (1924), pp. 113-124.

[2] *Arch. Camb.*, CXVII (1968), pp. 18-71 deals with excavations between 1938 and 1950. Edmund J. Mason has conducted further excavations in the cave as yet unpublished. The present name was given to the cave in 1938.

[3] *ibid.*, pp. 56-8.

[4] *Western Mail*, March 29th, 1978.

[5] *B.B.C.S.*, XXVII (1976-78), pp. 631-2.

Ystradgynlais (E), Ystradgynlais Higher (C)
SN 81 N.W. (8376 1601)

Sites of Uncertain Status

(RU 1) Gwernyfed School playing fields

Excavations in 1951 revealed the bases of four iron-smelting and forging furnaces consisting of oval, flat-bottomed hollows dug into the original ground surface and clay-lined, the dimensions of three of which were recovered: *No. 1*, 0.99 m by 0.84 m by 0.23 m deep; *No. 2*, 0.69 m by 0.46 m by 0.3 m deep; *No. 4*, 1.52 m by 1.07 m by 0.46 m deep. The lower infillings of the furnaces were deposits of iron slag and charcoal and the upper fillings contained Roman pottery including some samian and amphora sherds, probably of the later first century A.D. A flat iron chisel, used probably for forging, was associated with one furnace.

Fragments of finished ironwork were also found. The artefact associations strongly suggest a first century, Roman date for the installation.

Linear grass marks of uncertain character are visible on aerial photographs of the playing fields.[1]

Brycheiniog, IV (1958), pp. 63-4, 67-9, 71.
[1] C.U.A.P. CBG 19, 21.

Aberllynfi
SO 13 N.E. (171 372)

Other Remains

In addition to the localities described above, Roman or probably Roman remains have been found at the following places:

(i) Maes-gwyn Farm

A silver coin of Maximin (A.D. 235-238).

Arch. Camb. (1854), p. 132.

Llywel (E), Traean-mawr (C)
SN 83 S.E. (86 30)

(ii) Ystradfellte

A gold coin of Vespasian (A.D. 69-79) from the neighbourhood of Ystradfellte.

Archaeologia, IV (1786 ed.), p. 8.

Ystradfellte
SN 91 S.W.

(iii) Nant Cwm-du

The rim of a samian vessel of form Dr. 37 in East Gaulish ware has been found here, late second or third century A.D.

N.M.W. Records (August 1965).

Defynnog (E), Senni (C)
SN 92 S.W. (942 215)

(iv) Defynnog parish

A coin hoard in a pot was ploughed up in 1758, 4.8 km (3 miles) S.W. of Y Gaer, Brecon. The coins are described as "copper medals" and included one of Otacilia, wife of Philip I (A.D. 244-249).

Archaeologia, II (1773), pp. 23-4.

Defynnog (E), Maes-car (C)
SN 92 N.W.

(v) Llangamarch Wells station

A coin hoard in a pot was found in peaty ground near the station in 1871. The pot was described as a handled urn. Only two of the coins were recovered, both described as 'Second brass', but presumably ordinary *antoniniani*, of Victorinus (A.D. 269-271).

Arch. Camb. (1872), p. 165.

Llangamarch (E), Treflys or Penbuallt (C)
SN 94 N.W. (*c.* 936 473)

(vi) Vaynor

A hoard of seven bronze Roman coins was found in the parish in 1945. It included three *folles*, of Maximinus II (A.D. 305-313), Maxentius (A.D. 306-312) and Constantine I (A.D. 307-337). No further details.

J.R.S., XXXVI (1946), p. 133.

Vaynor
SO 01 S.W.

(vii) Llechfaen

A fragment of a pipe-clay figure of a cockerel was found in a field 0.8 km E. of the village. Fragments of pottery and brick were found near by. The figure has been regarded as Roman[1] but Mr. G. C. Boon regards it as post-medieval, as he does all the objects with it.

[1] M. J. Green, *Roman Cult-Objects* (Oxford: BAR, 1978), p. 72 and O.S. Record card SO 13 SE 21 who give the location as Talgarth contrary to N.M.W. records.

Llanhamlach
SO 02 N.E. (08 28)

(viii) Bryn-mawr

A coin of Constantine I is recorded from this area.

N.M.W. Records.

Llangatwg or Llanelli (E) Bryn-mawr (C)
SO 11 S.E./21 S.W.

(ix) Rhiangoll valley

A *sestertius* of Postumus (A.D. 260-69) is supposed to have been found N. of Cwm-du but doubt has been cast on its provenance.

N.M.W. Records (April 1963).

Llanfihangel Cwm Du or Talgarth
SO 12 S.E. or N.E.

(x) 'Tresco', Bwlch

A *sestertius* of Claudius I (A.D. 41-54),? British copy, was found about 0.3 m deep in the garden at the E. end of the house in 1980.

Brecon and Radnor Express, October 30th, 1980, p. 10; *Western Mail*, November 4th, 1980, p. 3.

Llanfihangel Cwm Du
SO 12 S.W. (1483 2208)

(xi) Dderw tumulus

A possibly Roman potsherd was found lying on the old ground surface below the earthen mound (now destroyed).

Arch. in Wales, 16 (1976), p. 17; *Inv. Breck.* I, i (forthcoming).

Glasbury (E), Pipton (C)
SO 13 N.W. (1386 3748)

(xii) Cairn at Tŷ-du

The exact location of this Bronze Age cairn is uncertain. Late Roman and Byzantine bronze coins were represented in 1863 as having been found with the Bronze Age remains but there is no mention of these coins in earlier accounts. The coins are part of a larger group spanning the whole Roman period and the sixth and seventh centuries A.D. There is no good reason to believe that any were found at the cairn.

Arch. Camb. (1863), pp. 377-8; *Arch. Camb.* (1871), pp. 327-30 where, for no good reason, the issues of Constantine and Claudius Gothicus are held to have come from the cairn. For full details of the cairn see *Inv. Breck.*, I, i (forthcoming).

Llaneleu
SO 13 S.E. (*c.* 18 34)

(xiii) Pontithel

A coin of Antoninus Pius (A.D. 138-161) was found here in 1961.

N.M.W. Records.

Aberllynfi
SO 13 N.E. (*c.* 164 366)

(xiv) Garn Coch

Six Roman coins, five of Constantine I and one of *Urbs Roma* type, have been found washed out of this Bronze Age cairn. A typical small Constantinian hoard.

Arch. Camb. (1854), p. 148. For full details of the cairn see *Inv. Breck.*, I, i (forthcoming).

Llangatwg
SO 21 N.W. (2123 1771)

(xv) Pen y Wyrlod

A coin of Crispus (A.D. 317-26) was found by an "unauthorised searcher" during an excavation of this Neolithic long cairn. Also found were some blue beads, possibly Roman.

Arch. Camb., LXXVI (1921), pp. 296-299. For full details of this site see *Inv. Breck.*, I, i (forthcoming).

Llanigan
SO 23 N.W. (2248 3986)

(xvi) Hay-on-Wye

Roman coins have been recorded here.

Camden's *Britannia* (ed. Gibson, 1695), p. 590; *B.B.C.S.*, IV (1929), p. 247 suggests that the reference may be to Clyro, opposite.

Hay (E), Hay Urban (C)
SO 24 S.W.

Suggested Sites and Finds

The following have been suggested as Roman sites or finds but certain evidence is lacking:

(i) Trecastell

A. H. A. Hogg has suggested the possibility of a fort mid-way between Y Gaer, Brecon and Llandovery, perhaps at Trecastell. No surface evidence for such a site has been found. Reputedly Roman coins were found in the garden of a house opposite the castle mound at *c.* 8827 2906 but no further details could be obtained.

> *Arch. Camb.*, CXXII (1973), p. 13.

Llywel (E), Traean-mawr (C)
SN 82 N.E. (8829)

(ii) Dol-y-gaer

A cornelian seal was found near here in the seventeenth century. No further details. It is possible that this was Roman. RR 7 runs nearby and 1.5 km N. is the Roman fort of Caerau.

> Lhuyd, *Parochialia*, pt. 3, p. 46. The same ref. records that "A piece of Gold was found at Castellan" in the same parish.

Llangamarch (E), Treflys (C)
SN 94 N.W. (*c.* 9248)

(iii) Builth Castle

Several authorities have suggested that a road connecting Y Gaer, Brecon and Castell Collen Roman forts crossed the River Wye at Builth.[1] Some have speculated on the possible existence of a fort at this place which is of considerable strategic importance as its later history shows. The reasons for doubting the existence of the road are given on p. 173. Nevertheless, C. J. Spurgeon[2] has drawn attention to an unexplained right-angled earthwork beyond the counterscarp bank of the bailey on the N.E. side of Builth castle. The scarp is much slighter than the works that belong undoubtedly to the castle and may pre-date them. A Roman date is suggested. A supposedly Roman coin was found on the castle site but no further details are available.

> [1] See RR 6.
> [2] *Brycheiniog*, XVIII (1978-79), pp. 48, 52, 58 f.n. 5.

Builth
SO 05 S.W. (0439 5103)

(iv) Bronllys Castle

It has been suggested that the Norman castle here was raised over the site of an earlier Roman military installation approximately half-way between Y Gaer, Brecon and Clyro (Rads.). The rectangular form of the castle bailey is noteworthy. However, besides the intermediate position between two known sites, and the suitability of the location for a fort or fortlet, there is no other evidence to support the suggestion.

> *Arch. Camb.*, CXXII (1973), map p. 9; *Trans. Radnor. Soc.*, 5 (1935), p. 76.

Bronllys
SO 13 S.W. (1489 3474)

Omitted Sites

These have been suggested as Roman sites or finds but their authenticity is very doubtful or has been disproven:

(i) Caerau, Llanddulas

Careful inspection of the various earthworks claimed to comprise a 6 ha Roman fort and possibly an earlier 8.5 ha installation failed to substantiate the identification. The resemblance to a Roman fort apparent on aerial photographs is most probably the result of a fortuitous combination of geomorphological features, the remains of a post-Roman boundary system earlier than the present field system and some relatively modern earthworks.

Roman Frontier, p. 200; first noticed on A.Ps. by J. F. Jones, *Carmarthen Antiquary,* III, pts 3-4 (1961), p. 128; R.C.A.M. Records, Brecknockshire Earthworks, SN 84 S.E. for detailed refutation; C.U.A.P. BAK 54, 59.

Llanddulas
SN 84 S.E. (8770 4050)   16 vii 82

(ii) Castell Madoc

This site has been demonstrated to be a medieval ringwork,[1] not a Roman fortlet.[2]

[1] *Brycheiniog,* XII (1966/7), pp. 131-2.
[2] *J.R.S.,* XLVIII (1958), p. 95.

Llanfihangel Fechan
SO 03 N.W. (0253 3703)

(iii) Heol-y-gaer

There is no satisfactory surface or aerial photograph evidence for a Roman fort supposedly occupying a spur 700 m W. of Heol-y-gaer farm. Obsolete later field banks seem to have been identified mistakenly as fort defences.

Trans. Cymmr. (1958), pp. 82-6; *J.R.S.,* XLVIII (1958), pp. 130-1; *Brycheiniog,* IV (1958), p. 121; C.U.A.P. ABI 94.

Glasbury (E) Tre-goed a Felindre (C)
SO 13 N.E. (184 392)

Index of National Grid References

This index gives the six-figure grid reference and corresponding monument number or page for every surviving structure mentioned in the Inventory, apart from roads and trackways for which the arrangement would be unsuitable. Its purpose is to simplify direct reference to the entry corresponding to a site located according to the National Grid, for which the proper name may be unknown or difficult to determine.

The references are classified according to the main categories of the Inventory, and lead not only to the descriptive entries of authentic sites, but to alternative categories where doubtful character has occasioned cross-reference in the text. Many rejected sites have been included under categories to which field archaeologists might be inclined to refer them on their own assessment.

The index for this part of the Inventory contains no direct reference to the other part which should be separately consulted.

Hill-forts and Related Structures

G.R.	INV.	G.R.	INV.	G.R.	INV.
SN 845 157	HF 1	SO 029 303	HF 33	SO 112 214	HF 43
SN 848 478	HF 3	SO 032 246	HF 28	SO 114 327	HF 55
SN 862 368	HF 2	SO 039 113	HF 20	SO 123 242	HF 46
SN 915 080	HF 4	SO 041 251	HF 29	SO 127 243	HF 47
SN 917 139	HF 5	SO 052 505	HF 38	SO 127 379	HF 59
SN 922 263	HF 9	SO 054 352	HF 35	SO 131 316	HF 52
SN 969 306	HF 11	SO 055 240 p. 124	'omit' (i)	SO 155 326	HF 53
SN 971 261	HF 8	SO 056 284	HF 30	SO 160 277	HF 49
SN 981 319	HF 12	SO 059 148	HF 21	SO 164 273	HF 48
SN 984 375	HF 15	SO 065 239	HF 25	SO 173 207	HF 41
SN 985 353	HF 14	SO 069 240	HF 26	SO 175 375	HF 57
SN 987 177	HF 6	SO 082 291	HF 31	SO 176 240	HF 45
SN 987 329	HF 13	SO 089 194	HF 22	SO 177 378	HF 58
SN 988 575	HF 17	SO 091 195	HF 23	SO 178 300	HF 50
SN 990 280	HF 10	SO 093 351	HF 34	SO 193 162	HF 39
SN 993 246	HF 7	SO 097 217	HF 24	SO 195 184	HF 40
SN 999 386	HF 16	SO 101 313	HF 51	SO 223 132	HF 61
SO 002 242	HF 27	SO 102 217 p. 124	'omit' (ii)	SO 224 153	HF 62
SO 009 366	HF 36	SO 106 347	HF 56	SO 225 206	HF 64
SO 014 294	HF 32	SO 110 235	HF 44	SO 228 125	HF 60
SO 020 380	HF 37	SO 110 326	HF 54	SO 228 185	HF 63
SO 023 112	HF 19	SO 111 209	HF 42	SO 237 411 p. 124	'omit' (iii)
SO 028 099	HF 18				

Roman Forts

G.R.	INV.	G.R.	INV.	G.R.	INV.
SN 924 501	RF 1	SO 003 296	RF 2	SO 168 219	RF 3

Other Roman Military Works

G.R.	INV.	G.R.	INV.	G.R.	INV.
SN 828 312	RMC 1	920 499	RPC 1	SN 923 163	RMC 3
SN 828 312	RMC 2	920 501	RPC 2	SO 000 298	RPC 3
SN 919 507	RMC 4				

Roman Civil Sites

G.R.	INV.	G.R.	INV.
SN 837 160	RCS 1	SO 069 258	RV 1

Roman Sites of Uncertain Status and other Roman Remains

G.R.	INV.	G.R.	INV.	G.R.	INV.
SN 86 30 p. 184	(i)	SO 08 28 p. 184	(vii)	SO 171 372	RU 1
SN 9 1 p. 184	(ii)	SO 1 1 p. 185	(viii)	SO 18 34 p. 185	(xii)
SN 9 2 p. 184	(iv)	SO 1 2 p. 185	(ix)	SO 2 1 p. 185	(viii)
SN 936 473 p. 184	(v)	SO 138 374 p. 185	(xi)	SO 2 4 p. 185	(xvi)
SO 942 215 p. 184	(iii)	SO 148 220 p. 185	(x)	SO 212 177 p. 185	(xiv)
SO 0 1 p. 184	(vi)	SO 164 366 p. 185	(xiii)	SO 224 398 p. 185	(xv)

Suggested Roman Sites

G.R.	INV.	G.R.	INV.	G.R.	INV.
SN 877 405 p. 187	'omit' (i)	SO 025 370 p. 187	'omit' (ii)	SO 148 347 p. 186	(iv)
SN 88 29 p. 186	(i)	SO 043 510 p. 186	(iii)	SO 184 392 p. 187	'omit' (iii)
SN 92 48 p. 186	(ii)				

Glossary: General

Words adequately defined in the Shorter Oxford Dictionary are not included unless they have been used in a more specialised sense than is given there. The list is further limited by the exclusion of proper names and terms of cultural significance, as well as typological definitions of artefacts, which can be ascertained from standard works. Definitions are only given in the list when reference to an appropriate section of the Inventory will not suffice. Terms special to Roman antiquities are indicated by (R): only the principal features of forts are included.

Agger (R)—A continuous raised bank; the rampart of a fort, but also the visible mound of a road.

Clavicula (R)—A curving continuation of the ditch and/or rampart of a camp projecting inwards or outwards to protect a gate.

Counterscarp bank—A subsidiary bank crowning the outer slope of the ditch of a hill-fort, etc.

Lynchet—A roughly levelled area formed by cultivation on sloping ground; the boundary between one field and the next on a slope.

Marching camp (R)—See p. 150.

Milliary (R)—1000 strong.

Opus signinum (R)—A lime concrete containing fragments of brick etc., smoothed and used to form a floor.

Pillow mound—A ridged, artificial mound, thought to have served as a rabbit warren.

Practice camp (R)—See p. 150.

Praetentura (R)—The area of a Roman fort in front of the headquarters buildings.

Praetorium (R)—A building of domestic character, usually regarded as the commandant's house, placed at one side of the *principia* in a Roman auxiliary fort.

Principia (R)—The headquarters building of a fort, centrally placed fronting the main cross-street.

Quingenary (R)—500 strong.

Retentura (R)—The area of a Roman fort behind the main cross-street.

Signal station (R)—A small embanked enclosure with single entrance, part of a system for signalling between forts. (For various types see R. G. Collingwood and I. Richmond, *The Archaeology of Roman Britain* (London, 1969), pp. 60-6.)

Vallate (uni-, bi-, tri-, multi-)—Of hill-forts, indicates the number of main lines of defence, each consisting usually of bank and ditch.

Glossary: Welsh Place-name Elements

Only the singular form is given.

Aber	Mouth of river; confluence	**Heol**	Track; road
Afon	River	**Llan**	Sacred enclosure
Allt, Gallt	Hillslide; slope	**Llech, Llechfaen**	Slab
Bach (fach, fechan)	Small; minor	**Llwyn**	Bush
Bedd	Grave	**Llys**	Court
Brenin	King	**Maen**	Stone
Bwlch	Gap; pass	**Maes**	Open field
Cae	Field	**Mawr (fawr)**	Big; great
Caer (Gaer)	Fort	**Moel (Foel)**	Bare mountain
Carreg (Garreg)	Stone	**Mynydd**	Mountain
Castell	Castle	**Nant**	Stream
Cefn	Ridge; back	**Ogof**	Cave
Celli (Gelli)	Grove	**Pant**	Hollow
Clawdd	Hedge; bank	**Pen**	Head; summit
Coed	Wood	**Pwll**	Pool; pit
Cors (Gors)	Bog; fen	**Rhiw**	Ascent; slope
Craig (Graig)	Rock	**Rhyd**	Ford
Crib	Narrow ridge	**Sarn**	Causeway
Crug	Rocky hillock	**Tor**	Rocky height
Cwm	Narrow valley	**Twyn**	Knoll; small hill
Dinas (Ddinas)	Settlement; fort	**Tyle**	Hill
Esgair	Ridge	**Ty**	House
Ffos	Ditch	**Ystrad**	Dale
Garth	Enclosure		
Glyn	Valley; glen		

General Index